SHIFTING SCENES

GENDER AND CULTURE

Carolyn G. Heilbrun and Nancy K. Miller, EDITORS

GENDER AND CULTURE
A SERIES OF COLUMBIA UNIVERSITY PRESS
Edited by Carolyn G. Heilbrun and Nancy K. Miller

In Dora's Case: Freud, Hysteria, Feminism
Edited by Charles Bernheimer and Claire Kahane

Breaking the Chain: Women, Theory and French Realist Fiction
Naomi Schor

Between Men: English Literature and Male Homosocial Desire
Eve Kosovsky Sedgwick

Romantic Imprisonment: Women and Other Glorified Outcasts
Nina Auerbach

The Poetics of Gender
Edited by Nancy K. Miller

Reading Woman: Essays in Feminist Criticism
Mary Jacobus

Honey-Mad Women: Emancipatory Strategies in Women's Writing
Patricia Yeager

Subject to Change: Reading Feminist Writing
Nancy K. Miller

Thinking Through the Body
Jane Gallop

Gender and the Politics of History
Joan Wallach Scott

Dialogic and Difference: "An/Other Woman" in Virginia Woolf
and Christa Wolf
Anne Herrmann

Plotting Women
Jean Franco

Inspiriting Influences
Michael Awkward

Hamlet's Mother
Carolyn G. Heilbrun

Rape and Representation
Edited by Lynn A. Higgins and Brenda R. Silver

SHIFTING SCENES

*Interviews on
Women, Writing, and Politics
in Post-68 France*

EDITED BY
ALICE A. JARDINE AND ANNE M. MENKE

COLUMBIA UNIVERSITY PRESS   NEW YORK

Columbia University Press
New York   Oxford

Library of Congress Cataloging-in-Publication Data

Shifting scenes : interviews on women, writing, and politics in
  post-68 France / edited by Alice A. Jardine and Anne M. Menke.
    p.   cm. — (Gender and culture)
  Translated from the French.
  "Interviews with fifteen women writers and theorists working in Paris"—Introd.
  Includes bibliographical references (p.   ) and index.
  ISBN 0-231-06772-0
  I. Women authors, French—20th century—Interviews. 2. Women and literature—
France—History—20th century. 3. Politics and literature—France—History—20th cen-
tury. 4. French literature—Women authors—History and criticism—Theory,
etc. 5. French literature—20th century—History and criticism—Theory,
etc. 6. France—Intellectual life—20th century. I. Jardine, Alice.
II. Menke, Anne M. III. Series.
PQ307.W6S55 1991
840.9'9287'09045—dc20
90-24486
CIP

Printed in the United States of America
c 10 9 8 7 6 5 4 3 2 1

WE DEDICATE THIS BOOK TO EACH OTHER.

Contents

"In 1983 I started a series with the title 'To the Revolution.' I was in a protest show against the Whitney Museum's exclusionary policies; [the show was comprised] of postcard-size works. . . . I included a print of a woman's upper body with her hands above her head holding a snake. I was going to call this 'Woman with Snake' but the curator suggested 'To the Revolution' after a dance by Isadora Duncan. I used this generic title because I wanted to continue depicting woman as activator, to get away from this 'lack'—the loss and castration of the tongue. I wanted to depict women finding their voices, which partly reflected my own developing dialogue with the art world, that somehow I had a tongue and at least a part of the language of that world, there was an interchange. I'm speaking of equality, and about a certain kind of power of movement in the world, and yet I'm not offering any systematic solutions."

—Nancy Spero in an article by John Bird
(1987)

SHIFTING SCENES

Introduction

THE WOMEN interviewed here have helped shift the scenes of feminist literary and cultural criticism in major ways over the past quarter of a century—both in France and around the world. Many of them have done so through the introduction of the psychoanalytic scene into this critical effort. This "other scene"—the scene of the unconscious—that so resists representation has both literally and figuratively undermined many of the more voluntaristic and pedagogical assumptions of feminist theory and practice.[1]

Of course, there is a more generalized theatricality to this process,

[1] For a sense of the ways in which the encounter between the analyst and the analysand most literally disrupts the mimesis of traditional forms of representation, see Luce Irigaray's "The Gesture in Psychoanalysis," in Teresa Brennan, ed., *Between Feminism and Psychoanalysis* (London and New York: Routledge, 1989).

which, while it may find many of its origins in the "family dramas" of psychoanalysis itself, cannot be contained as such. For that theatricality extends to the *transdisciplinary* ways in which the relationships between subjectivities and the constitution of those subjectivities are foregrounded in the work of these women. It extends as well to the "presentations of self" they so carefully orchestrate as they continually (re)place themselves on the world stage. *Elles font des scènes:* they "make scenes"; they write and speak with a passion usually effaced from any but the most "poetic" of writing—especially from academic writing as it is practiced in the United States. Like poetic language (and they have all written poetically in some form), their "scenes of writing"[2] provoke our resistance, our fascination, our sense of otherness in ourselves. Like Roman Jacobson's "shifters"—the technical term he used for those small words that move around our time-space coordinates (I, you, us, them, here, there, etc.),[3] these women will not hold still for anything like a "portrait."

For these reasons and others, we have chosen not to present these writers as "personalities," but rather as "shifting scenes" of the postmodern theater in which many of us, as feminists, are increasingly unsure of who and where we are (actresses or audiences?) with regard to the master narratives of patriarchal history.

The voices that are orchestrated here—those of Chantal Chawaf, Hélène Cixous, Catherine Clément, Françoise Collin, Marguerite Duras, Claudine Herrmann, Jeanne Hyvrard, Luce Irigaray, Sarah Kofman, Julia Kristeva, Eugénie Lemoine-Luccioni, Marcelle Marini, Michèle Montrelay, Christiane Rochefort, Monique Wittig—emanate from thinkers who would never, under any circumstances, gather in the same room for a discussion. The text that follows is a provocative, challenging continuation of the work in which these women have been engaged in the fields of literature, psychoanalysis, philosophy, and feminist and critical theory. The notoriety of these women and the polemical nature of their comments earmark their responses as a decisive intervention in current feminist debates. These debates include the relationship between gender and writing, psychoanalysis and feminism, writing and the mass

---

[2] See Jacques Derrida, "The Scene of Writing," in *Writing and Difference,* Alan Bass, trans. (Chicago: University of Chicago Press, 1978).

[3] Roman Jacobson, *Shifters, Verbal Categories, and the Russian Verb* (Cambridge, Mass.: Russian Language Project, Department of Slavic Languages and Literatures, Harvard University, 1957).

media, and women and the institution, as well as the debates on sexual difference and essentialism: the tensions and contradictions inherent in speaking for and as women. *Caveat lector:* this is *not* a collection of "cozy chats" with "famous writers," complete with pictures, in magazine prose.

This book of interviews with fifteen women writers and theorists working in Paris owes its existence to the invitation extended to us in 1985 by Joan DeJean and Nancy K. Miller. They were organizing a special issue of *Yale French Studies* devoted to "The Politics of Tradition: Placing Women in French Literature."[4] We were asked to contribute an article on twentieth-century women writers.

Our initial response was, "How can one possibly write an article on the literary canon at the end of the twentieth century?" The question of literary history did not at first seem to us to be the most compelling one, in light of the postmodern sensitivity to the need to reconceptualize History. We are, of course, committed to revising the canon. Nevertheless, we must first question the epistemological assumptions upon which such an endeavor is based, for they are inevitably implicated in the phallocentric thought and binary logic that organized the canon in the first place. For example, it did not seem to us that *being placed in French literature,* that is, in a by definition overwhelmingly Western, white, Christian, male canon is what writers who have been excluded from it are struggling for today.

Nonetheless, it is now clear that the very work that has most convincingly elaborated postmodern, post-structuralist theory—and helped create new contexts for marginalized writers—could itself rapidly disappear if the power of institutions and their ideologies to (de)legitimize certain kinds of knowledge is not taken seriously. Thus it seemed important to us, particularly at that moment in time, to find a way to map some of the fields of force operating between the new topologies of knowledge and the archaic power structures upon which they continue to rely.

To do this, we decided to turn away from History with its third-person pronouns, past tenses, and "fixing" of narratives—and to turn toward Discourse itself with its implications of the "I" and "you," its emphasis on the "now," and its insistence on process. Despite the com-

[4] Joan DeJean and Nancy K. Miller, eds., *The Politics of Tradition: Placing Women in French Literature.* Special issue of *Yale French Studies* (1988), vol. 75. Reprinted as *Displacements: Women, Tradition, Literatures in French* (Baltimore: Johns Hopkins University Press, 1990).

plicated status of interviewing (looking to the author as an authority on texts), we decided to assume the contradictions and put our questions about the literary tradition to some of those intimately involved with these issues: women writing in France today.

As we were deciding whom to interview for this project, it soon became clear that we would be forced to reproduce for ourselves the very process of canon formation the special issue of *Yale French Studies* was calling into question. We knew that we were beginning with and would be limited by our own knowledge, subjective preferences, ideology, complicated personal and professional relationships, and a resistance to pluralism as well as to party lines. We opted to proceed by foregrounding as much as possible the usually implicit assumptions and biases that inform the organization of a body of knowledge.

We decided that rather than attempt to cover the field of all women writing in French today, we would focus on those women writing in Paris whose work has been perceived in the United States as "French feminism."[5] This group of women is comprised of both fiction and theory writers who by now have already had a marked impact on feminist theory in the United States, either directly or indirectly, and whose work is located within the fields of force mentioned above. These women are working primarily within the domain of language and address the kinds of issues raised by post-structuralist thought. Of particular interest to us were the political and intellectual effects of representing the women in question as "French feminists."

The framework we imposed upon our choice of whom to interview produced the anticipated canonical problems of inclusion and exclusion. It precluded inviting certain women, for example, those involved in the social sciences, or those whose work has not yet been translated enough to become central to the American theoretical debates we are addressing, although this important work is clearly feminist. Two such women are the sociologist Christine Delphy, whose analysis of housework, *Close to Home: A Materialist Analysis of Women's Oppression,* is now available in English, and the philosopher Michèle Le Doeuff, whose work is only now being translated.[6] Our framework also paradoxically led to choices

---

[5] See Elaine Marks and Isabelle de Courtivron, *New French Feminisms* (New York: Schocken, 1981).

[6] Christine Delphy, *Close to Home: A Materialist Analysis of Women's Oppression,* trans. and ed. Diana Leonard (Amherst: University of Massachusetts Press, 1984). See also "For a Materialist Feminism," *Feminist Issues* (Winter 1981), 1(2):69–76. See, for example, Mi-

to interview some women who strongly contest their ties to feminism and/or their status as "women writers." Of the writers we did invite to respond to our questions, several simply refused (including Nathalie Sarraute and Marguerite Yourcenar) or never responded (Françoise Sagan); Simone de Beauvoir's death in 1986 precluded our invitation and her decision. We will not, in the space of this introduction, present in detail the work of the fifteen women in question, most of whom need no introduction to an English-speaking audience already engaged in these debates. We have, however, provided short biographical sketches of the contributors, which appear at the end of the book, as well as a selective bibliography of these women's texts.

The interviews were based on six questions (five that were repeated in each interview, and one specially designed for each writer). As we formulated our questions about the relationship between women and the literary tradition in France, we tried to make apparent our own resistance to the entire problematic of canon revision. We wanted to remain in between; to show that we were "representing"—albeit in no simple way—a desire not entirely ours. This required complex rhetorical moves on our part—moves that often led to long pre- and postinterview explanations of our double-talk.

We asked the women the following five questions. QUESTION 1: What does it mean to you to write at the end of the twentieth century? QUESTION 2: Is it valid/of value to write as a woman, and is it part of your writing practice today? QUESTION 3: Many women writing today find themselves, for the first time in history, at the center of such institutions as the university and psychoanalysis. In your opinion, will this new placement of women help them to enter the twentieth-century canon, and if so, will they be at the heart of this corpus or (still) in the footnotes? QUESTION 4: Today we are seeing women produce literary, philosophical, and psychoanalytical theory of recognized importance, and, parallel to this, we are also seeing a new fluidity in the borderlines among disciplines and genres of writing. Will this parallelism lead only to women being welcomed alongside men, or to a definitive blurring of these categories? QUESTION 5: Given the problematic and the politics of the categories of the canon, and given the questions we've been dealing with, do you think your oeuvre will be included in the twentieth-century

chèle Le Doeuff, "Women and Philosophy,"trans. Debbie Pope et al., in Toril Moi, ed., *French Feminist Thought: A Reader* (New York: Blackwell, 1987), pp. 181–209 as well as her book *L'étude et le rouet* (Paris: Seuil, 1989).

canon, and if so, how will it be presented? In your opinion, what will the content of the canon be? Each woman was then asked a sixth question relating to her own work.

The interviews, originally conducted between May 1986 and November 1987, eventually took on every conceivable permutation of oral and written forms over the ensuing three years. The majority of the interviews, conducted in French, took place in person in the homes of the women interviewed. However, Catherine Clément, Claudine Herrmann, Luce Irigaray, and Michèle Montrelay wrote their texts. Jeanne Hyvrard read from a prepared text and also answered extemporaneously, while Monique Wittig's interview took place in English over the telephone. Every writer was given and many took advantage of the opportunity to rewrite the text and to review the translation, to the point that few of the texts closely resemble the initial exchange. Excerpts of these interviews first appeared in *Yale French Studies* (1988), vol. 75, and were reprinted in *Displacements: Women, Tradition, Literatures in French*, coedited by Joan DeJean and Nancy K. Miller.

The responses demonstrate a wide range of concerns that are only tangentially related to the question of the canon. Many of the concerns expressed were in fact the direct result of reactions to our initial questions: the women interviewed often were interested not in answering the questions but in questioning them and then relating them to other issues that seemed more urgent to them. Isn't the question of the literary "canon" hopelessly passé in our high-tech, media culture? What can be the meaning of a national ("French") canon in an increasingly transnational world? Why bring up "writing" (as fiction, as *écriture*) in the context of its enemies (criticism, the institution, the mass media)? And, for many, there was the question of why we wanted to concentrate on the metaphysical category of "women" when the crucial field of force is the construction of sexual difference through notions of the feminine and the masculine.

We understood some of the resistances these women brought to our questions; for example, there is the issue of what it means to write at the end of the twentieth century. For most of the women, this time frame led to discussions on the relationship between writing and the mass media. For Cixous, the mass media constitute a curse on writing. Clément decried the tendency of the media to distort women writers, while Collin felt that the presence of the mass media makes writing an archaic practice that she nonetheless enjoys. Hyvrard sounded a different note. She has profitably enlisted the mass media in her frustrated efforts to teach economics to technical high school students. Whereas Hyvrard sees a common televisual mental space as a prelude to a planetary identity, Cixous rejects it as a screen operating to hide what is happening in less well known parts of the world. Hyvrard celebrated the potential of cybernetics to escape binarisms, but Kristeva felt that the mass media made information uniform and rendered the question of the canon obsolete. Montrelay noted the power of the media to suppress certain types of discourse, such as psychoanalysis, and Rochefort felt it constituted a barrier between a book and its public.

Some of the women's reactions were unexpected. We had felt that our project raised American questions, which were translations of an American academic desire, projections having to do with a canon that is ultimately perhaps not as French as it is American (French literature as it is taught and read in the United States). Our combined desire was to problematize this American desire. The responses of the women in France forced us, however, to acknowledge our strong (if reluctant) complicity with this American desire. We were surprised. It was hard for us to understand that so many professed indifference to inclusion of their own work in the canon. Most of these writers, after all, are far from being widely taught in French universities. And inclusion was not the only problem: for many of these women, the word "canon" does not refer to the literary tradition, and few of them see it as an area of feminist concern.

These collected responses demonstrate a strong resistance to the notion of the "canon" itself. For even when the writers did admit that such a thing exists, they wondered why anyone would want to be *in* it. One of the most often repeated points was that there is no *one* canon—especially in the twentieth century.

Perhaps the canon is, in fact, a myth (in the strong Barthesian sense of that word). To construct an image of one canon is to deny process—canons change continually. To construct an image of *one canon* is inevitably to become involved with the law—and the sacred. Do we want to do away with the canon or bring women into it? Either way, to fight the battle in these terms is to accept the sacred in its relationship to the law. The implication of this insight is that the primarily Anglo-American war with the canon is an (undeclared) holy war, an ecclesiastical battle. It does seem to us that these unavoidable associations for the French of the "canon" with the Church, the sacred, and the law have become naturalized in English.

However, while we eventually acknowledged our complicity with the

American desire to revise the canon, complicity was most certainly not one sided. If there was a combined desire on the part of these women in France, it was to expose the "American," even "irrelevant" nature of our questions. Yet it seems to us that the strong when not passionate tones of these women's responses betray a reluctant acknowledgment of their oppression as women by the literary establishment and an often covert recognition that they are not indifferent to the effects of these highly theoretical matters on the destiny of their own work, especially in the United States.

Most, if not all these women, after all, are well known in various circles of the U.S. academic world. Duras, Rochefort, and Wittig are widely read fiction writers. Cixous, Clément, Herrmann, Irigaray, Kofman, Kristeva, and Wittig figure prominently in American feminist theory. The texts of Irigaray, Kristeva, Lemoine-Luccioni, and Montrelay are relied upon in works of psychoanalytic theory and analysis. Chawaf, Cixous, and Hyvrard are studied as examples of a new feminine stylistics. The analyses and editorial work of Françoise Collin in *Les Cahiers du GRIF,* the feminist journal she founded, are appreciated in the United States and all Western Europe. Marcelle Marini's books on Duras and Lacan, as well as her contributions to American anthologies of feminist criticism, draw students to France to study with her. Cixous, Hyvrard, Irigaray, Kofman, and Kristeva also entice American students to Paris, while Herrmann and Kristeva teach regularly here in the United States. Most of these women have been invited numerous times to lecture in the United States.

The openness the American academy has demonstrated to these women's work contrasts quite sharply with the battles they have waged with French institutions, especially the university. Indeed, if there was one theme shared by those interviewed, it was a resistance if not a violent opposition to the oppressive force of university discourse. The tendency of the institution to ring the death knell for creative thinking and writing was repeatedly decried. Many of the writers maintain that women in the university today run a real danger of becoming more male than men—and all agree that the French university system is hopeless on both scores.

Some of the key struggles fought with the French academic and publishing institutions surfaced in the interviews. The greatest difference between France and the United States was identified as the contrasting reception of "feminism" in and outside the academy. Here in the United

States, a large number of universities have Women's Studies programs; books that claim to be feminist, some even by male feminists, are widely published and read; and, despite the growing evidence of an antifeminist backlash, feminist scholars are present in increasing numbers at the university level.

Only four of the women we interviewed have, however, what would qualify in the United States as traditional academic appointments: Cixous, Kofman, Kristeva, and Marini. The resistance these women's work meets with is epitomized by the fact that they have all fought long, arduous battles for recognition by the French academic institution. These battles are ongoing; for example, Kofman was denied tenure again in 1989 despite her numerous publications. Collin and Irigaray no longer have university positions; Hyvrard teaches economics in the secondary school system. Herrmann has taught both in France and in the United States (at Boston University); Kristeva has a rotating appointment at Columbia University.

The interviews attest to the largely hostile reception of feminist or even feminocentric work by the French academic institutions. Collin noted that the centralized organization of French schools has a paralyzing effect on feminist research and indeed all creative work. Herrmann attested to the complete lack of a feminist tradition in the French university, going so far as to argue that there is no place in it from which to stage a feminist critique of French literature. Kofman, whose recent denial of tenure provoked passionate response in the French media, stated that she and any of her students who attempt to analyze women are just not taken seriously.

Despite the resistance within the university to what these women write, each has published extensively, and nearly all of them have written both fictional and theoretical texts. Their prolific production can in part be explained by the cult of the intellectual in Paris and by the existence of a sophisticated audience for theoretical work. This audience is formed from the general public, nourished by the widespread media coverage of literary and theoretical texts, and relied upon by all French publishers. It is worth mentioning that editorial practices in France are significantly different from those in the United States. Writers in France are encouraged to combine their particular expertise with an inventiveness that includes experimenting with language. This, combined with the rarity of recourse to manuscript review by outside readers, leads to less editorial homogenization and intervention.

Despite their underlying political rivalries, many of the women spoke highly of one publishing house in particular, Editions Des femmes founded by Antoinette Fouque, which publishes primarily work by women. Cixous, one of the women interviewed who publishes with Des femmes, described it as more of a hearth than a publishing house. A few of the women also conceded that the university and publishing institutions do serve some useful functions. Collin insisted that the publishing institution helps women to be heard, and Irigaray stated that the academy can help relay thought to larger audiences. Kristeva noted that the increased presence of women in these institutions is a positive but not secure gain, and pointed out that the university does maintain a certain classical culture in danger of extinction in this age of mass media.

Marini offered publishing as an alternative to university-recognized work, and along with Irigaray and Kristeva, she spoke of the importance of research groups and facilities in France. One example of such a group is the Centre National de la Recherche Scientifique (CNRS), a national research foundation in Paris, not directly affiliated with a university, that provides funding and facilities for research. These research groups, whether organized formally like the CNRS or informally like the ones referred to by Kristeva and Marini, offer French women a space that is less rigidly defined and more conducive to the kind of work they feel needs to be done.

Another aspect to the less than friendly reception of feminist work is the perceived lack of solidarity among French women, signaled by Chawaf. Cixous feels that women in Parisian universities are not interested in women's issues. Many of the women interviewed stressed the importance of work elaborated alone (Collin, Duras, Rochefort, and Wittig) rather than a need for a collective identity as women, an identity that, Irigaray insists, has not yet been defined. There was even a strong resistance to any association with such a collective identity, whether as women or as feminists. Hyvrard stresses the central role feminism has played in her own survival, yet she considers it as only part of a larger set of problems she situates on an international scale; given the rivalries present in the nonunified Women's Movement in France from the outset, she finds a "Holy Alliance" of feminists unlikely. Lemoine-Luccioni finds it repugnant to speak of women as a category, Kofman stresses the metaphysical nature of such a category, and Montrelay emphasizes that she never was a feminist writer. If in the seventies there was a feminist movement in France, then its moment has passed, according to Clément, Duras, and Marini; and Duras and Herrmann sound a pessimistic note about the extent to which men were changed by it. Kofman and Roche-fort, however, point out that the feminist movement will at the least prevent women's work from disappearing again.

There was therefore a strong resistance on the part of these women to being categorized, in terms of either their own status or that of their work, as "French," as "women," or as particular kinds of "writers." Many of these women are *not* French by birth, have not particularly felt oppressed as women, do not consider themselves writers, etc. This resistance is not, however, only a result of "personal stories." Their resistance is also grounded in a complex postwar French intellectual history: from the thorough questioning of identity (including national identity), to the theoretical work on the impossibility of maintaining the binary oppositions essential to identity (e.g., man/woman), to the complex reconfigurations of what "writing" is and does. Thus it is extremely difficult for women writers in France to accept even the terms of our American feminist debates.

Indeed, since Simone de Beauvoir's celebrated declaration in 1949 that "one is not born, but rather becomes a woman," all the women interviewed here have struggled to shift intellectual debate—including debate about sexual difference—from its deadlock with/in binary terms (same/other, man/woman, oral/written, etc.). It is hardly surprising, then, that those interviewed felt the need to situate themselves carefully within our at times intentionally provocative, at times unintentionally facile formulations and characterizations. For example, the question of discipleship, of the relation women intellectuals in France have to the long-standing tradition of male "master thinkers," met with contrasting responses. Lemoine-Luccioni foregrounded her "indebtedness" to La-can, while Kofman reacted strongly to our characterization of her as Derridean.

As their comments on feminism might suggest, another factor con-tributing to these women's reluctance to be categorized is the compli-cated relationship women in France have to the feminisms that surfaced during the social and political turmoil of 1968 in France. From the particularities of the antifeminist tradition in French institutions to the splintering of the MLF (the Women's Liberation Movement) in the late 1970s, there have been widespread misgivings about feminism.[7] Whether

[7] The MLF, or "Mouvement de Libération des Femmes," was the name the French press gave in 1970 to various radical women's groups that had surfaced since 1968. The name was used by the general public to designate the women's movement in France until it became the official trademark of the group "Psychanalyse et Politique" in 1979. See the

feminism is the appropriate analysis of the oppression of women in French society, and whether it can provide the needed solution, has been the subject of heated debate. Indeed, many of these women, especially those with strong ties to and rigorous training in psychoanalysis, have insisted instead upon the repression of the feminine in Western culture and the untoward consequences that have resulted from this repression for both men and women.[8]

Thus by U.S. feminist standards, the attitudes toward women expressed in these interviews range wildly. In fact, women meet with sharp criticism from many sides. Chawaf speaks of the degradation in writing by women, although Duras claims that the most important books and films being produced today are by women. In contrast to the rivalry among women alluded to by Chawaf and Duras, Collin feels that women are an important way to relay other women's work. Rochefort tells of women's sexism, Kofman finds few truly innovative women in philosophy, and Wittig states that to say that writers have been excluded from the canon because they are women partakes of theories of victimization. Lemoine-Luccioni is convinced that it was no coincidence that Freud, Lacan, and Einstein were men.

Despite the reluctance of many interviewed to be categorized as women—most strongly expressed by Wittig's decision not to respond to our "writing as a woman" question—and the refusal to posit the specificity of woman, most women did nuance their position on woman and women. Chawaf said it was both a privilege and a problem to be a woman; Cixous found it impossible not to respond as a woman, even if she, along with Kristeva, worried about being obligated to do so. Clément feared the distortion women writers suffer at the hands of the mass media. Collin and Marini insisted that while there were times when they did write as women, other subject positions are available to them, which are necessary for creative work. Herrmann felt that what is personal in her writing comes from her woman's language and experience. Irigaray linked what she terms the incomprehensible split between the one who is a woman and the one who writes to the pseudoneutrality of the law of tradition. Kofman, while denying that she writes as a woman, does

---

three introductions by Marks and Courtivron to *New French Feminisms*, as well as Maïte Albistur and Daniel Armogathe's *Histoire du féminisme français* (Paris: Des femmes, 1977).

[8] Elaine Marks first formulated the oppression/repression analysis of American versus French feminisms. See "Women and Literature in France," *Signs* (1978), vol. 3, no. 4, pp. 832–842

state that one can't separate a text from the sexual positioning of its author and does classify her work as feminist. Rochefort places her emphasis on experience. According to her, biology has nothing to do with it: she compares writing as a woman to writing as a Buddhist, a samurai, or a coal miner.

Central to the postwar French intellectual scene that serves as the backdrop for these women's work is French psychoanalytic theory, particularly as elaborated by Lacan in his rereading of Freud and pursued and transformed in the work of current analysts. Among those we interviewed, Irigaray, Kristeva, Lemoine-Luccioni, and Montrelay are practicing psychoanalysts, while nearly all the other women have published texts dealing with psychoanalysis. Many have themselves been analyzed.

They do not, however, all share the same opinion of the analytic institution. Cixous registered her dismay that some American feminists have attempted to get rid of Freud, and referred to his discoveries as our richest treasure, while Clément, her coauthor of *The Newly Born Woman,* reminds us that psychoanalysis and the university are "female careers" that operate as a ruse of History. Collin described the diminishing importance of psychoanalysis and the essentialist impasse to which it led, but credited psychoanalysis with taking sexual difference seriously. Hyvrard and Kristeva echoed Collin's sense of the limits of analysis. In Hyvrard's case, these perceived limits led her to write "Traité du désordre" (Treatise on disorder), whereas Kristeva has responded by participating in an encounter between psychoanalysis and neuroscience.

Irigaray urged that if we are not seduced by theories and problems of male genealogy, then psychoanalysis may be of great use to us in our task of defining our identity as women and establishing our own genealogies, and that it can free us from our confinement within patriarchal culture. Kofman feels that her own analysis played a large role in her writing, but that the institution of analysis in France represses originality. Lemoine-Luccioni, on the other hand, assured us that she has never experienced any prejudice against her as a woman in analytic circles, and that in her field women have occupied whatever place they wanted without difficulty. Marini cautioned that psychoanalysis works too well as an interpretive grid for reading literature. Montrelay, on the other hand, praised psychoanalysis as one of the highest and most valuable forms of human freedom, noting that it is the object of censorship in the media and of persecution in totalitarian states.

The importance of psychoanalytic theory to the work of most of the women interviewed is evident in their remarks on sexual difference and sexuality. Blurring sexual difference was advocated by some women but resisted by others. Kofman described that gesture as a feminist strategy in her own work. Marini spoke of sexualities in the plural and discussed the different types of writing that result from the varying expression of these sexualities. She felt that the lack of sexual differentiation can be useful. Kristeva worried that blurring sexual difference would lead to the death of desire; she advocated calling upon our bisexuality.

Three women speak of male homosexuality in their analysis of the role men play in patriarchal institutions. Chawaf described some men's negative response to work by women writers as repressed homosexuality, as did Duras, while Lemoine-Luccioni suggested that the male homosexuality of certain institutions explained their resistance to the admission of women.

Two American writers have offered alternative analyses of such male responses. Eve Kosofsky Sedgwick speaks not of male homosexuality but of "male homosocial desire," and of the way male bonding operates across the bodies of women. Craig Owens cautions against confusing such male bonding with homosexuality, calling attention to the homophobia such an analysis disguises.[9] This sensitivity to homophobia, as well as to heterosexism, is evident in Wittig's work. In her interview, Wittig discusses lesbians not in terms of their sexuality but as a sociological group, as people trying to escape the class of women.

The emphasis on Freudian- and Lacanian-inspired psychoanalysis in the work of some of these women may puzzle or alienate certain American readers. This type of psychoanalysis is intrapsychic, and privileges the (oedipal) family, agencies, and drives. Many feminists have criticized the work of Freud, Lacan, and some of the analysts we interviewed as static, sexist, male-oriented, and pessimistic, leaving no room for change or intervention and relying too heavily on biological metaphors, to the point of engaging in essentialism. Some feminists look instead to intersubjective psychoanalysis (e.g., developmental psychology and object relations) to address issues of the mother-child bond, child development, individuation, and autonomy.

[9] Eve Kosofsky Sedgwick, *Between Men: English Literature and Male Homosocial Desire* (New York: Columbia University Press, 1985); Craig Owens, "Outlaws: Gay Men in Feminism," in Alice A. Jardine and Paul Smith, eds., *Men in Feminism* (New York: Methuen, 1987), pp. 219–32.

The criticisms leveled at "French psychoanalysis" are, however, just as puzzling to the French analysts/writers as Lacanian analysis is to many American feminists. French analysts/writers would insist that by rereading Freud via Saussure, not to mention Marx, Nietzsche, and Heidegger, we can thoroughly investigate how we are constructed. Instead of assuming that we are either "men" or "women"—which these French women find essentialist—we can examine the constructions of femininity and masculinity in both sexes and therefore change them. In addition, far from ignoring the question of the mother and child, writers and theorists such as Chawaf, Cixous, Hyvrard, Irigaray, and Kristeva in fact have rendered the question of the maternal and the preoedipal central to their theoretical systems and fictional explorations.

Some of the perceived differences between these analytical approaches may stem from the fact that once thinking is imported, translated, and edited to conform to another semantic and syntactic (ideological) system, it runs the risk of being rendered less complex. That risk is compounded when the thinking is intended for pedagogical and/or practical applications, and by the time lag between the writing and translating of texts. Despite these difficulties, there have been a number of attempts to address the concerns of both intrapsychic and intersubjective psychoanalysis. Some examples include the work of Jane Gallop, in *The Daughter's Seduction* (Ithaca: Cornell University Press, 1982); Juliet Mitchell and Jacqueline Rose, in their introductions to *Feminine Sexuality: Jacques Lacan and the école freudienne* (New York and London: W. W. Norton and Pantheon Books, 1985), and Jessica Benjamin in her book *The Bonds of Love: Psychoanalysis, Feminism, and the Problem of Domination* (New York: Pantheon, 1988).

It is in hope of furthering such interdisciplinary work on women, writing, and the politics of theories—feminist and/or psychoanalytic— that we have gathered these fifteen women together in this book. For the debates addressed by them here provide timely material for English-speaking readers. They offer an opportunity to listen to an influential group of writers work to shift the scenes of writing, psychoanalysis, feminist theory, and literature through their ongoing engagement with questions of self-representation, institutional affiliation, and posterity.

WE ARE extremely grateful to the fifteen women who agreed to allow us to "canon"-ize—in the musical sense of compose—their voices here.

MANY OTHER people also made this project possible in its multiple stages and forms.

We are grateful to the Harvard Graduate Society for a grant for translating and editing expenses.

We would also like to thank all the women who translated these texts: Patricia Baudoin, Lauren Doyle-McCombe, Heidi Gilpin, Katherine A. Jensen, Deborah C. Jenson, Christine Laennec, Mary-Kay Miller, Carrie Noland, Janice Orion, Leyla Rouhi, and Margaret Whitford.

We are also grateful to Thérèse Chevallier, Emily Eakin, and Susan Fuerst for typing the manuscript at various stages; to Bettina Brandt and Stephanie Hull for assisting us in compiling the annotations and bibliography, and to Deborah Jenson for writing the contributors notes. Special thanks to Marti Hohmann for her editorial acumen.

Due to the significant amount of translation and transformation of these texts—for which we thank all those who assisted us—errors may remain. We of course accept final responsibility for any and all inadequacies.

NANCY SPERO graciously allowed us to use her "To the Revolution" for our cover, for which we warmly thank her, as well as Josh Baer and Regina Joseph at the Josh Baer Gallery in New York City.

Anne Menke would like to thank Stephen Pogue for his unfailing support; her daughter Alexandra Menke Pogue for her *joie de vivre;* and Nour Hachache, Peggy Sue Hight, Tyra Goodman, and Tara Khodabashi for their loving attention to Alexandra, which made this prolonged project possible. Alice Jardine is grateful to the many students at Harvard University who inspire her to continually question the place from which she speaks, and to Richard Ledes for introducing her to Nancy Spero's work.

Our various editors, Joan DeJean, Carolyn G. Heilbrun, and Nancy K. Miller, and our executive editor at Columbia University Press, Jennifer Crewe, were extraordinarily supportive during the preparation of the manuscript for the Gender and Culture series, as well as for the *Yale French Studies* article that preceded it. We are also grateful to Karen Mitchell, our fine copyeditor. We wish to extend special thanks to Nancy Miller for her expertise, guidance, and friendship during both projects.

ALICE A. JARDINE AND ANNE M. MENKE

1
Chantal Chawaf

TRANSLATED BY CHRISTINE LAENNEC

Question 1: What does it mean to you to write at the end of the twentieth century?

—It brings up the possibility and the necessity of seeking out new directions. For literature, which functions through writing, has not tried to verbalize certain spaces that are without words, without a grammar —those spaces one could call the preverbal. The verbalized representation of these spaces through literary languages should increase our consciousness as well as our knowledge of women, the feminine, life, and men. It should open up communication between women and men, and among women.

Excerpts from this interview, translated by Anne M. Menke, appeared in *Yale French Studies* (1988), vol. 75.

—(AM) So, in your opinion, these things haven't yet been done, they still need to be done. Do you think we are in the process of accomplishing them?

—I think that part of this work hasn't been done at all. There's a gigantic repression [operating] that is becoming more acute, that almost amounts to an interdiction of speech, especially in the realm of affects and the body.

—(AJ) I would say that's the case more and more. And we're almost at the end of the twentieth century.

—The early seventies saw the birth of multiple creations by women who rejected the barriers that prohibit us from speaking. This feminine-feminist surge seemed to be on the offensive, and people responded to us as if we were attacking something. And then we gave our response. I think that instead of playing war games on a battlefield, attacking, defending, and attacking again, we have to adopt a different strategy. This is indispensable if we want to survive and continue to be free to create and explore. We have to retreat and become part of a resistance [movement] in order to make and safeguard a space [for writing the body].

The bestselling books being published in France today are by women writers, but there is no new writing, no real writing of the body or the affects in this feminine merchandise-literature. The cultural movement [that consisted] of a feminine inquiry into feminism with a definition of it and of the carnal has been coopted, taken away from women. And now other women are writing [books] that deny the evolution of feminine thought. There is a degradation of feminine expression and feminine speech in the novel, in what we still dare to call literature. This degradation completely closes off [the possibility of writing] authentic literature, that is to say, living expression, which goes beyond the feminine problem, the problem of women, and touches upon the problems of art, creation, and the freedom to create. Here one must question (or suspect?) publishers and the media. They publish very little of this work, [even though it is] being written. We must be able to communicate in our work. But the possibility of doing this is in danger of being curbed. That is exactly what wasn't the case in the early seventies.

Question 2: Is it valid/of value to write as a woman, and is it part of your writing practice today?

—It's a privilege today to be a woman—there is a lot to be said on that subject—but it's also a problem of identity. This is because of the experience a woman has of her body, her relationship to her mother or motherhood—even if she doesn't experience all this as a mother. Women are not necessarily mothers, but they do nonetheless have a relationship to their mothers that is completely different from the mother-son relationship. Women, as Robert Stoller has shown, remain closer to the feminine because they don't need to distance themselves from it so as to become virile.[1] The body, pregnancy, the world of the flesh, of affects, the entire world of generation, of the prenatal, the preverbal, the pregenital, origins—even if she never becomes a mother, a woman is better informed about all this than any man ever will be. If she gives birth, obviously she lives out motherhood as no man does. If she nurses a child, no man has that experience. So women also have a connection to life as it is being made in a way men don't. Ethically, metaphysically, there's a whole current of thought [in women] that opens onto life, that opens onto a symbolization of living things.

On the other hand, the son, in order not to become effeminate, separates himself from his mother and must separate himself from her precisely in order to consider himself a man, to consider himself masculine. Therefore, very early on he must do this work of detachment that will be encoded into his culture, into all his symbolic and cultural work, into all his thought and behavior. And so already there is something there in complete opposition to the world of origins. One will remain, the other will have to distance himself. Distance himself from what? From this feminine body that contains life, where life begins biologically, from which life comes.

As soon as we begin to think biologically, we have a tendency to limit life to the experience women have of the body, as if biological difference were not symbolized, as if it had no opening or had not become civilized, as if it could remain something barbarous or wild, something without language—what Lacan calls feminine jouissance, the body without words.[2] Whereas here, precisely, women have a marvelous opportunity to give a language to this body that has been deprived of words. The body has been too limited—it has been limited to nothing

[1] See, for example, Stoller's book *Sex and Gender: On the Development of Masculinity and Femininity* (New York: Science House, 1968).

[2] See Juliet Mitchell and Jacqueline Rose, eds.; Jacqueline Rose, trans., *Feminine Sexuality: Jacques Lacan and the école freudienne* (New York: Norton and Pantheon, 1985).

but organs: when one speaks of the body, right away, in the case of both men and women, one refers to their sexual difference or to their sexual organs. That limits the body, and the body stops there. But the body is immense, infinite, living, and imaginary. The body is the very possibility of thinking about the condition of living, it's the vocation of giving life and of preserving life, it's a responsibility in itself, an entire ethics, an entire consciousness.

Man has reduced the body to pure eroticism, to relationships between men and women—so-called love relationships—to precise, specific moments that are completely separated from life and the social. And I think that what has been marginalized and through religion put in opposition to the spirit—the body, the flesh—all that has been stamped with guilt and shame and needs to be socialized. I won't even mention how woman in certain religions or writings is considered impurity itself or the devil. Something of that has remained in people's minds: that fear, that fear of woman, that fear of the body and of life. Men and women humanly share this precious body, life, affectivity. I think that woman, by virtue of her different sexual experience, can initiate man into what frightens him, into this feminine that he has completely separated from his own identity and society, a society in which we all live. I believe that there's an immense empty space that has been blocked and inhibited because it was frightening and because man knew it less well. It brought man back to the problem of his identification with the mother and his love for the mother, while also bringing him back to the fear and threat the mother represents for the son's virility and masculinity. And that's a knot that needs to be untied.

[All this constitutes] a cultural work site for the twenty-first century, a symbolic work site where building must take place within language. When I gave a lecture at an American university, a man told me, "Oh yes, I like what you said very much"—he claimed that he understood everything. And then he said to me, "Yes, but this preverbal, this body, this affectivity, this feminine—you can't symbolize them! You have to go through the phallus, through the father." According to this theory, women can only be fantasized, that is, socialization and culture occur exclusively through the phallus, through the name of the father, whereas the body, feminine jouissance, woman, and the mother all obstruct symbolic language. So the body is relegated to the body, jouissance to feminine jouissance, and woman is identified with this body and jouissance. And if woman enters into language, she can only enter into it as something that is fantasized, [or exists] only in fantasy.

But fantasy is the imaginary separated from reality. And so language would separate woman from her reality. For woman to enter into language, for the body to enter into language, woman would have to be separated from the reality of her desire, in all its intensity. We would only be imagined, imaginary. But then where does that leave us? Hesitating, real, desiring, we have no language. Why? Because we are supposedly not representable. Lacan says that what is desirable about the penis is the phallus, whereas woman in her hollowness, in her invisible sexual organ, is much less desirable. A famous psychoanalyst says that the female organ is much less desirable than the male organ and that's why, in his opinion, the male organ calls forth representation and symbolization. No one wants—it would seem—to represent the female sexual organ. And so representation goes through the phallus. This amounts to a masculine identification. We cannot have other representations except through this intermediary and by turning away from ourselves and our own bodies.

I vehemently protest this—and I'm not the only one. Why are we not representable? Why should this uterus that carries life, that gives life, pleasure, and suffering, that is eminently anchored in life, not be representable? I'm thinking about the Greeks, for whom the logos and discourse signified order and moderation—as opposed to immoderation, barbarism, wildness, and cannibalism. The latter surely referred to the body, with its desires, its preverbal, with what precedes education, its drives, original life, and its not-yet-organized intimacy. In short, the ambivalence of what is alive and living on the level of the affects was and is frightening. And according to our civilization, it should not and cannot enter into language, which is order and moderation. For the Greeks, immoderation is unrepresentable, it is *the* unrepresentable, it is the unnameable. Life at its origin, carnal life, is the definition of what is barbarous, wild, and overflowing, in opposition to discourse and the logos.

We, as women today, in our logos and discourse, have to articulate the excess, desire, the uncensored body, and life—not an idealized life, but life just as it is, with its problems, anxieties, and frightening aspects. We must do so because it is precisely this fear of life that has kept life outside culture. Where has life been located? On the side of madness, jouissance, love quickly made and just as quickly forgotten, and eroticism. This misplacement of life has authorized all the disdain, all the sadisms, masochisms, and pornography, and, finally, all the hatred of the body. It has also led to linguistic trafficking about the body, wherein one calls love what often hides the most abominable refusal of life, the body, and the other: perversity, what Robert Stoller calls "the eroticization of hatred."

—(AJ) I just finished coediting, with Paul Smith, a collection of essays on men and feminism.[3] There are ten articles by men, and ten by women, in which the authors try to articulate to some extent what the effect is of men discovering, or beginning to discover—some men, very few, a minority—these spaces, these connections. First, they discover feminism; they listen, they understand at the symbolic level, they understand at the political-social level, and they learn to speak the language of sociopolitical feminism. And if they have the stamina, if they don't turn away, if they don't try to escape it, if they continue to think, some of them even begin to be attentive to this further struggle that is really a symbolic, political, and economic one: that is, they start to discover that other space of which you have been speaking. And there are quite a few men in this collection who are trying to speak that space, and who on the level of discourse are becoming "more women than the women."

—I'm not surprised.

—(AJ) But the men in this collection are American and British. I don't have the impression that they represent the same phenomenon as in France where a certain generation of male theorists—Derrida and company—has discovered the feminine and has talked about it "without women."[4] In this collection at least, it's not exactly that particular theorization of the feminine that is at issue. It's more a question of a real experience. And these men get angry, and, as they try to understand, they even change physically. They change their lives, they change their discourse, they become very feminine. But at a certain point when I or other women in the collection try to say, "But I am the woman here—" then they get really angry! They get angry and they say, "But no! You are a man because you are trying to say that I cannot be a woman!" And thus the discourse begins to spin, within an incredible whirlpool where we end up arguing about who is more woman than women? But where are women in all this?

—(AM) "Cherchez la femme!"[5]

---

[3] Alice Jardine and Paul Smith, eds., *Men in Feminism* (New York: Methuen, 1987).

[4] See Alice Jardine, *Gynesis: Configurations of Woman and Modernity* (Ithaca, N.Y.: Cornell University Press, 1985).

[5] *Cherchez la femme* is an old French expression with several meanings. While *chercher femme* signifies to get married, *cherchez la femme* means to search for the emotional

—(AJ) Cherchez la femme, yes. But at the end of the twentieth century! And I wanted to ask this question: have you found, in your context, that there is a small minority of men who are discovering the spaces of which you have been speaking? And if so, have you come up against the problem of having to insist upon your position as the woman?

—Yes, there is a risk in men discovering their femininity. The verbal and cultural expression of the feminine, in the unconscious of a man, sends him back to the mother, to the primitive symbiosis that he formed with her. Returning to the mother risks devirilizing and feminizing man who, through education, has had to silence what in him originally belonged to the feminine. Yes, I know what you are talking about, I'm familiar with it. Which is exactly why it's important to define the feminine and to make clear to women the importance of making themselves known as women, of helping [other] women to make themselves known to men, and the necessity of helping men to find their own femininity, to express it and to be able to distinguish it from our femininity as women. They have their body, we have ours; they have their affectivity, we have our affectivity. That is how we can encounter one another. If we encounter one another it is because we are different. It's from the starting point of that difference that men and women can love one another. Otherwise, it starts to become perverse: centering everything around the self, around oneself. There is no longer an other. Men who want to coopt everything continue, in fact, to reject the other. They have always rejected it, they are still doing so.

—(AJ) I find that to be true as well. Another effect of this perversity is that there is a refusal on the part of men to explore a masculinity that would not be a traditional metaphysical masculinity eroticized only in a certain way, etc. There is a violent refusal to explore an other or to create another masculinity. Because in finding femininity these men feel they have solved the problem, there's no more work to do. Everything is settled.

—There's a repressed homosexuality speaking and that's it. It doesn't go any further than that. . . . Antoinette Fouque[6] said that people have always talked about female hysteria and penis envy. But Antoinette said

investment in something, and is also a synonym for the adage, "Behind every great man, there's a woman." It was, incidentally, also the name of a French television game show.

[6] Antoinette Fouque, a psychoanalyst, was the spokeswoman for the controversial women's group "Psychanalyse et Politique" (Psychoanalysis and Politics) founded in 1968. She was instrumental in the establishment of the Editions Des femmes publishing house.

that we should talk about male hysteria and uterus envy. I was happy to hear that, because I've never ceased to notice the jealousy that man has of the feminine and woman, of the womb that can bear and give life. They say, "Yes, but even so, it would be nice if men could get pregnant too." They have a problem that, far from being resolved by our work, is being exacerbated. They can't take it any more.

—(AJ) And that's called. . . .

—Envy. They envy us. They have always envied us. Men have never stopped envying women. That certainly explains a lot about misogyny. And here we are, more creative than ever: we think, we reflect, we act, we do a lot of things that they do too. And we continue to bring life into the world. And we continue to have our jouissance. I think that, even sexually, men envy the pleasure of women. . . . I think what we are talking about is the feminine richness of women, which is a problem, which is *the* cultural problem. It's time for us to symbolize this feminine and to have an aesthetics and our [own] culture; it's time to teach men to love us. We need to do this in order to permit ourselves to love them, so that instead of all this death and hatred there will be something of life that wins out: that, for me, is to some extent the literary motivation of the twenty-first century.

Question 3: Many women writing today find themselves, for the first time in history, at the center of such institutions as the university and psychoanalysis. In your opinion, will this new placement of women help them to enter the twentieth-century canon, and if so, will they be in the heart of this corpus or (still) in the footnotes?

—It's not enough to be a woman or to be of the female sex in order for the work that we're doing to change things. On the level of the feminine and in relation to this cultural problem of women, women who work in the institution must work concurrently from another angle different from that of the institution. Unfortunately, this is not the case for all the women who have entered the institution. They often go into the institution only because they have abdicated something, they have renounced something, and they are soaking up this somewhat phallic culture.

—(AM) So in your opinion it can be harmful for women to enter the university?

—No, on the contrary, it's completely necessary. Only, you have to have an awareness and a lot of courage, and maybe a fighting spirit, a strategic mind, a whole diplomacy, and subtlety. But sometimes certain women repress or destroy their affects, their bodies. And then they are lost. What they do will not bring anything new, it won't enrich anything.

— (AJ) With regard to these issues, what do you think is happening within the institution of psychoanalysis in France today?

— (AM) That brings us back to what you were saying earlier about the problem of whether we have to go further than Lacan. If one no longer refuses the entrance of woman into the symbolic, will the fact that there are now quite a few women psychoanalysts change anything?

— It should change something if these women want it to. If they desire it. But do they want that, do they desire that? Because women's unconscious moves toward the feminine, but sometimes women's unconscious moves toward the masculine as well, toward the seduction of the father. That's when it turns completely against women.

Question 4: Today we are seeing women produce literary, philosophical, and psychoanalytical theory of recognized importance, and, parallel to this, we are also seeing a new fluidity in the borderlines among disciplines and genres of writing. Will this parallelism lead only to women being welcomed alongside men, or to a definitive blurring of these categories?

— It seems to me that if everything went well it could change things. And that if it doesn't change anything, if it puts women on one side and men on the other, it would be because there hasn't been any communication between men and women, because something in all this work on the feminine hasn't been assimilated. Partitioning, separation, is always dangerous.

— (AJ) In the United States a lot of women, especially intellectual women, have noted that they are not being read, that men just don't read them.

— (AM) Do you have the impression that this is what's happening in France?

— I have the impression that when a woman's work goes in a direction that renews or changes something, then men don't read it. But when the work goes in a conformist, reactionary direction, men read it right away; they don't even pay attention to the fact that a woman wrote it. Conformist women often link up with men's old fantasies. Otherwise, let's just say that men feel as if women's books don't concern them, they concern women. Men don't read women's books. And even if men want to be positive, their response to a book that deals with the feminine is to say: "Oh yes, that's very good for women, that must please women, women must like that!"—but they don't think that the book concerns them just as much as it does women. Men remain outsiders.

—(AM) So there's a refusal to listen to what women are saying?

—Yes, I think so—I'm trying to speak in more general terms. To judge from my individual experience, it's nonetheless true that when men are interested in what you are doing, then they change, and something happens. Men are transformed, something opens up and is transformed, and that's encouraging. But in order for these men to come to you, there is an entire social barrier, which comes very close to being a barrier of power, interest, economy, and politics that needs to be removed. It is much more difficult to remove that barrier than to move a man individually. It is easier to participate in changing an individual through our work than to participate in changing a culture, mentality, or society: those things that constitute and inhibit men.

—(AJ) Do you get letters or responses from the men who read you?

—Oh yes. I have had reactions from some young male writers, from the new generation of men who are looking for themselves. They think they can find themselves with our help. Some of them are fascinated by a kind of writing like my own; they are partly envious of it, and keep a close eye on it to try to get hold of it. They try to steal it and appropriate it for themselves. . . . These men try to reproduce my writing, and that's a little stupid because it's necessarily less authentic. Instead of expressing themselves, instead of understanding that what they have to do is come up with an equivalent, these young male writers in fact lose their own expression, the liberation and symbolization of their own femininity and of everything they don't yet know about themselves. And so they continue not to know themselves, and they end up still being in competition with us. I see that all the time; I've experienced it a lot and it's not at all positive.

Question 5: Given the problematic and the politics of the categories of the canon, and given the questions we've been dealing with, do you think your oeuvre will be included in the twentieth-century canon, and if so, how will it be presented? In your opinion, what will the content of the canon be?

—For us to be happy (I'm speaking in the plural) to be included in the canons of the twentieth century—personally, in order for me to be happy to be included in it—it would at least have to be a canon that was faithful to what I have tried to do and to what I've tried to change, to what has changed through what I've written. If it's a canon that completely coopts you in order to classify you as a continuation of the nineteenth century or as pastiche, then I'm not at all interested in being part of it. I want nothing to do with it. I have a chance of being included only if the canon-makers acknowledge that what I'm trying to do really goes beyond me as an individual. I will be included only if people recognize that there are new things to bring into existence precisely on the symbolic level, that what I am doing is valuable, necessary work—but it will also depend on society and on social evolution. Unfortunately, I don't know. Really, I think that if you continue [to write], it's because you have confidence and people accept you. You have to be fierce, you really have to have a lot of courage. We all need a lot of courage. And we also need solidarity among women, which unfortunately, in France at any rate, is far from being the case.

—(AJ) The same is true elsewhere I think; certainly it is true in the United States. I think that today there are, among the many quandaries of the moment, a couple of problems causing a lot of confusion for feminists: the potential relationship of men to feminism, as we've mentioned. But there's also the question of women's relationships with other women. Several articles and books have been written recently about the necessary de-idealization of feminism's "all women together"—articles, for example, about competition and anger between women. This particular question was forced upon me through personal experience. I had no idea that things would come to that.

—Me neither! I began publishing ten or eleven years ago—I was full of naïveté, illusions, and love for women, and I continue every day to lose a few more of those illusions. Women are formidable! They don't realize the damage they are doing to themselves in order to gain themselves. They don't realize that they lose themselves in losing others. They always need to step on toes, to push away everything that comes from other women; you'd think that anything created by another woman bothers them. And I see this—I have specific examples in mind—happening all over. And personally, I'm just the opposite. I just don't understand. Women detest one another. Not in general, obviously, there are exceptions and I'm talking about France, but women's interactions with one another can be just awful, nothing but a narcissism that is hateful to the other, a refusal to admit the other's work, a misunderstanding of it. And if the other one's work ever talks about women or lets women speak. . . . There are many women writers, even great women writers, who hate women.

Question 6: Do you think that it's possible to talk about the specificity of women's writing today?

—It's still too early. And I'll tell you why. There aren't enough women [writers]—not in France anyway. We shouldn't partition things, especially not between France and the United States, but I have to do it to some extent to answer your question. In France, there aren't enough women who have proven that they have a specific work to do, artistically or culturally, work that can also be done in other cultural or artistic realms, in film. Literary work remains marginal; there aren't enough women working to express the feminine whose work can be spoken of and made known. It's also dangerous [to speak of women writers]. Recently someone told me what a critic had said to him about me: "Oh! No man could write what she writes." I think that's dangerous. And he thought he was paying me a great compliment. It's very dangerous because, first of all, I don't agree: any man could write the masculine equivalent of what I am writing. Any man could write about all this work on the affect, all this deciphering, this verbalization of living life that I'm doing in realms that are still nonverbalized or that belong to the preverbal, and therefore to the archaic. Men have to do it just as much as we do, they know it as much, they have it as much, they have a body just as much, and they are just as human as we are, so they can do it too. Furthermore, another woman, any other woman who does this work, who creates, is different. Each woman is different, no two have the same face: style is the individual.

—(AJ) You mean style isn't the man (à la Lacan)?!

—A woman's style is the woman! Style is the woman. But there are as many styles as there are women. So it's dangerous. Rather than specificity, I would prefer to say that there are realms into which literature hasn't been introduced or which haven't been introduced into literature. These realms have been left to hospitals, psychoanalysis, and psychiatry. They have been called regressive, but they are essentially the realms of the body, the feminine, desire, and the enigma of fusion with the body of the mother. These realms haven't been expressed yet. They cannot be, for they don't yet have the means to be symbolized because they are missing a tongue, a language. And that expression is for us to do, we have yet to do it. Personally, that's what interests me so much— in the end it goes beyond this specificity of women, because any artist, any creator can do it. But obviously, as women there is a certain experience, a certain proximity that we have to the body, and to the mother. The regressive is the return to the maternal: men know the regressive just as well as women do; but obviously who knows this return to the maternal, the maternal itself, better than we do? Who knows this woman's body better than we do? As women, we have more information about it and therefore we can express and convey more than men can about this realm. But men will have to do it in an equivalent form, in the realms where we cannot do it. Men have to deal with the whole question of the masculine affect: everything men experience and feel but don't necessarily put into words. If they do put it into words, then they will have information that we don't have and that we are missing. Whence the interest for both men and women to work in this direction, which is the same one: the return to the original, which I call regressive, and which only verbal language, by giving it words with which to speak, can help evolve.

—(AM) Is there a difference between what women write and feminine writing [*écriture féminine*]? For example, when Hélène Cixous wrote—a long time ago now—about feminine writing in "Laugh of the Medusa,"[7] she insisted that the sex of writing does not correspond to the writer's biological sex, and she gave more examples of men who practice feminine writing than women. Does this mean men write feminine writing "better" than do women?

—I don't think so. That's an opinion that touches on the transsexual, that's a question of transsexualism in language.

—(AM) Yes, that's what I wanted to be clear on. For you there's a difference.

—To go back to where we began, if we circumscribe the feminine in the realm of the body, if therefore in the realm of the body we don't evade the genesis of the body, we will take the body in its entirety and not chop it up, we will accept it. There will be tolerance, because the work to be done is to tolerate what has been classified as unrepresenta-

[7] Published in Elaine Marks and Isabelle de Courtivron, eds., *New French Feminisms* (New York: Schocken Books, 1981).

ble, unnameable, because it was rejected as frightening. So we should welcome this body in its entirety. The body is also biological, however. Now we have to spiritualize the biological, and that's a work in itself to be done, to spiritualize precisely those things that belong to the categories of wildness, regression, sickness, symptoms, etc. Because the body is lacking spiritualization, it's lacking a language. Therefore, to say that a man writes feminine writing better than a woman does, that is, to say that he can write better than a woman, is perhaps only saying that there will be a writing that will better express his own femininity than a woman will express her male femininity. But to say that he writes woman better, that he writes the body of a woman better than a woman can write it, well, no. A woman can translate herself better. She will more genuinely want to make a place for woman's body in the symbolic and in literary work. No, no, no, because a man doesn't have the same knowledge, the same consciousness, he is necessarily separated. His work would be a work of separation and what I am talking about is a work of union, where language, writing, and the body would be united at last. And who better than we women can do this work with regard to a woman's body?

The biological is a word that has made people terribly afraid and it really is frightening and will continue to be frightening if nothing comes to take it out of its own frightening physical-chemical realm, because from that perspective it seems very inhuman and very dehumanized. We must civilize and spiritualize the biological, and introduce it into culture. We separate it out completely from the spirit and thought, and as long as there is this language separation, there will be a division of the living, there will be inequality between affects and sensitivity on one hand and culture and the social on the other.

— (AJ) I find that a certain feminism has participated in this by saying that we can't talk about biology, we can only talk about culture. I think that even if politically I agree that we can have access to the biological only through culture. . . .

— But exactly: a culture has to be made that will find access, through the word, to the body of language, that will find access to the source of the life of words, of the meaning of a sentence: access to the body and its perceptions, to which language must give words.

— (AJ) It is strange to think that feminism may have participated in this fear of speaking of the body by refusing (at least until recently) to speak of biology.

—But look at what is happening today with respect to biology in science. If the biological isn't backed up by much thought and work on sensitivity, affectivity, and the human, it will be more separated than ever. Then the body may well dominate—and the opposite will happen: the spirit will no longer be able to do anything against the body or matter. And that will be terrible. I think that, on the contrary, we men and women have to unite, we have to get rid of partitions and break down barriers. Men and women together need to envisage the word "fusion," which frightens everyone even though it underlies all desire, even though it is what constitutes desire. And this desire for fusion can be symbolized, even if it is a desire for symbolic fusion; it will continue to respond to desire and generate life to avert misfortune. We have to work toward a living rapprochement, the rapprochement to the body, for language to become humanized.

2

Hélène Cixous

TRANSLATED BY DEBORAH JENSON AND LEYLA ROUHI

Question 1: What does it mean to you to write at the end of the twentieth century?

—I haven't followed this question to the letter, I haven't taken into account the end of the twentieth century. The theme of endings isn't in me. *Famishment [faim]*, yes, but *finishing [fin]*, probably not.[1] I can respond, on the other hand, to the question of "writing in the twentieth century"—at any rate I can try to let myself be questioned by an era. In terms of textual production, the end of the twentieth century is the age of mass media, the age of the greatest possible threat to their opposite,

Excerpts from this interview, translated by Deborah W. Carpenter [Jenson], appeared in *Yale French Studies* (1988), vol. 75.

[1] *Faim* (hunger) and *fin* (end) are homonyms, whence Cixous's play on words.

which is writing. The language of mass media, the discourse of mass media, has fallen on us like a curse in the last generation. It may be that for me, writing at this point means more than it did when I began.

When I started writing in the sixties, I was pushed by a subjective total need, entirely absorbing and stemming from my earliest childhood, to enter the land of writing. At that time I was in a state of anguish, that is to say of joy; I wasn't in touch with the sociocultural scene at all. I was filled with the desire to find myself in a world that wasn't marked by one century or another. I realized fairly rapidly, even while I believed that I had entered writing in its eternity, that this timeless writing was being threatened from all sides by the events of the time, the violence of the age, a violence that goes by the name of mass media and that wages war on us by all audiovisual, journalistic, and editorial means, thanks, in effect, to this sort of gigantic structure so profoundly hostile to a true culture and its ceaseless development. There is a dragon now, and this dragon is directly threatening because it has developed a certain flattened-out, cliché-ridden language, a popular mass language. This is the shame of writing, the opposite of poetic writing and its enemy. The mass media not only produce a discourse that completely excludes everything that can be poetic language but furthermore combat poetic language as dangerous, demented, or obviously useless.

So I realized that writing meant both writing as I had always desired it, which was keeping hold of the unending meditation on the human passions, and a necessary gesture of defense: immediate defense of writing itself and of everything it represents, which is to say a certain kind of thinking that rejects simplifications, that wants absolutely to take into account all the contradictions that make up living. That is what your question made me think of.

Let me add that I prefer to keep in mind that I am still writing in the century "of the broken vertebrae," the century that produced the writings that most touch and nourish me with their torment and their beauty. I prefer to think that Tsvetaieva, Akhmatova, and Mandelstam were still alive when I was alive, that, without knowing it, I crossed paths with Clarice Lispector, that Kafka and Rilke were not far off, and that the same threatening sky hovered and still hovers over those I love.[2] Only the clouds change their shape, and the threat changes its intensity.

[2] The Russian poets Anna Akhmatova (1889–1966), Marina Tsvetaieva (1892–1941), and Osip Mandelstam (1891–1938) wrote their poems after symbolism was eclipsed by futurism, acmeism, etc. Tsvetaieva was never closely affiliated with any literary group;

This century is passing over us with claws outstretched, lacerating now Russia and then Germany, here France and there South Africa, sometimes half the world at a time. I feel that I am an inhabitant of a century in which a poet's life is a necessary miracle.

—(AJ) Do you see in this, and I don't mean to be overly dramatic, a question of life and death? Because personally, thinking of the mass media in the everyday sense of the term, I felt like interrupting and saying yes, they bring death, a certain death in language.

—Yes, definitely.

—(AJ) They flatten everything out, as in hospitals when a heart stops beating and the line goes straight.

—For me, in a certain realm that is once again the realm of writing in the proper sense, writing which labors to rescue the kingdom of languages, that is the enemy, and it's an enemy which scares me a lot because I see it gaining ground.

—(AJ) Yes.

—(AM) I wonder if the threat resides in the technique itself or in the manner in which it is used. For instance, if you think of certain films that are not specifically made to make money and that have no hope of doing so, maybe you could convey other things with these films. . . . Certainly you can do a lot of things that aren't being done.

—That's definitely true, you can. You can also write via very small publishing companies, you can bring out publications and circulate them through small groups, you can invent a "samizdat" for our country; obviously there are survival tactics. But that doesn't address the danger of the effacement of memory. Memory and love are disappearing. We bury the words that are our masters under heaps of stupid images. Children are raised not on milk, not on books, but on television. That is what we give them to drink. So the generations no longer know, we have forgotten. For me it's really the most dreadful threat; I feel memory disappearing. In the past—now I'm already someone who says "in the past"!—you could expect of a child that he had read a book; now you can't. This is very serious. Memory is the grounding, the ground on which the public, poetry, its writing, and its reading all grow at once.

Akhmatova and Mandelstam formed the core of the acmeist group. The Brazilian writer Clarice Lispector (1925–1977) wrote novels, short fiction, and children's literature. Among her most recently translated works are *The Hour of the Star,* trans. Giovanni Pontiero (Manchester: Carcanet, 1986), *The Passion According to G. H.,* trans. Ronald Sousa (Minneapolis: University of Minnesota Press, 1988), and *The Stream of Life,* trans. Elizabeth Lowe and Earl Fitz (Minneapolis: University of Minnesota Press, 1989).

So of course we can fight, and we must. But there are really very few means. We must blow incessantly on the ashes to uncover the spark.

—(AM) Yes. I wondered if maybe the fact that French television has been controlled by the government up until now is significant. Does the fact that there will be private channels, channel five for instance, change this situation?

—It will be worse; we were already on that downhill track. Channel five is an extra channel. There were already three French channels of very poor quality, since the commercial imperative dominated already, but there was in effect a spare, and now that will disappear. "Twentieth century" made me think of something else: I have always had a tendency to question history. I feel in touch with history, I've always asked myself about its relationship to writing as I conceive of writing, which is to say a poetic writing, a writing that wants to sing. How can the song be in rapport with the cry, the sigh, the groans that come from places made miserable by contemporary history? How can the song overcome or make audible the silence of the camps and the detentions? This, of course, is not specific to the twentieth century.

—(AJ) Is there perhaps a relationship to speed that is different?

—Maybe, but I wonder if it isn't also linked to the fact that the distances, the differences, the stillnesses are growing all the time. We could think we were making progress, but we're regressing. Of course, there are local instances of progress. In France, for example, it can't be denied that there has been progress in some details, for example in the condition of women. But the profound advance made by the MLF [French Women's Liberation Movement] has been repressed and put aside for later. (Perhaps for the twenty-first century? I'm not despairing. Strong thoughts, like great poems, end up resurfacing.) On the other hand, the gaps between democratic countries, the relatively free countries, and the other totalitarian or underdeveloped countries are so huge that we are faced with the question of the language we write in and the relationship we have with the rest of the world. For me this is essential because I've never identified myself exclusively with France. I feel that French is my language—which is also open to question because it's my Foreign French language—but I also feel a kinship with other countries. I have those countries in me; every time I write and say to myself "How lucky I am." I have an intense and terrible feeling of luck because I know that if it had been another land, another country, another language, that turned out to be mine, I would not have been able to write. In the fated peregrination of my family, I might have been born in Chile, or in Russia, or in a [South African] concentration lääger [camp].

This luck gives me a feeling of having escaped fate. It follows me relentlessly, like a reminder, and would be capable of producing in me a form of guilt. I don't feel guilty, but I do feel rich, and I'm always asking myself what a life without writing would be like, and god knows there are lives without writing. There are all the countries where people are illiterate, and you can't imagine a comparable misfortune. Then there are all the bans on writing internalized by women. Then there are the worst bans on writing such as those in the USSR, where they don't have the right to write, think, publish. Every time I write, I think of that. Of Akhmatova's poems printed in series of twenty copies. Of the poet deported for poetry. (And the appearance of a thaw doesn't make me change my mind: there have already been seventy years of dead silence [tombe] in the USSR. How can one forget that? And what will be born of so much silence?)

Because I am lucky, because I have, in my life, been helped as much as impeded, because my writing is heartily welcome in a place that is much more like a hearth than a publishing house,[3] I feel the more acutely for those "I's" and those "you's" who are ill fated. Imagine if I had been born in South Africa!

—(AJ) That is important, and I think that these two factors, mass media and history, must really be thought of together, because we live in a world where there are such distinct temporalities. . . . When I see, as I have recently in Senegal, for example, the immense power of the American culture industry. . . . It lands there as if it were from another planet, in the midst of a completely different history, and suddenly you have several extremely different temporalities coexisting.

—(AM) Paradoxically, you could argue that even with all their problems, the mass media through their simultaneity and the power of the image have almost forced a number of people to acknowledge other worlds. Without television and film, for example, we might have no image at all of countries entirely different from those in the West.

—Frankly, I don't believe so. Maybe I'm too harsh, but I think the mass media are a screen, because we think we see, but the screen screens it out. In showing us, they repress what they show us most of the time. There's nothing worse than that. Sometimes a spark gets through, but

[3] Cixous is referring to Editions Des femmes, which publishes primarily women's texts.

that's once in a million times; the rest of the time it erases what it displays. The media show you a war on television, it's so badly done that you don't understand anything, and that anesthetizes, it turns you into a spectator, and I find that to be another assassination. Look at the difference between what you've seen on television and what you will see there. . . . We need to rescue the voyage, we must go to these places. In saying that, I'm not accusing the means, but the ignoble *use* of the *means*. That said, the audiovisual medium is much easier to divert from artistic vocation than writing is. You learn nothing from television.

Question 2: Is it valid/of value to write as a woman, and is it part of your writing practice today?

—What does that mean, is it valid or of value?

—(AM) Is writing as a woman valid or valuable as a category in the first place: can you say that I am a woman, that I write as a woman? After all, in your own formulation of "l'écriture feminine," you have been careful to distinguish between the sex of writing and the sex of the author.

—(AJ) I would also add that there are women who responded to our letter inviting them to participate in this project by saying "I am not a woman, I am a writer, and I don't like to be categorized as a woman writer." So we are not asking this question in some overarching, general way—we know after all that you have worked extensively on the question of writing as a woman. But rather we are asking it in relation to this project: women and the politics of literary tradition.

—(AM) Yes, above all because the idea of bringing women into the canon presupposes that being a woman is something specific, that a woman's writing constitutes a separate category, or that writing as a woman means something. And we wondered: what does it mean? For the women who originally proposed this project, writing as a woman means something very specific.

—Yes, obviously. It's a delicate thing to answer because there too one is caught in exactly what I spend my time denouncing, words used as cages, and it's always dangerous. In any case there is a double bind; we can't avoid answering either, I don't believe in that. One of the dangers, one of the difficulties that women who write have encountered these last two decades consists in having to stand up to the *word* "woman," to the word "feminine," issuing from critical places. For example, when I began to write I wasn't involved in these problems, it was before 1968; in 1968 the women's movement began in France. These are questions that came looking for me, because after 1968 people began to talk about them. That created a climate for me. But I was working there in my corner, on literary textuality. So I only answered several years later. Not that I ever *refused* to answer. But the opportunity didn't arise for me until 1975. The opportunity, which is to say the direct call, [came from] Antoinette Fouque. You can rediscover a continent a generation late! Such was my case. I arrived at the movement that she had inaugurated seven years earlier. The concept of "contemporary" needs revising. It was a turbulent time. It was impossible, for *ethical* reasons, not to respond to the questioning. For it's true that it's *the woman* in me who writes, not only the poet. I couldn't not respond, because I would have felt that I was betraying a people to whom I belong. I belong as well to other peoples. My first people was the Jewish people, then the Algerian people, then the people of women, etc. I cannot but respond if one of my peoples is put in question. Then straightaway one enters into all the paradoxes, all the limits, and all the bad formulations of these questions. But there is one thing that I can't eliminate from my consciousness, and that's misogyny; I've always known that. At those moments I feel solidarity with all efforts, not to force misogyny back—because I've never seen misogyny step back, I've only seen it disguise itself—but in any case to analyze it and try to find the means to respond to it. There is a part of me that answers to the name "woman." I would not make use of a sentence like "I'm not a woman, I'm a writer," because not for anything in the world would I say "I'm not a woman." To me that means nothing. Yes, I am a woman. I admit that I don't even know what the utterance "I am not a woman" means when pronounced . . . by a woman?

—(AJ) I don't either. When one of the women invited to participate in this project refused on those grounds, I said, well, okay. . . .

—I've often heard women say that. It's a position like any other. For me personally it's nonsense, because I feel I am a woman. But what does that mean? It's something you live, you feel, you enjoy. Maybe there are women who don't take pleasure in it, who don't live it, who can't write it, or who place themselves elsewhere or identify themselves otherwise, and why not? There are lots of possibilities. It would also be terrible if you felt *obligated* to feel yourself to be a woman!

—(AM) But I think that for the women in question, being a woman and feeling that one is a woman would force them to be read as women, to be reduced to that category.

—I think that the woman who says "I am not a woman" says so because she feels threatened by the condition of women. She is not alone; we're all threatened by that.

—(AM) Absolutely.

—The woman who says that is withdrawing from the battlefield where people are taking blows. I will never say that, but there are moments when I want to say: "Listen, how about if we talk about something else. . . . " It's tiring, and it's even deathly boring.

—(AJ) That's just it. But you know the anthology compiled by Sandra Gilbert and Susan Gubar, *The Norton Anthology of Literature by Women: The Tradition in English?*[4]

—No.

—(AJ) It's an anthology of literature by women writers writing in English, "The English Tradition." There was a whole polemic in the papers among American women writers: some who said, wonderful, now there is a tradition, now it is anthologized by Norton, a major press; and others who said no, no, no, the point is to choose the best writers, not just women. That is a specific example of this gesture concerning the canon.

—That's the dilemma: how to struggle against exclusion without reproducing another type of exclusion. One has to be aware and proclaim the limits of each defensive gesture. The moment you defend yourself, unfortunately you become an attacker. But we can't all be Gandhis.

—(AM) We are actually putting together a little canon ourselves, in doing this project, and we came up against the problem of how to make choices.

—Conversely, this doesn't mean that one should eliminate the woman question from literature—it makes up part of it—only one must also address this question to men. It's an enormous problem. These questions are like mines, you step on them and they explode.

—(AJ) Yes, that's just the way it is.

—You have to be able to think above and beyond current events. We are all threatened with being prisoners of our time, that can't be denied. We must constantly work with current events. Confinement in the age

---

[4] Published in 1985 by Norton.

is what's the danger. Personally I don't feel imprisoned by the events of the time. I think there are moments of struggle. Then moments of stasis. And that one must also write from the standpoint of eternity. At least try to rediscover the roots of all these symptoms.

—(AJ) Well, personally, I know women who are very conscious of these larger problems, and yet they still feel completely engaged in a daily battle with the university. . . .

—That I understand.

—(AM) . . . . and with the publishing houses. So for many women, these are real and urgent struggles.

—I understand. And that is the terrible part, of course, that one is obligated. . . .

Question 3: Many women writing today find themselves, for the first time in history, at the center of such institutions as the university and psychoanalysis. In your opinion, will this new placement of women help them to enter the twentieth-century canon, and if so, will they be in the heart of this corpus or (still) in the footnotes?

—This question struck me as "American."

—(AJ) In what way?

—It may be that in American universities, American academics are doing some kind of feminist work. That makes me turn back to the French situation, which I don't know well. But I have the feeling that women in the French universities are not greatly interested in women's problems, only a tiny minority concerns itself with them. It seems to me that the majority of French university women are aligned with men. But that's my experience, which does not extend to all of France. It's a Parisian experience. So I don't think it is the women in universities who will contribute to making sure there is more room for women. Moreover, this question of the twentieth-century canon does not exist here. I can't answer it.

—(AJ) On the most elementary level, an example of the canon is *Lagarde et Michard*,[5] which probably will continue to exist, in spite

---

[5] André Lagarde and Laurent Michard, *Textes et Littératures* (Paris: Bordas, 1962). Hereafter referred to in these interviews as *Lagarde et Michard*. This series of volumes serves as one of the literature textbooks for all French schoolchildren. It classifies writers "by century as major or minor, classical or romantic, precursors or followers," as Joan DeJean and Nancy K. Miller so succinctly put it in their letter inviting us to participate in the *Yale French Studies* issue on the canon.

of everything, into the twenty-first century. So in the category of twentieth-century literature, and its presentation to students, one wonders if. . . .

—I should tell you that I haven't looked at *Lagarde et Michard*. . . .

—(AM) There aren't very many women: I think Colette and Beauvoir are in the twentieth-century volume, and that's it. Perhaps a little Georges Sand, but really that's all for the entire history of French literature.[6]

—(AJ) This is one of the things those feminists working on the canon are concerned with; after all, you must really begin with schoolchildren. Books such as *Lagarde et Michard* are meant for them.

—Maybe we should distinguish between institutional and noninstitutional handbooks. I think that there are handbooks in France that are really quite open but that perhaps don't have the circulation of *Lagarde and Michard*. I know many high school instructors who don't necessarily obey the institution and repression. They can assign texts very freely, even as concerns the reading lists that students present for the baccalaureate.

—(AM) Perhaps the question concerns us too, as students of French literature, and the manner in which the literary corpus was presented to us: there were no women, none at all. I came to France five years ago to read them, but that was the first time.

—Maybe the situation is worse in the United States.

Question 4: Today we are seeing women produce literary, philosophical, and psychoanalytical theory of recognized importance, and, parallel to this, we are also seeing a new fluidity in the borderlines among disciplines and genres of writing. Will this parallelism lead only to women being welcomed alongside men, or to a definitive blurring of these categories?

—Do you think there is a fluidity of boundaries between disciplines and writing genres?

—(AJ) I can't speak for France, but today in the States I can see the emergence of a certain kind of writing, often theoretical, that is not so much interdisciplinary as trans- or pluridisciplinary. This new kind of writing and its authors often encounter strong resistance if not outright rejection by such institutions as the university.

[6] I was exaggerating only slightly. The *six* other women writers are: Marie de France, Madeleine Scudéry, Marie-Madeleine de Lafayette, Marie de Sévigné, Germaine de Staël, and Marceline Desbordes-Valmore. For a discussion of contemporary women writers in the *Lagarde et Michard*, see Marini's answer to Question 5 in this volume. —A.M.

—Writing that, for example, would be literary, philosophical, and psychoanalytic at the same time?

—(AJ) Yes, but not like in France.

—(AM) No, it's not exactly the same thing; it's not as theoretical.

—(AJ) It's less theoretical, but at least there's an effort to transcend categories and to make the boundaries between bodies of knowledge more diffuse, as, for example, with current work in cultural criticism or popular culture. We were simply wondering whether this phenomenon has anything to do with the advent of women subjects into the "institutions" that govern our ways of knowing.

—I don't think so. It's a complex question, which I don't want to answer. I have the feeling that there is not, at least in France, any transfusion of scenes. Of course, there is a passageway that has opened up between the philosophical and the psychoanalytic and a translimitation with Derrida. But there is still, on the one hand, all that principally comes from a certain discourse in keeping with mastery and theorization, and on the other hand something that keeps free of mastery and has the right of fantasy; and that is writing. Certain philosophical texts are written in a modern kind of writing, but that doesn't make them literature. As to the second point, would this bring women alongside men, I don't think so. If suddenly everything opened up, if you had a sort of heterogeneous field where everything would come to meet everything—which in my mind doesn't exist—then women would be the losers. The "meeting" would give way to reappropriation by men.

—(AJ) Yes. I'm thinking of Women's Studies in the United States, where there is precisely this fantasized state, completely unrealized for the moment, but fantasized and idealized, in which there would be representatives of all disciplines and one could take everything one wanted from this place or that, and in which one could ask questions about women and around women. And what you find in reality is professionalization and expertise in the disciplines, but very little transfusion of knowledge.

—I don't believe that the borders between literary, philosophical, and psychoanalytic categories are going to suddenly lose their ground. On the other hand, it's obvious that neither is there any pure literature, pure philosophy, pure psychoanalysis. What interests me is the passage into literature of a portion of philosophy, the passage into philosophy of a portion of psychoanalysis, etc. The fact remains, though, that in each case one will always be dominant, and that one will be masculine.

—(AJ) Yes, that is a major question. I was thinking especially of the margins in America, of the margins around Derrida's work, for example; because within these margins there are actually men and women who write pluridisciplinary texts, but. . . .

—But let me tell you that it falls nevertheless on the philosophical side.

—(AM) Yes, that's true. To the point that those with no philosophical background have a hard time reading these texts.

—What is important is that philosophy overflow its own boundaries. And that it hear itself resound, as in the case of Derrida, in the strange language of poets.

—(AJ) One can talk about Hélène Cixous's texts in terms of their reception as fiction and literature first but also as a place where all these disciplines meet.

—There are all kinds of literary texts, and then there are literary texts that I don't want to call of philosophical substance because that's not the case, but whose plan or desire also has to do with thinking the world. Not only to echo or translate it, but to try to think it through. For example, the poets or writers who have been studied by the philosophers, by Heidegger as well as by Derrida, are the poets who connect the secrets of writing and the writing of the world. It's a certain "genre," if you will, be it Rilke or Hölderlin; in that area the tradition happens to be German. Maybe my rapport with that sphere stems from my being half-German; maybe it's my other language, I have no idea. But it is indeed a question. I feel the need to respond, I have the sense that writing is not totally irresponsible. I am not a philosopher; I have read a certain amount of philosophy, I have held onto some of it, not something that belongs only to philosophy but that pertains to all human thought. I have the same rapport with psychoanalysis. So if, when people read my texts, they notice the form less than a certain kind of message, that's what they find. Then perhaps there is also the fact that I teach. That said, I write in an absolutely nonphilosophical blindness. I progress from nonknowledge to nonknowledge, and I have a lot more questions than answers.

—(AJ) It weighs on one to be a professor!

—I don't know, but I don't think my seminars function on the level of mastery.

—(AJ) It's true that coming to your seminars one doesn't have the impression that one is dealing with a professor in the sense that. . . .

—In such a situation one must find a language for communication with very different people, and then propose an approach, propose a path, even if, for me, that path must remain completely poetic.

Question 5: Given the problematic and the politics of the categories of the canon, and given the questions we've been dealing with, do you think your oeuvre will be included in the twentieth-century canon, and if so, how will it be presented? In your opinion, what will the content of the canon be?

—I have no idea how to answer. This story of the canon is really an American notion, perhaps one that will come to exist in France, I don't know.

—(AM) Maybe it has to do with the way in which French literature is presented in the United States. We get the impression that the canon is established in France, but perhaps it's completely American?

—Perhaps it is your use of the singular that troubles me, because in my opinion what there is in France is not "the" canon, but categorizations that are ideological and vary from one theory to another. Yes, one always attempts to code, but there is an infinite variety of codes. I don't know.

—(AJ) We were a little wicked to ask this question, it's true, because it is precisely a matter of each person's fantasies. How your texts will be read in the twenty-first century, it's a question that. . . .

—I have never asked myself that question. My question is: how "I" shall read in the twenty-first century, i.e., the remaining unknown I. Enjoying the entirely altered aspect of that old twentieth century is something I shall look forward to when I am dead.

Question 6: From Hélène Cixous, the theoretician and the practitioner of l'écriture féminine, to Hélène Cixous, historical dramatist à la Shakespeare: this trajectory has provoked strongly opposed reactions.[7] Some see this displacement of the feminine in favor of giving man back his place at the center of the story/history as a splendid success; others are worried that in the process of this return to History the "repressed feminine," barely glimpsed these last few

[7] We are referring to Cixous's play *L'Histoire terrible mais inachevée de Norodom Sihanouk, roi du Cambodge* [The Terrible but Unfinished History/Story of Norodom Sihanouk, King of Cambodia], produced under the direction of Ariane Mnouchkine, Théâtre du Soleil, Paris, 1985.

years, already seems to be disappearing. How have you experienced this trajectory?

—There, in contrast, I have something to say. Here is how I live what I prefer to call my "path." I've followed a particular path, not diverged from it, and along the way my orientation hasn't changed. It is this same path that has only moved closer, little by little, to my early preoccupations. I've told that story in texts such as *La Venue à l'écriture*. My arrival in writing started by means of a look at the world when I was very small, a way of perceiving violence and worldwide tragedy. I was filled with worry when I was three or four years old; I was worried about the world, about human beings. When I was a child the first people I belonged to, because the age dictated it (the forties), was the Jewish people, who were threatened with disappearance. Then I realized that I couldn't identify myself totally with the Jewish people because it was too much of a father-son people (even if I like fatherson). Little by little I sought out "whom I resemble," "with whom I assemble." That doesn't mean I have a need to be part of a group. I am someone who is "called" by calls. I feel calls. Distress signals question me. I will always be a woman and I will always respond in that way. But that isn't my only definition.

A great presence has always haunted me, that of the history of peoples, and I've never known how to respond sufficiently through writing. So, I carried out personal activities in certain movements, through certain actions, but never political parties. And in my texts there are always echoes of this obsessive concern.

If you look back, in all my texts that work on what I call the scene of the unconscious you can find the same torment: while you write, or while Dora[8] makes a scene, there are successively Algeria, Vietnam, Greece, Iran without their own scene. That has never ceased, and it is written. But each time it was written as remorse, as the scene I couldn't quite make appear, until I realized that to make these scenes appear, I had to change genres. One must have the other scene.

In my work there is a first period that, in my opinion, is absolutely inevitable for anyone who writes. One must face oneself, one's ego, its hells and its paradises, in order to arrive, finally, at these moments of status quo, of peace with the self, that allow you to move as freely as possible toward the other. What I myself have always sought and desired

[8] See *Portrait de Dora* (Paris: Des femmes, 1976).

is the other. You have to traverse the ego to get to the other and others. There is a moment where any work of writing and reflection, which can be an analytic undertaking for some, should reach the stage of efface-ment of the ego, of tranquillity with the ego. This is not simple, certainly not for any woman. From that moment on, one can become the stage of the world. Then, in that season of tranquillity with the ego, the question of the other and others, which has always been my passion, can be brought up. Three years ago, in order to present [this idea to] my seminar I employed the word "precarious." What matters to me is what is fragile. That's what seems to me to be the vocation of writing: what is simultaneously necessary, rare, alive, and precarious. In certain texts I've worked on the objects for which no one has any time. I've worked on an insect, on a feather, on a moment of meditation, on a fruit. I wrote a book called *Limonade tout était si infini* about one little sentence by Kafka, a sentence that fell straight from life, on a scrap of paper, and I would like to reach the moment where a work could be a sentence, one simple sentence, without beginning or end and bearing within it the whole secret of life and death. Mythical moment, poetic temptation.

These are such imperceptible things. If not writing, what will take care of them? And yet they are so necessary.

For me women are also this precarious people, at once totally present and totally absent, one that can be forgotten at any moment, or remem-bered at any moment. There is a logic in my choices and my behavior. And with that, I went one step further and I came to the others—not only women, but not to the exclusion of women—and in this case it was Cambodia, a country that has all the same characteristics of fragility. A people at once cultivated, sensitive, and what's more, and this I find seductive, very capable of jouissance. Cambodia was paradise, and at the same time it was threatened with disappearance, holding on by a breath. This seemed to me to be my own story on a broader scale, more varied, more open, more urgent. More immediately effective, because theater has an immediate effectiveness that writing doesn't. Writing has a long-term effectiveness, a deferred force. Being able to move forward with two kinds of writing is my particular good fortune.

Obviously, I didn't sacrifice women to Cambodia. That would be totally contradictory and appalling. One should be careful of that kind of thought. In the United States some years ago, at the moment of the apogee of feminism, I found with astonishment that American feminists wanted to get rid of Freud under the pretext that he was misogynist, etc. That's the same kind of naïveté. Since he was a man, he should be chucked out. Instead of working to separate the good grain from the chaff, one was burning the entire harvest. In completely exiling Freud one exiled the treasures of the unconscious, our richest realm. You might as well say that you're leaving life, leaving the world. At the time I used the following metaphor: I guess one mustn't take a plane because it wasn't we who invented it. One should take what there is, not deprive oneself of the world, but on the contrary, take the maximum and give the maximum. A period must be reached in which women do what they have never done and what only men have done, not to compete with men or beat them at their own game, but to do *in a woman's way* something that goes beyond the war of the genders/genres. It would be terrible if theater and history, which have so far been the work of men, were also prohibited. I, a woman, am writing this story/history. And that colors my whole narrative.

Theater can be reduced to being feminist theater, but that is not my perspective at all. Conversely, it must not be a kind of theater—here one would return to the institution, to classicism—that reproduces the exclusion of women. As a woman I have a great deal to do to back and invent this scene—in particular to concern myself with the role of women in theater, which is generally minimized, both in practice, on the part of the actors, and in the written works, and in particular in Shakespeare, whom I am nevertheless unwilling to give up. When Shakespeare is presented, there are few women's roles, and actresses and women suffer from it.

So what have I done? I've tried to concern myself with a people, charming and gentle (as Rimbaud would say), that is in danger of death at this moment, even in agony. A people of great tenderness, with a strong femininity. In order to create, one needs to be able to identify with someone or something. I can identify with the Khmers; I couldn't identify with a people who put women behind veils. That is a problem that exists for everyone. And then I paid attention, with all my strength and with all the possibilities of theater, to the place of women in this work. I tried to make space for them, because if one starts to relate history the first thing one finds is the absence of women. In the History of Cambodia there were no women. I saw that the Queen Mother of Sihanouk had a quite extraordinary presence. Quickly I pushed her into the story/history, doubled her, and accompanied her with another role, that of Mom Savay who did not really exist. Similarly, as I had to bring the people to life, I decided that they would be women. It was a calculated choice. I did the maximum to make their presence felt. I wanted the last scenes to be carried by women, by bringing the last words out of the mouths of women and passing the messages of life through them. I had such a need to convey feminine presence that I didn't give out parts equally. The men are more negative than the women. Maybe that's the reality. Where I've cheated a bit is that among the Khmer Rouges there were some monstrous women, who played a very important role, one that was actually equivalent to that of the men. There were women worse than Lady Macbeth, worse than Goneril,[9] among the Khmer Rouges. I confess, I cheated in the other direction, I minimized their part. Why? Because if I had remained faithful to historical reality, it's women who would have paid for it. It might perhaps have pleased some of the public to see the ignominy of the Khmer Rouge women. I don't want to feed the misogyny that is always ready to grow. So I did my secret little work, and I think that the public could feel it. I could sense so well that when people were leaving the show they felt strongly for the two old women. They are loved and they steal the show. On the one side there is Sihanouk who is of immense importance, and that's as it should be; but on the other, it's the old women who are loved.

—(AJ) Some people haven't been pleased to see a man, a king, at the center of the story/history. I had the impression rather that Sihanouk's kind of madness, this impossibility of doing everything at the same time, of being there for everyone, of listening to everyone . . . was in some way, dare I say, feminine? Yet people picked up on "the man at the center."

—It's a limited view because once again femininity and masculinity are not automatically distributed between men and women. I would not have put Khomeini on stage because I can't imagine that he has the smallest grain of femininity in him. It's enough to see Sihanouk to feel that the feminine is inside him, and I would add that he is aware of it, proudly and honorably, because among the Khmers there is no repression of the womanly. Sihanouk is a great statesman, and also a multiple, complex being, who contains a little of everything. To say that he is only a king, that he is only a man, is to fall for what is most superficial and misleading in our opinions.

---

[9] Goneril is King Lear's eldest daughter.

—(AM) Yes. People could say, this is Shakespeare, it's the story of a people told through one man, a king. But something else takes place inside the theater thanks to the placement of the Cambodian people. When one steps into the theater, the first thing one sees is the Cambodian people positioned in a kind of gallery all around the spectators. We, spectators, watch their history. And silently this people watches us watching their history. The effect is incredibly strong; it's uncanny. This effect would be lost if one read the play: it must be seen.

—Maybe it's the title that leads us to consider Sihanouk as pure phallus, I admit that. But the project is to tell the story of a people. It so happens that this people has a permanently present figure, from 1941 to 1986, Sihanouk, who traverses everything. He's like the river. He can't be denied and yet that doesn't eliminate the people.

—(AM) And furthermore, if you work with the myths of a people, you know that's how it takes place.

—Absolutely.

—(AM) In order to work with the myths of a people, above all in order to show their aspirations, it is absolutely necessary to have a center. In this case it so happens that a prince is at the center.

—One should work in a flexible and metaphorical way: take Sihanouk as the metaphor for a people. And don't forget that in theater small and great should swap places and be represented in an equivalent way. The characters of theater are always kings and princes. The man of the people is a king. I take the word prince or king figuratively, as meaning someone exceptional, who has to carry an entire destiny, whatever it may be. That's something the theater teaches us. Dora is a princess. In my first little texts, I had fun writing the legend of psychoanalysis, and for me Dora wasn't just anybody. She has become one of the myths of the twentieth century.

When I wrote my little play on India, I changed the names: I called the heroine of *La Prise de l'école de Madhubaï* Sakundeva when in reality Phoolan Devi was the queen of the Dacoits—she was an untouchable but was called queen by her band. This isn't because I'm obsessed by royalty, but because I think that peoples should be made up of kings. That's what the French Revolution should have been: not knocking down all men but on the contrary raising everyone up. And the force of art should be to invent characters so necessary and right that they become the future queens and kings of our imagination. That is how it was with those inventions torn from nothingness and now known as

Falstaff, Don Quixote, Prince Myshkin, or Nastasya Filippovna, or . . .
Selma Lagerlöf's Margareta Celsing.[10]

[10] Prince Myshkin and Nastasya Filippovna are characters in Dostoevsky's novel *The Idiot*. Margareta Celsing is the main female character in the Swedish writer Selma Lagerlöf's 1891 novel translated as *The Story of Gösta Berling*.

3

Catherine Clément

TRANSLATED BY CARRIE NOLAND

Question 1: What does it mean to you to write at the end of the twentieth century?

—I will answer this question in two contradictory ways.

Writing at the end of the twentieth century, just as during the first century A.D. or the fifth century B.C., has always "meant" the desire to achieve immortality, whether by means of the simple inscription of a trace or the elaboration of a work attributed to a single individual. From this point of view, writing at the end of the twentieth century suggests to me that the human race has not been able to reconcile its anguish over the death of each individual member, nor has it come to terms with its own eventual disappearance.

On the other hand, writing has its own history, its achievements, adventures, and regressions. The act of writing cannot be dissociated from the history of writing. For me, writing is at once a precise memory and a radical forgetting of this history.

But the real truth is that, in order to respond to your question, I had to work out a rationalization of a process that I never question on my own. I *have* to write.

And it just so happens that I live in the twentieth century.

Question 2: Is it valid/of value to write as a woman, and is it part of your writing practice today?

—Your next question demands a response similar to the one I just gave you: writing as a woman is a valid stance for me—and I happen to be a woman. As far as the process itself is concerned, I have no specific answer. On the other hand, women writers come up against obstacles analogous to those faced by women in other professions: drawing up contracts and establishing subsidiary rights, for example, can cause certain problems. What is most striking is that, more than any man, a woman writer is immediately distorted by the media, which composes a fictitious "portrait" of her, flattering or unflattering, but always linked to her status as a woman.

Question 3: Many women writing today find themselves, for the first time in history, at the center of such institutions as the university and psychoanalysis. In your opinion, will this new placement of women help them to enter the twentieth century canon, and if so, will they be in the heart of this corpus or (still) in the footnotes?

—The growing importance of women in institutions like the university and psychoanalysis is real; but we must not forget that we are talking about "female careers," that is, those professions, whatever they may be, that permit women to arrange their own work schedules. Having worked successively in the academic profession, then as the editor of a column in a French weekly, then as director in a ministry, I can testify to the difference between "female careers" and "male careers": it is considerable. The existence of more flexible professions is a ruse of history that enables women to find time to write, and therefore to publish.

It is only publication that allows women writers to enter the canon of the twentieth century. The step has not yet been taken that will allow women to enter as full-time writers, capable of making a living by the pen.

Now, to be a writer should mean that one can live on what one earns from writing. The real entry into the canon of the twentieth century will not be achieved until women no longer need to engage in "female careers" in order to practice their craft.

Question 4: Today we are seeing women produce literary, philosophical, and psychoanalytical theory of recognized importance, and, parallel to this, we are also seeing a new fluidity in the borderlines among disciplines and genres of writing. Will this parallelism lead only to women being welcomed alongside men, or to a definitive blurring of these categories?

—It seems to me that the question of the borderlines between disciplines is distinct from the question of the participation of women in these disciplines. To give a different answer would imply that women have a natural tendency to cloud the issue, that they are confused, incapable of intellectual rigor; the danger of such a response is obvious.

Question 5: Given the problematic and the politics of the categories of the canon, and given the questions we've been dealing with, do you think your oeuvre will be included in the twentieth-century canon, and if so, how will it be presented? In your opinion, what will the content of the canon be?

—Entering into a canon does not depend upon one author, but rather on the collective that defines the canon and its rules. Therefore, I cannot give you an answer regarding my own work, especially since I make an effort to break away from the rules of literary production in France when I write my novels and essays. As far as the essays are concerned, I take special care to make sure they bear on many diverse fields so that I cannot be easily categorized. I have written books on psychoanalysis, ethnology, the opera, bull fighting, India, Brazil, and culture and aesthetic theory. I have a secret canon whose contours may appear clearly only in the years to come.

Question 6: In 1975, you and Hélène Cixous wrote The Newly Born Woman, *which, especially since its translation in 1986 into English, has become a classic in the United States. Indeed, it is one of the key texts introducing North*

Americans to the debates known as the "new French feminisms." What do you think of this canonization of your text in the United States? What in your opinion was the fate in France of the ideas presented in "The Guilty One," "Sorties," and "Exchange"?

—I cannot account for the lateness of the American publication of *The Newly Born Woman,* nor for its success. The period during which Hélène Cixous and I wrote this book coincided with the emergence in France of a current of thought that has been effaced.[1] The ideas that we presented in that text have not aged; however, the social effect has changed considerably. Women's writing has developed over time—not a tremendous amount, but enough so that in the context of today's France our book seems to belong to a certain historical moment. What remains vital and pertinent is what Hélène Cixous says about her own way of writing; but since the French publication of *The Newly Born Woman* she has written and published a good deal. As for my own ideas, they have been fully corroborated by the research in ethnology conducted recently by women (Jeanne Favret-Saada,[2] for example) and by the research of the "new historians."

One could turn the question around and ask it in the following way: why is it that *The Newly Born Woman* wasn't published in your country until eleven years after its publication in France? And to what do you Americans attribute its success?

Your response matters to Hélène Cixous and me because the Women Writers' series that was inaugurated by *The Newly Born Woman* has long been suspended by its editor, Christian Bourgois.

[1] Clément appears to be referring to the immense vitality of women writers and theorists in France in the seventies. Her "sense of an ending" is echoed by many of the women interviewed here.

[2] See, for example, *Les Mots, la mort, les sorts: La sorcellerie dans le Bocage* (Paris: Gallimard, 1977), trans. Catherine Cullen as *Deadly Words: Witchcraft in the Bocage* (New York: Cambridge University Press, 1980).

4

Françoise Collin

TRANSLATED BY HEIDI GILPIN

Question 1: What does it mean to you to write at the end of the twentieth century?

—I am indeed writing at the end of the twentieth century, but I do not know what it would have been like to write in the eighteenth or nineteenth century. I only know that writing in a civilization that has become essentially audiovisual doubtless can seem archaic. But I love this *archaism,* which for me means not something outmoded but something originary: safeguarding our relationship to language, which is timeless. Language, in its exteriority, preserves interiority, and in its public character, remains interindividual. The communication of writing

Excerpts from this interview, translated by Patricia Baudoin, appeared in *Yale French Studies* (1988), vol. 75.

takes place through both an author and a reader, a woman author and a woman reader, and demands their participation. I have sometimes had the urge to paint or to make films. But when I was young, isolated as I was, writing was the most immediate mode of expression and creation [available to me]. Writing does not require extraordinary means: a piece of paper, a pen—any woman or man can have access to that. That is doubtless why, in Europe at least, women write much more than they paint, build, or make films.

But the choice of writing is not simply linked to circumstances: as a little girl, I was fascinated by words, I wanted them. I found a sort of strength in them that allowed me to resist my environment. As soon as I began my first narrative, I knew I could never give in to the traditional form of the novel, because novels give an illusion of coherence, of a totalizing of existence that follows a dominant progressive line. What I was interested in was giving voice to dispersion, nonhistory, the not-one, the chaos that my experience seemed to be. Now, at the same time, I was interested in philosophy, that is, in rationality. Speaking a kind of reason that does not unify has given direction to all my endeavors, including, later, the creation of a journal (*Les Cahiers du GRIF*),[1] a plural work par excellence. Perhaps this has something to do with the affirmation of a woman subject; perhaps it later enabled my participation in feminism.

—(AM) Have you ever used a computer to write? I ask this because obviously everyone once wrote by hand, then many used typewriters, etc. Is writing in front of a machine a different experience from writing longhand for you? Do you ascribe a particular value to the nonintrusion of the "rational" machine?

—The graphic nature of handwriting has never really obsessed me. I am not one of those writers for whom the relationship to a sheet of paper, a pen, or a pencil is important. Quite the contrary, since, from the first, I wrote at a typewriter—right off. The typewriter balances and gives rhythm to the development of my sentences. Writing longhand, I rush too much: I write so badly anyway that I can't even read my own handwriting. The typewriter pacifies me, it slows down time.

I haven't moved on yet to computers, for financial reasons first—computers are still expensive in Europe—but also because of a certain

[1] *Les Cahiers du GRIF,* published in Brussels, is one of the earliest and most widely recognized feminist journals in Europe. Françoise Collin has been the editor since founding the journal in 1973.

fear of losing what my relationship to my mechanical typewriter offers me.[2] I do, however, cross out a lot in my writing, and I often compose by collages, as one would in a film. I work by cutting and pasting or Scotch taping. No doubt the computer would make things easier for me, but I know I would constantly be using the printer because I need to see the text on paper.

—(AM) The typewriter can be seen as an interesting intermediary between the writer and her/his text.

—My old mechanical typewriter—a 1950s Smith-Corona—is hardly an intermediary. It's like an extension of my body. In fact, something happened to me that was nearly tragic: three years ago, my apartment was broken into, and my typewriter was stolen. The loss of my typewriter more than any other object was most painful. But a sort of miracle happened: a friend of mine found and gave me an identical typewriter, which had been his father's: same make, same old model. I think that is the most beautiful present I've ever received. I'm still using that typewriter today, just as I used the first one. When I am on vacation or traveling, and I have to use another one, I feel resistance, an unease. That's why I'm leery of switching to computers.

—(AJ) We're getting off the topic here, but this is interesting vis-à-vis the woman writer's relationship to writing and the body as it has been so emphasized in France. For example, with a computer, changes can be made on the screen. But if you correct that way, you lose the "first text."

—Yes, I need to keep my first versions. Sometimes I come back to them because they were better, or because later I've dropped interesting passages. I do think that it would be painful for me to lose these first texts right off. Fairly often, as a matter of fact, even when the text is finished, I keep my drafts. I only throw them out reluctantly so they don't crowd my drawers.

—(AJ) That brings us back to the twentieth century, for isn't the computer intrinsically related to the dominant logic of our twentieth century: what matters is the final product, not its process?

—I'm not sure that the dominant logic of the twentieth century is operative where literature and art are concerned. It seems to me that, on the contrary, modern art does or can integrate process into the final

[2] Since this interview took place, I acquired a computer. It's been in my office for three months, but I haven't had the courage to learn how to use it. For now, it's still a hostile presence. [Collin's note.]

result; such a practice is in direct opposition to industrial production, which is strictly interested in the final product. For example, a text can present different versions of the same narrative or event. Or it can let "holes" show through in its continuity and thereby reveal its dispersed character, its nonhomogeneous nature. This even occurs frequently in the structure of modern narratives, as opposed to nineteenth-century novels; it also occurs in philosophical texts that have dropped the pretense of becoming a system, of claiming total coherence as their sole criterion. (Someone such as Maurice Blanchot, on whom I have worked a great deal and written a book,[3] makes this heterogeneous character apparent). I am very interested in these detotalizing practices.

Question 2: Is it valid/of value to write as a woman, and is it part of your writing practice today?

—That's a difficult question. In the first place why ask a woman that question? Would one ask a man if he writes as a man? And, then, what does "as a woman" mean? Since you are asking me the question, it has to be because, for a woman, writing as a woman is not an obvious proposition; your question would seem to imply that one could be a woman and not write as a woman. [The question of] writing as a woman would then be aiming at how in the act of writing, a woman manages her relationship to her sex or to the difference between the sexes. Of course when I write, it is always a woman who is writing, but that doesn't imply that I always write "as a woman," even if criticism can detect something feminine in the text. (Of course, it can also detect something feminine in writing by men.) But neither my body nor my historical situation (of being a woman) is as such the determining factor in the act of writing. Each time, consciously or unconsciously, she who writes fixes her place of enunciation—and that of her audience. The writer's place of enunciation is certainly not neutral, but it isn't unique either. Choosing the place one writes from is part of the act of writing. And writing probably spreads out from several places of enunciation, which in turn authorize several valid modes of critical reading.

Thus it's the whole question of the writing subject that is being asked. Who is writing when I am writing? The writing subject is not a subject prior to writing, is not a subject who is already present before writing and who would only be searching within her/his words for her/

[3] *Maurice Blanchot et la question de l'écriture.*

his expression. Writing is not only the expression but also the constitution of its subject, or subjects, because whoever writes is not one man or one woman. That's why writing is an opening of meaning that reading keeps reopening, and not the production of one meaning.

The "as a woman" of a woman who writes is managed differently in each case. As far as I am concerned, when I write within the framework of feminism, for women, I stress the "as a woman." When I write a poem or fiction, the "as a woman" is less present (even if obviously it is still a woman who is writing). In daily life, by the way, the "as a woman" isn't always present in the same way either: when I walk around in a city I like, when I look at a landscape, when I listen to music, the "as a woman" is attenuated to the point of disappearing. It is emphasized, however, when I hear "macho" comments, when I participate in a feminist action, when I get together with my women friends. . . . There are different ways of taking on and signifying one's situation, and even one's bodily experience. Sometimes the sexual dimension dominates, sometimes age, sometimes national or linguistic allegiance. And writing can, at different times, take on one or more of these elements to a greater or lesser degree. As for feminist criticism, it approaches a text, a work, from a reading grid based on the difference between the sexes. That's what characterizes it and makes it effective. But a reading grid never exhausts the text. It makes some of its aspects apparent, but can't constitute an evaluative norm.

I am wary of the notion of "feminine writing," developed in recent years, insofar as it claims to define what is really feminine. Feminism is not, for me, an ontology, or a metaphysics that would define woman as being, but a political and poetic movement that incites women and each woman to be, without any prejudice concerning what this being should be. There is in feminism, in France anyway, a metaphysical or naturalist current that claims to define women on the basis of their physiology or their morphology, as if the body were an objective given, the fundamental shared basis of a sort of species (feminine specificity): that is right in line with Freudian positivism. The body is not a given but a relationship; it signifies itself in language, and it is taken up again in the workings of meaning. The difference between the sexes is incontrovertible, but the determination of what each sex *is* remains open.

And there is still less a concept of feminine writing or of woman's writing that describes what this writing *is*. There can be a sociology of writing by women, which analyzes its specific conditions of emergence and diffusion in a given society; there can be a feminist criticism of writing, which approaches a work from the point of view of gender characteristics: that does not imply that one can define woman's writing as belonging to all works by women and specify them as such.

Writing "as a woman" is thus a certain way of situating myself in writing, which is more obvious in my feminist thought than in my fiction or even in my philosophical writings. It is a way of oversignifying my gendered position. Elsewhere, in my other writing, it seems to me that I have allowed my moorings to drift, that I don't have any voluntary, predetermined notions as to my place of enunciation or my destined reader. For one can truly write only if one does not predetermine one's space. (This space can indeed be quite "feminine"—that doesn't matter.) To write is to lift all censorship, if possible, all self-censorship. It is always about producing what one didn't know before writing.

—(AM) Only in France can one imagine that writing "as a woman" could be a form of censorship. In the United States, it's the opposite: writing "as a woman" is something extra, a kind of freedom, an opening-up. . . .

—Perhaps because there has been, in France at any rate, a theorization of feminine writing, of feminine art, that has been linked to a theorization of the female body, and that has occasionally seemed restrictive to those women who weren't experiencing their bodies in that way and who weren't writing in that feminine register. Personally, at certain times I have felt, perhaps wrongly, the weight of that censorship and, as a writer and as a feminist, have had to free myself from it. All the same, I don't think that such theory was or is absent from the American feminist horizon. One does find there the idea of a "feminine specificity" that one keeps trying to define. But it is true that in France the relationship to theory is somehow sacred: if theory enters into conflict with experience, experience is wrong. In the United States, theory must account for experience, but if it doesn't work, or no longer works, you get rid of it without regret. I suppose that's what's called American pragmatism. (So in Europe, the bankruptcy of Marxism induced an irreversible trauma among intellectuals, as if the end of an ideology were the end of the world, as if no leftist politics was possible anymore if it wasn't based on a system.) It seems to me that in the United States the feminist movement has incited women to create and write in diverse registers, even more than to define the nature of the feminine. Or rather that each woman has defined that nature in her own way.

—(AJ) What authorized you to write? I think that if I were asked this question, I would have difficulty answering it: for there is still today a tension for me between my desire to risk writing in the strong sense (as "uncensored," as you emphasized before) and my desire to keep writing in the way I have so far (more "academically")—a way that, at least for my generation, was largely if not totally authorized by the entrance of feminism into the academy.

—I wrote and published before the advent of feminism. So I can't say that, as far as I'm concerned, feminism authorized me to write. I don't know what authorized me; I probably authorized myself. In the first stages of feminism, I even felt guilty for writing the way I did, since writing is always about recoiling into one's uniqueness and one's solitude, and so also in a way about not participating in collective action. I don't feel that way anymore today, for we have understood that there is no living collective that isn't made up of singular individuals. One has to speak in one's own name in order for one's voice to exist and for it to enable dialogue.

Regarding my feminist thinking, I believe that all the women who read my work or with whom I engage in dialogue not only authorize me but make me feel like continuing and going further. (As you do at this moment by interviewing me.) For my other types of writing, in philosophy and fiction, of course my male and female readers, when they assert themselves, also encourage me—and the role of, among others, the male or female publisher has an important symbolic value. Nor can one deny the force public success gives one, for example. But there is also self-justification in writing, a sort of obscure necessity, an "authorization" that comes even before publishing, which is no doubt related to the secret pleasure words give, a pleasure that often cannot be equaled by the pleasure given by people. This is already experienced in the pleasure of reading. Even if writing needs others, if it requires a reader, it also is fascinated with solitude.

Question 3: Many women writing today find themselves, for the first time in history, at the center of such institutions as the university and psychoanalysis. In your opinion, will this new placement of women help them to enter the twentieth-century canon, and if so, will they be in the heart of this corpus or (still) in the footnotes?

—It is true that the women who wrote in preceding centuries did so on their own, without benefiting from the security of a political, social, or scientific institution (even if the salons, for example, can be said to have functioned similarly in the eighteenth century). Their texts represented a *coup de force*. Today, at least for certain women, their writing is made official and authenticated by a title or affiliation. This situation certainly helps them to be heard and to take their place in the arena of intellectual exchange. Even more so because in our society one who is only herself or himself is nothing; you need a label, a validation certificate. (Unfortunately, for many this label replaces thought, but it affords social recognition.) This new position of women certainly enables them to be better heard. I don't know if it will ensure that their texts will survive the test of time. It gives them a chance anyway. An institutional backing does increase the social circulation of a text, but it doesn't guarantee its value. . . . The institution and one's relationship to the institution, moreover, are more complex than they seem. There is, to be sure, the university, or, since Lacan, psychoanalysis—a new space of power—but there is also the world of publishing, the mass media, and even systems of social relations, an entire network that determines the space of intellectual power and its scene. There are those who have moved in, others who are camping out on its steps, and others who come and go. There are passing heroes—dictated by fashion—and there are those who are left behind or excluded.

—(AJ) France, for us, during the last two decades or so has been about works of fiction, philosophy, and psychoanalysis, but it does seem that it is the women most influenced by psychoanalysis who remain the best known, particularly in the United States.

—Psychoanalysis did indeed occupy an important place in French thought over the course of the 1960s and under the influence of Lacan. That place is diminishing today. An entire current of feminist thought, which we call "essentialist,"[4] sprang either directly or indirectly from psychoanalysis to the extent that it ratified the distinction between man and woman, masculine and feminine, on the basis of biological and morphological difference. That's the type of feminism that "went over" best in the United States, and it's all the more paradoxical given that it's completely opposed to Simone de Beauvoir's position (also very successful in the United States), since, as is known, for her "one is not born, but rather becomes a woman."

---

[4] Collin is probably referring in large part to the writings and practice of the group "Psychanalyse et Politique." For a recent consideration of the essentialist debate in both countries, see the first issue of *Differences* (1989), vol. I, no. I.

One always has a somewhat schematic, even caricatured vision of what is foreign. Only a few big names are known, and those are rendered sacred. But the reality on the scene is completely different. Thus in France an entire current of research exists, derived directly from Simone de Beauvoir and indirectly from Marxism, that considers the feminine to be a historical product of oppression.

As far as I am concerned, I think that any attempt to define woman remains imprisoned in metaphysics, and that the common world of women cannot have resulted from either belonging to a common "species" (or race?) or even from their common oppressed position but instead arose from a decision, which one can call political, to mutually recognize and name one another, to mutually cause one another to become subjects.

But thought, in France as elsewhere, is not made of dominant "currents" alone; it is made of countless texts and work from various authors, each one following his/her path, which cannot be organized by labels.

To come back to psychoanalysis, whose influence is not so strong today as in the past, I think it had the merit of taking seriously the question of the difference between the sexes. At the same time, however, it continued to be marked by late-nineteenth-century positivism, to which Freud was linked, in trying to found this difference on an organic duality that determined access to the symbolic. This position oriented the feminism that derived from it.

—(AJ) To come back for a moment to the question of the relationships between creativity and the institution, there are perhaps some cultural differences here, from one country to another. In the United States, there is, at least today, a sort of institutional subculture; which is to say that the institutions themselves, either out of distraction or for some other reason, let slip through, let enter works and especially people who do not identify with the institution or, for that matter, are even anti-institutional. My impression is that in France, this phenomenon is less widespread. Do you think American institutions, the university in particular, leave one more freedom?

—The institution, wherever it is, is always necessarily permeable to whatever is outside it, but often with some delay. Nonetheless, American institutions are probably more flexible, more open than the French ones. As far as the university goes, the American university's relative autonomy clearly enables each university to negotiate its programs and to choose its professors, whereas in France, the university is centralized and every change must come from above, and thus [be implemented] in every university in the same way—which is paralyzing. This development has, by the way, been very harmful to feminist research. In the United States, indeed, all that's needed is one or two determined people, in a given university, to take an initiative or to develop a sector. Here that is unthinkable. Nevertheless, it is useful to point out that from time to time parainstitutional initiatives open up the institution. I am thinking of the Collège International de Philosophie in Paris, where there is a place for seminars, problematics, and people—including non-French ones—not all of which could be integrated into the university. This college is controlled by "institutional" people but leaves some place for others. For France that's already daring. . . . What May 1968—whose twentieth anniversary was just celebrated—has enabled us to imagine is indeed completely covered up today. But I think that's somewhat the case all over. In the United States as well, it seems specialization and competitiveness have taken over.

I think that the size of the American territory, its division into states, also furthers institutional diversification and the multiplication of codes and fashions. This is perceivable at the level of literature and the publishing world. Not all publishers are working out of New York—all writers don't flock there to live—whereas Paris exercises a centralizing effect on all France, and even on the francophone world.

The American scene should not, however, be idealized: it seems to me it also includes effects of fashion that are somewhat paralyzing. I am thinking in particular of America's reception of French thought, or even of French feminist thought, which amounts to a few names being repeated in any and every context. I am thinking of the "deconstructionism" vogue, which, ever since Derrida, has hit all the French departments, and today even the Women's Studies departments. I am thinking of the invitations extended to intellectual stars, who are being fought over with dollars. As if thinking were a product one could buy at a fixed price, according to the laws of supply and demand. Besides, one could even wonder if feminism hasn't become just a new gadget of American society, if feminist research hasn't become a new kind of lobby. The point of this is not to judge it negatively but to point out that each national culture does indeed have its own way of functioning, with advantages and disadvantages.

But, as I said earlier, the advantage of the United States is its diversity and also its capacity for responding to new practices.

Question 4: Today we are seeing women produce literary, philosophical, and psychoanalytic theory of recognized importance, and, parallel to this, we are also seeing a new fluidity of borderlines among disciplines and genres of writing. Will this parallelism lead only to women being welcomed alongside men, or to a definitive blurring of these categories?

—I am not at all convinced that feminism is responsible for this fluidity of borders between genres, which we used to dream about during the seventies, and which you are alluding to now. All in all, "feminist research," for example, finally adopted the style and tone of traditional scholarly works, with a similar concern for erudition, references, and critical apparatus—to the extent, by the way, that this research wanted to be recognized by the institution. The "transdisciplinarity" that had been the aim at the outset was left behind: there is feminist research in history, philosophy, psychoanalysis, and sociology. On the other hand, women are writing novels, poems, and plays.

No doubt some books, some authors, both men and women, don't get locked into these limitations, but this phenomenon isn't new. There have always been "essayists" who write without becoming locked into a specialty. (Among our contemporaries, one could mention Barthes or Blanchot.) They—men and women—create their own frame of reference, their own code.

I don't know if feminism furthers the emergence of such "outside the framework" texts. What is being looked for in feminism is first of all a common space, which didn't exist before but which today is a space being inscribed within the public arena. Feminism has a recognition problem: the internal recognition of women by women and the external recognition of women by the university, publishing, and social institutions. The subversive nature of the feminism of the seventies is losing some ground.

—(AJ) It seems to me, however, that in the United States more than in France, and yet often on the basis of this same French thought, we are producing works where the disciplines are mixed, where the boundaries are blurred: between psychoanalysis and philosophy, for example, or through the emergence of a new "cultural criticism."

—In France too, of course, one can find references to Lacan and to Derrida, to Kristeva and to Bataille in the same book—a sort of "nouvelle cuisine" of thought. But this "nouvelle cuisine" also has its own specific codes, its highly considered authors, and its fashionable topics.

And some men and women attempt to escape from cumbersome scholarly language, to let a certain pleasure of writing play even in their theoretical texts, a pleasure that exceeds the need for efficiency alone. But this is not primarily a feminist issue or an issue stemming from feminism. Nor is it a true abandoning of codes: it is only a more subtle manner of defining them and playing with them. The work that distills its own code is a rare one.

—(AJ) I am still wondering how the gender of the author affects this question of boundaries and the reception of works. When men blur the boundaries, when one does a little cooking, puts in a little Derrida, a little Lacan, I personally, quite often, respond to it negatively. On the other hand, when a feminist takes these same texts and does the same thing with them, when she is in the kitchen, the cooking is often quite good, it's different. I was wondering if there isn't something . . .

—(AM) It is different when women do that. Yet what I hear over and over again is women being accused of not being able to master any one thing. If a woman quotes several theorists, it's because she hasn't understood anything. A woman has to specialize; she doesn't have the right to quote everyone. But if it's a man, everyone knows right away that he has read and understood everything. He has the right to do that and to write that way, to blur the boundaries between disciplines if he wants to. Women can do it only among themselves, in the kitchen.

—Yes, and unfortunately, many women nowadays absolutely want to prove themselves, to show that they "know," out of a concern for the recognition I was just talking about. And beneath the weight of erudition and theory, thought risks being smothered. The competence of a specialist is certainly admirable and enviable, but it can replace neither thought nor action. It cannot absorb feminism. Personally I am always seduced by the rigor of knowledge and competence—which is not to be confused with formal erudition—but I also have a profound admiration for "wild," free writings that emerge from original, even self-taught individuals: writings often doomed to the margins, even to being forgotten. There is no overarching criterion: each woman, in the way that is hers, must look for the rigor that suits her. But it is true, as you say, that men are given credit for the transgression of forms, whereas for women, it is often considered an inability to attain the norm. We have to avoid giving in to this unwitting blackmail. There can be true creation only if one accepts that one may not please, if one accepts that one may not be recognized, or at least if the desire to please or be recognized isn't the determining factor. That is, of course, difficult.

Hannah Arendt, in analyzing the situation of the Jews in nineteenth-century societies, says that they were constantly moved from the position of pariah to that of "parvenu," from exclusion to assimilation.[5] That's our problem too. I don't have a lot of sympathy for parvenus. But then again, the position of pariah is not enviable either. How can one stop being a pariah without becoming a parvenu?

Question 5: Given the problematic and the politics of the categories of the canon, and given the questions we've been dealing with, do you think your oeuvre will be included in the twentieth-century canon, and if so, how will it be presented? In your opinion, what will the content of the canon be?

—That question makes me laugh. What's the twentieth-century canon? Is there a twentieth-century canon? How would you define it? And if there is one, is the way you would define it today the same as the way it will be defined in the future?

History is constantly reshaped and reread in line with the present. Works that seemed important in their time disappear completely and sometimes reappear later. And it all depends on the point of view one adopts. The reading of history itself is work in constant motion and depends upon those who read.

To speak of a twentieth-century canon is to believe that there is a single point of view for "History," in its entirety, in a Hegelian manner. I don't share that opinion. We think, speak, act in the uncertainty of the Last Judgment, at the mercy of what is imposed upon us today. There is no Last Judgment. I don't know if what I have written and accomplished will be taken up by the women or men who follow me. I did what I had to do, what I was able to do, at a given conjuncture, and on the basis of my own abilities. In so doing, no doubt I made something move—through my fiction, through my articles and essays, and through the journal I founded and led, the *Cahiers du GRIF*. I don't know what will happen to this work. That [decision] belongs to the women who will come after me. In any case, I answered the call of my time, of my generation. I never asked myself about the "canon." Of course, each writer hopes that what he or she has written will be read and reread, will make sense, that its heritage will be welcomed.

—(AM) More simply stated, then, will today's women writers be read later? Will they be read after their deaths?

[5] Hannah Arendt, *The Jew as Pariah: Jewish Identity and Politics in the Modern Age*, ed. Ron H. Feldman (New York: Grove Press, 1978).

—That will depend on the women and the men who come after. I hope so. I hope we haven't worked in vain. That we won't be submerged. That it won't be necessary for women to start all over. I dare to think that our words will not die with us. But I don't know which ones will be strong enough [to act as] beginnings for the next generations. Whatever the case may be, and even if everything I've accomplished ends up submerged, that's what I was able to do within the framework of my limited existence. I cannot prejudge the desire of those who come after me; I cannot outguess or constrain them. We will leave a heritage, but that heritage is, as René Char (whom Arendt cites frequently) says, "without a last will and testament."

Question 6: According to you, then, what is finally the relationship between writing and the institution?

—I am tempted to answer first that there is none, or that it can only be destructive, but I do have to nuance that a bit. The institution constitutes a source of encouragement, of support, and especially a significant channel for writing, but it can't do anything for creation proper. It also happens that it can paralyze creation, harden it or falsify it. Creation, like thought or fiction, needs the "social element" that the institution provides, but creation cannot succumb to the social. Thought runs the risk of becoming professorial thought, of giving in to scholarly display; fiction runs the risk of giving in to publishing demands or to the ease of success.

For women, as for men, there's a difficult balance to negotiate that everyone must negotiate in her/his way. There are those who, totally drunk from recent success and publicity, become dependent upon it. Others, by choice or out of necessity, resist as much as they can any sort of institutionalization, do not give in to publicity, don't even go after it, and pursue their work outside the surrounding intellectual and/or worldly brouhaha. It seems to me that women who for so long were deprived of a public arena, who have only just arrived there, can be pretty easily tainted by their own success. In discovering the intoxicating strength that an institution can offer them, they may sometimes tend to risk forgetting its relativity or its misdeeds.

Getting back to creativity, I think that important work, first and foremost, is elaborated in solitude, far from the noise of the world. Work requires retreat, an at least momentary indifference to the social, even if an institution is needed for the work's financing or publication. I

hold the "wild ones" in high regard, those men and women who tena-
ciously pursue their own trajectory without worrying too much about
its institutional inscription. But that is only possible for women if others
relay the information, if they read, comment on, and make known what
has been elaborated in silence. All women's creative forms are then in
solidarity with one another, and together they are responsible for the
survival of the "matrimony." Without these relays, works die or disappear. Without them, women who create end up discouraged and stop
believing in what they are doing. During the first part of the twentieth
century, one often saw women supporting other women—I am thinking of Alice B. Toklas alongside Gertrude Stein. Today, the system of
relays is rather more collective than interindividual, more public than
private. And above all it is based on a sort of exchange in which each
woman, in playing the role of relay for another, finds in that role a
chance to affirm herself. It seems to me that what neofeminism has
created is, for the first time, the conditions for a direct line of filiation
and symbolic affiliation of women. For the first time relationships are
being woven among us through our texts, our works: they are objecti-
fied, with attention and respect, through a mixture of agreement and
disagreement. The other woman is no longer perceived as a devouring
and threatening maternal figure, or as a rival daughter figure. What we
say and what we write is, for the most part, received in its truth and
beauty, which each one of us can take up again and share. Our product
detaches itself from us: it mediates our relationships. It seems to me that
that's the most important thing we've learned in the last few years.

But I think that it's a first step, and that the second step would be to
have *everyone* recognize our creations and what they offer not just to
women but to humankind. The ruse of the two-sexed world (whose
dominant facet is, of course, masculine) is to recognize the validity of
our creations, but for women only—which is to say that it finally refuses
to acknowledge that the world in general may have something to learn
from women. It is a subtle form of negation that we have perhaps made
easier by isolating ourselves in order to consolidate ourselves. To be
sure, women's individual literary works can be recognized by the world
of men or the two-sexed world, and even find a place there—one thinks
of Marguerite Duras, for example—but the innovation that the thought
and voice of women can introduce into this world is often evaded. The
two-sexed-but-male world annexes some works by women but also pro-
tects itself from them.

In the same way, "feminist research" today, even in the midst of important developments, runs the risk of being confined to a women-only world, as if it had no value and no effectiveness for all knowledge, as if it were only annexed to it, as one of its specialties. That is why I think that today the strategy for feminist research must be to ensure its presence in all university departments and research centers, rather than grouping it into a specialized department that runs the risk of being marginalized.

5
Marguerite Duras

TRANSLATED BY KATHERINE ANN JENSEN

Question 1: What does it mean to you to write at the end of the twentieth century?

—Writing . . . I've never asked myself to be aware of what time period I was living in. I have asked myself this question in relation to my child and his future activities, or in wondering what would become of the working class—you see, in relation to political considerations or issues. But not as concerns writing. I believe writing is beyond all . . . contingency.

Question 2: Is it valid/of value to write as a woman, and is it part of your writing today?

Excerpts from this interview with Alice Jardine, translated by Heidi Gilpin, appeared in *Yale French Studies* (1988), vol. 75.

—I have several opinions about that, several things to say. Perhaps I should give a personal example. I don't have any major problems anymore in terms of the reception of my books, but the way men in society respond to me hasn't changed.

—(AJ) That hasn't changed at all?

—No, each time I see critics who are . . . Misogyny is still at the forefront.

—(AJ) Only in France or . . .

—I haven't read the foreign papers. *The Lover,* you know, has been translated in twenty-nine countries. There have been thousands and millions of copies sold. I don't think that in America there's been as much [misogyny] . . . because a lot of women write articles [on my work]. I don't think there's been any misogyny, strictly speaking, aimed at me in America.

—(AJ) I have the same impression.

—No, actually, there is someone at the *New York Times* who doesn't like me at all, because I was once rather nasty to him. It was after a showing of *India Song.* The auditorium was full, I remember that, and at the end the students were really pleased and gave me a big ovation. The audience was asked to speak; I was there to answer. So this guy got up, you know, from the *Times,* very classic, old. He began, "Madame Duras, I really got bored with your . . ."

—(AJ) He said that?! in public?

—Yes, it was a public thing. So I said: "Listen, I'm really sorry, but it's hardly my fault. There must be something wrong with you." He just looked at me. (Usually this works well.) "Please excuse me, but I can't do anything for you." It was really terrible. Since then, people tell me, "I can't invite you anymore because he'll never forgive you." It doesn't matter to me. I'm very happy.

—(AJ) I have the impression that misogyny, in the most classic sense of the term, exists in France much more than in the United States. Even if it's on the tip of American men's tongues or the tip of their pens, they stop themselves now because there's been so much . . . They swallow their words because they know what will happen afterward if they don't; whereas here in France, it seems to me that they get away with it. No one says anything. And that's why, for me, to write as a woman in France begins to have a very different meaning. . . .

—But I have safety valves. That is, from time to time, I write articles about critical theory, and that scares the critics.

—(AJ) I can imagine.

—But . . . it scares women too. It has to do with *écriture féminine*. There are a lot of women who align themselves with men. Recently, a guy did a whole page in a journal about me to say that I don't exist, that I'm . . . I don't remember what. So in that instance, I said that he was the victim of great pain at the thought of my existence. And I can't do anything about that.

—(AJ) It's not worth the energy.

—No. It's not a question of energy. It's just that in France, if you don't pay attention, you can get eaten up.

—(AJ) As a woman or as a writer generally?

—As a woman writer. There are two potential attacks: those from homosexuals and those from heteros.

—(AJ) And they're different?

—At first, no; but in the end they each think that they do such different things, although it's not true at all. They do the same things. It's about jealousy, envy . . . a desire to supplant women. It's a strange phenomenon. I write quite a lot about homosexuality . . . because I live with a man who's homosexual . . . as everyone knows . . . but I write outside all polemic. You see, *Blue Eyes, Black Hair* is outside any polemic. Homosexuals are often not interested in their experiences, they think they've said everything there is to say. That's a limitation. They're not interested in knowing what a woman can get from that experience. What interests them is knowing what people think about homosexuality, whether you're for or against it, that's all.

—(AJ) You have been describing men's reactions to your work as a woman writer. I too have been intrigued by the question of how men respond to woman and women. My latest book, *Men in Feminism,*[1] coedited with Paul Smith, is a collection of articles addressing the complicated relationship men have to feminism, and women have to feminist men. My book *Gynesis*[2] intervenes in this debate by examining how the metaphor of woman operates in several key French texts by men from the last twenty-odd years, for example, those by Blanchot, Deleuze, Derrida, and Lacan.

—You know, even before those writers, there was Beauvoir. She didn't change women's way of thinking. Nor did Sartre, for that matter. He didn't change anything at all. Is *Gynesis* coming out in France?

—(AJ) Yes. One of the interesting problems that has come up with

[1] *Men in Feminism* (New York: Methuen, 1987).
[2] *Gynesis: Configurations of Woman and Modernity* (Ithaca: Cornell University Press, 1985).

my translator is how to find an expression for the term "man writer." In the United States, you see, we're trying to deuniversalize: we say woman writer. We try to give terms genders. But in French, it doesn't work at all. If my translator uses "man writer," everyone will say it's horrible.

—It's too late.

—(AJ) Yes, it's too late. But I can't just put the gender of the writer in the footnotes either. When I say "writer," I mean "man writer" because that's how the universal returns.

—Because "writer" historically means male, is that it?

—(AJ) Yes, the universal.

—But even when they were making distinctions between men and women writers twenty-five years ago, in newspaper headlines, there were no women writers or men writers. There were "novels by women," "novels by men," and books by women or books by men. But that was always a minor distinction, always in a footnote.

—(AJ) It's odd, in French you can get woman out of the universal, but not man (you can say woman writer [*femme écrivain*] but not man writer [*homme écrivain*]).

Question 3: Many women writing today find themselves, for the first time in history, at the center of such institutions as the university or psychoanalysis. In your opinion, will this new placement of women help them to enter the twentieth-century canon, and if so will they be at the heart of this corpus or (still) in the footnotes?

—I think that the women who can get beyond the feeling of having to correct history will save a lot of time.

—(AJ) Please explain.

—I think that the women who are correcting history, who are trying to correct the injustice of which they're victims, of which they always were and still are victims—because nothing's changed, we have to really get that: in men's heads everything's still the same. . . .

—(AJ) You really think so?

—I'm sure, yes. The women who are trying to correct man's nature, or what has become his nature—call it whatever you want—they're wasting their time.

—(AJ) What you're saying is really depressing.

—I think that if a woman is free, alone, she will go ahead that way, without barriers; that is how I think she'll create fruitful work.

—(AJ) All alone?

—Yes. I don't care about men. I've given up on them, personally. It's not a question of age, it's a question of intellectuality, if you like, of one's mental attitude. I've given up on trying to . . . to put them on a logical track. Completely given up.

—(AJ) It's true that in the United States, after so many years, especially in the university, after so much effort to change what and how we read, what and how we interpret, etc., the new generations may be feeling a sort of exhaustion and boredom with that struggle.

—That's what I think.

—(AJ) Yes, but it's really complicated . . . this desire not to be always criticizing, always in negation.

—Yes, it's an impasse.

—(AJ) I have always believed in the importance of this struggle, but I recognize more and more why young women can say that the struggle isn't for them.

—I'm certainly not leading it.

—(AJ) But you did lead it at a certain period, didn't you?

—No. Maybe you're thinking about a woman from the women's movement who interviewed me.[3] I don't remember anymore. I said there was a women's writing, didn't I?

—(AJ) Yes.

—I don't think so anymore. From the position I have today, a definitive one, the most important writer from the standpoint of a women's writing is Woolf. It's not Beauvoir.

—(AJ) Yes, but for me, there's more of a schizophrenia to it, because when I think of my intellectual, institutional, political life, Beauvoir is the one who plays the part of the phantasmatic mother . . . I must do everything, read everything, see everything . . . but in my desire for writing, it's Woolf. They go together.

—Yes, exactly. It's not all of Woolf. *A Room of One's Own* is the Bible.

—(AJ) And in my imaginary, Marguerite Duras, you are there with Woolf.

—Yes, well, still. You know, when I was young, I was very free. I was part of the Resistance during the Algerian War. I took a lot of risks, I risked . . . even with Algeria, I ran the risk of being imprisoned. Maybe it's in that sense that I'm still free.

—(AJ) That is, because you've already taken risks.

---

[3] Duras is referring to Xavière Gauthier's interview with her, published as *Les Parleuses*.

—Because I haven't written on women. Or very little. I see women as having pulled themselves through. That is, they've taken the biggest step. They're on the other side now. All the successful books today are by women, the important films are by women. The difference is fabulous.

—(AJ) So perhaps, according to you, we have to turn away somewhat from the reactive struggle and move instead toward creativity.

—Yes, that's what I think.

—(AJ) Do you think this is going to happen by itself? I'd like to believe it, but I'm not sure.

—I believe that a book like *The Lover*—which was a slap in the face for everyone, for men—is a great leap forward for women, which is much more important. For a woman to claim international attention makes men sick. It just makes them sick.

—(AJ) I didn't see it like that from the United States.

—That's how it was. I don't know how it was for Americans because I got an important American prize . . . and six Americans voted for me. You see, there were 700 voters, then 500, then 300, and finally 70 and then less—you know at different stages of the competition. In the end, there were nine voters. The six Americans all voted for me. The three Frenchmen (France has never had a prize in America) all voted *against* me.

—(AJ) You're kidding?

—Some papers, and probably they were right . . . said that they didn't want a writer from the Left to have the first American prize. But that's not it. It's because I was a *woman* writer. Of course, we must recognize that those three people were on the Right. I think that women on the Left are less alienated; whereas on the Right, so many women with government responsibilities are just followers. It's striking how visible that is.

Question 4: Today we are seeing women produce literary, philosophical, and psychoanalytical theory of recognized importance, and parallel to this, we are seeing a new fluidity in the borderlines among disciplines and genres of writing. Will this parallelism lead only to women being welcomed alongside men, or to a definitive blurring of these categories?

—I don't know, it's dangerous. Because men's criteria have been tested a long time, and men manipulate them astutely and diplomatically. Men aren't politicians, they're diplomats, and that's a degree lower.

Question 5: Given the problematic and the politics of the categories of the canon, and given the questions we've been dealing with here, do you think your oeuvre will be included in the twentieth-century canon, and if so, how will it be presented? In your opinion, what will be the content of the canon?

—(AJ) This is an indiscreet question. . . .

—No it isn't. I don't know what it will be, I don't know, how can I say this, who will be deciding. The only thing that reassures me is that, now, I've become a little bit of an international phenomenon—even a pretty big one. And what France won't do, other countries will. So I'm safe. But those are the terms that I have to use. I'm not safe in France. I'm still very threatened.

—(AJ) You think so really?

—Yes, I'm sure, I know, I'm sure.

—(AJ) For me though, coming from the outside, that's incredible, incomprehensible even.

—But they never attacked Simone de Beauvoir.

—(AJ) What do you mean?

—They never attack Simone de Beauvoir. They never attack Sarraute. But in my case, I've been involved in men's things. First, I was involved in politics. I was in the Communist Party. I did things that are considered in bad taste for a woman. That's the line England took for a long time. In England, they said that Marguerite Duras could never be a novelist because she was too political. Now, my literary oeuvre, my literary work has never gotten mixed up with politics. It never moves to rhetoric. Never. Even something like *The Sea Wall* remains a story. And that's what has saved me. There's not a term, not a trace of dialectic in my fiction. Well, there might be some in *The Square,* perhaps, a kind of theory of needs from Marx that was figured in the little girl, the maid who did everything, who was good for everything, but that was the only time, I think.

—(AJ) But still, your book *Les Parleuses* has come out from Nebraska press with a great deal of success.

—How was that translated?

—(AJ) *Woman to Woman.*

—Isn't that a little outmoded now, *Les Parleuses?*

—(AJ) Not in the United States. Here maybe. No, not even here; people recognize that there are really beautiful things in it.

—The speaking women, that is?

—(AJ) Yes, the image of two women engaged in speaking to each other.

—You know, when I gave that title to my publisher, he was afraid it would have a negative effect. But I said I wanted it because others would say that women just gossip.

—(AJ) Right. . . .

Question 6: And a last question just for you: we are asking you these questions about the future destiny of the work of contemporary women, when, in fact, your work seems to have been canonized already. Actually, you are one of the few people who has been able not only to see her work emerge from an unfair obscurity into the limelight but who has seen it attain worldwide recognition. How has becoming a celebrity influenced a vision that was intentionally critical and other?

—You know, *The Lover* came late in my life. And even its fame wasn't something new for me. I had already had two things make it on the worldwide scene, and so I was used to that phenomenon—of something operating totally independently of you. It happens like an epiphenomenon, it takes place in inaccessible regions. You can't know why a book works, when it works that well. First, it was *Hiroshima, mon amour,*[4] which was seen all over the world. And then I had *Moderato cantabile,* which must have had the same effect as *The Lover,* for it was translated everywhere. Such a small book that was a worldwide hit, it's strange. Well, I was no young girl in the face of those events. As for the end of your question, "a vision that was intentionally critical and other"—that doesn't have anything to do with it. I understand the implication in your question that being famous somehow intimidates, inhibits. No, no, on the contrary. . . .

—(AJ) But there's a mythology that says that being famous is a defeat in mass culture.

—Yes, I know that. . . . That reminds me of what Robbe-Grillet told me one day. He said, "When you and I have sold 500,000 copies, that will mean we don't have anything else to say." Well, so I don't have anything else to say—and he has another book.

[4] Screenplay and dialogue by Marguerite Duras, directed by Alain Resnais.

6

Claudine Herrmann

TRANSLATED BY PATRICIA BAUDOIN

Question 1: What does it mean to you to write at the end of the twentieth century?

—Writing seems to me to be dangerous in a world where the future of humanity is in jeopardy. I wonder sometimes if our descendants will know how to read and if books won't be a passing stage of the general evolution of things.

Writing should, logically, be what our editors think it is: addressing the present, at least, or perhaps the coming year. Still, things don't exactly happen that way for me. When I write, it seems to me (although I'm willing to admit readily that this point of view is irrational) that I

Excerpts from this interview, also translated by Patricia Baudoin, appeared in *Yale French Studies* (1988), vol. 75.

meet with what escapes from time, with what is external to the entropy that surrounds me and possesses me. It is surely not that I imagine myself addressing posterity or that I'm basking in excessive illusions about the durability of what I write, but the very act of writing displaces me inside and gives me the impression of communicating with what is invisible and what cannot be destroyed. In that respect I'm probably much like other writers who came before me, the only difference being, perhaps, that I'm not trying to place that feeling back into a system. Naturally, time is recaptured when the book appears and you have to deal face to face with what is now called "promotion." But that, too, is the twentieth century.

Question 2: Is it valid/of value to write as a woman, and is it part of your writing practice today?

—Although the books that have shaped my thought were mostly books written by men, I know that today if there is anything in me personal and worth expressing, it is necessarily related to my experience and my woman's language [*langage de femme*], simply because I have no other. Even what is imaginary is transmitted through my own circuits and becomes feminized along the way. I became conscious of that with speech long before writing: in the speeches I gave as a young lawyer, I tried so hard to imitate the forms of discourse then in fashion. As I tried, however, to express in my own language what I really thought, the result would surprise me. That's what happens when I attempt to borrow a male concept: it becomes other. Sometimes I do an exercise that consists in narrating an essentially virile scene, a naval battle, for example. You'd be surprised to see how it turns out.

Question 3: Many women writing today find themselves, for the first time in history, at the center of such institutions as the university and psychoanalysis. In your opinion, will this new placement of women help them to enter the twentieth-century canon, and if so, will they be in the heart of this corpus or (still) in the footnotes?

—I don't know exactly what the word institution means here. Are we talking about having a place in "society" or about belonging to the labor force? Nearly all women who have written in the past held positions of importance in the society of their times. Today, positions are most often linked to employment—but it doesn't matter: what is essential for a writer is to be in touch with the world. For some women writers, and not the least among them, that contact can be rather tenuous. I'm thinking of Emily Dickinson.

Question 4: Today we are seeing women produce literary, philosophical, and psychoanalytical theory of recognized importance, and, parallel to this, we are also seeing a new fluidity in the borderlines among disciplines and genres of writing. Will this parallelism lead only to women being welcomed alongside men, or to a definitive blurring of these categories?

—I think personally that the production of *women*, to the extent that women will not be satisfied following (or waiting on) men, will be inscribed alongside men's productions, except in the exact sciences, if there are any left.

Question 5: Given the problematic and the politics of the categories of the canon, and given the questions we've been dealing with, do you think your oeuvre will be included in the twentieth-century canon, and if so, how will it be presented? In your opinion, what will the content of the canon be?

—I have absolutely no idea where my work (which I hope only to complete), will stand. I wonder fruitlessly about whether it will ever appear in a canon. That word for me has nasty connotations, and I don't particularly care to be catapulted into the world of the official. I do, nonetheless, like having women and men readers, and I do recognize that the usefulness of the canon lies in how it multiplies reading possibilities. I hope I'm insulting no one by saying that this canon is a necessary evil. Besides that, the future raises this question for me: there will certainly be more and more books and less and less time to teach them, because of the growth of other areas of knowledge; so, where do we cut back? I have no idea. Nevertheless, I hope that in this mythical canon, there will be proportionately more women than there are today.

Question 6: In the United States, if there is a lively literary criticism, it is feminist criticism. Here in France, on the other hand, your book The Tongue Snatchers *figures among the rare serious contributions in this domain. Why has the meeting of literature and feminist theory inspired so few French women?*

—Entrance into the French university system takes such a toll on everyone that it becomes difficult to attack it once one has entered its fortress: it has shaped your mind, dominated (or seduced) your intelligence, and if you were not ready to be smitten, you would not have spent the best years of your life taking exhausting and competitive entrance exams. Today you can be critical of the impressive corpus of French literature only in accepted forms. Now, feminist criticism, as I see it, is radical and works [against resistance] without courtesy, like a lever. . . . What's more, to show yourself as culturally feminist presents the—justified—fear of displeasing those who will have to vote on your advancement. The French university is tied to its tradition, and I can guarantee that it has no feminist tradition. . . . As for imagining that someone from the outside could launch into such a critical adventure, don't even think it, for in France there is a solidly entrenched idea according to which outside the university there is no true knowledge. This reminds me, strangely, of the saying "Out of the Church, far from salvation" [*Hors de l'église, point de salut*]. It is, by the way, the Sorbonne that, a long time ago, used to point out the dubious points of faith. Today, it has got its hands on knowledge, for the better perhaps, but also for the worse.

Follow-up Question 1: We would like to hear more about your experience as a woman writer: (1) how are your "training" as a lawyer and your fictional writing related, if they are? (2) and what compelled you to write The Tongue Snatchers *with respect to your desire to write and your "discursive stance" as a woman?*

—Compared to linguistics and literature, the law teaches that a single word can change the fate of an individual or even a people. Although the rigidity of legal language can be irritating, it gives to those who know how to handle it a verbal avarice that I find a resource in these times of verbal inflation. With my training, I hope that I have learned how to give to each word a definite meaning.

But the work of a lawyer does not consist only in dealing with the law; it also means dealing with speech—and spoken language differs profoundly from written language.

One does not compose a speech meant to persuade a listener instantly in the same way one composes a written text that can be thought over and reflected upon by the reader. Associations of words and ideas that occur in a conversation are different from those that take shape quietly, before a blank sheet of paper.

I must admit, however, that *The Tongue Snatchers,* many chapters of which were discussed in a seminar taught at Boston University, retains some elements of spoken discourse. That is, perhaps, what gives it its movement.

A writer rarely knows why she wants to write a certain book rather than any other. I spend much time figuring out what I would like to write, but little time wondering why.

Follow-up Question 2: You are the only one, among the women we are interviewing, who really does divide her life between the United States and France. From this "in between" space, how do you see the "women's movement," the present state of feminist theory, etc.?

—I think that these days feminism is rather worse off in the United States than in France, first of all because here in the United States we are in the midst of a major political reaction, and because this reaction, this "return to traditional values" (as if such a thing existed), affects all minorities—but also because here all these phenomena acquire a greater magnitude. I see American life in all its aspects as a gigantic pendulum.

For example, there's the question of the judicial system in the two countries. Once a statute has been passed in France (let's say, a law that legalizes abortion), it is very difficult to change it. The two chambers have to vote, and it is very unlikely that they will take a stand against public opinion. With the common law system, on the other hand, a small group of judges whose position is not dependent upon an election can entirely reverse the jurisprudence we have now with a single decision. They may choose not to do it, but the choice is theirs—and they have already done it in a few discrimination cases. The Supreme Court and the Reagan administration are generally doing their best to limit civil rights (only Congress occasionally resists).

But on the other hand, I find that women themselves are partially responsible for the setbacks we are experiencing. On both sides of the ocean, some women are in despair while others believe that the fight is over. New generations, in fact, believed too quickly that the fight was won and that all they had to do was pursue brilliant careers. Every day I see an astute flattery, a delicate way of reassuring the establishment emerging in lectures and works that claim to be feminist: we are being good girls, some women seem to say, and very scholarly. We are only doing feminist criticism; really, there is no need to worry. . . . We accept the system. . . . We are really not out to change society. . . . In fact, take a good look: it is to you, who are still our masters, that this discourse is addressed. . . .

I was invited, not long ago, to give a lecture before an American academic audience. During one of the discussions led by a woman who had organized a feminist study section, a professor rose to state that Madame de Lafayette's works had been written by a man.[1] I wanted to refute such a secular absurdity, but I found that I was refused the opportunity to speak. Later, thanks to the fact that a New York storm kept me indoors at the airport, I questioned the young woman president.

—Why?

—What can I say, she responded, my career depends on "them."

But cowardice doesn't pay: I have heard that not as much attention is being paid to Women's Studies. And why should we be surprised at this, if everything Women's Studies had in it that was violent and volcanic has been made palatable? In my opinion, feminism is not a "fad" (as I've heard President Silber [of Boston University] call it); it will survive but only if it continues to be fought for. Otherwise, the fragile territories that we have conquered will soon be lost as they already have been several times during the course of history.

But I'm not despairing: the real hope comes from all the obscure women who have become aware of themselves and who work in the shadows: I'm thinking of all those who learned that they really exist and

---

[1] Not only was the *Princesse de Clèves* first published without the name of its author, but Mme de Lafayette repeatedly denied having written it; a letter she wrote to Ménage in 1679 settled the matter for most. Antoine Adam, in his introduction, "Le Roman français au XVIIe siècle," to *Romanciers du XVIIe siècle* (Bibliothèque de la Pléiade; Paris: Gallimard, 1958), explained "that it was out of the question for a woman of [Mme de Lafayette's] rank to figure on the title page of a book" (p. 51). See also Joan DeJean, "Lafayette's Ellipses: The Privileges of Anonymity," in *PMLA* (1984), 99(5):884–902; Marcel Langlois, "Quel est l'auteur de la Princesse de Clèves?" *Mercure de France* (1936), vol. 15; and Bruce A. Morrissette, "Marcel Langlois' untenable attribution of *La Princesse de Clèves* to Fontenelle," *Modern Language Notes* (1946), 41(4):267–70.

that creation is possible for them. It is those women who will, perhaps, survive for the future.

FURTHER THOUGHTS: what I see happening on the two sides of the Atlantic Ocean is not so different—except for technicalities. There has been no deep change in mentalities: on the one hand, men are no more concerned than they were before with family tasks; on the other hand, most women who have added a job to their previous work are exhausted, and, for that reason, rarely advance to the best positions.

Younger generations tend to take for granted all the opportunities that are now theirs and do not realize that success can be measured only in the long term. What has been won can be lost again if it is not thought of and fought for. Most women who participated in the last feminist wave seem to be rather disenchanted, although research and meetings of small groups continue in France as well as in the United States. An important colloquium on sex and gender took place in Paris during the spring of 1988 and such activities as archiving women's films or publishing women's books continue at the Centre Simone de Beauvoir and at the Librairie des Femmes.

I must admit I'd been hoping that relationships between men and women would improve, that understanding between the sexes would deepen. But it seems to me that men, generally speaking, were very quick to take advantage of what was believed to be an improvement in women's condition: if women can earn money, can avoid children or have abortions, does that not mean for some men that they as men can assume less and less responsibility and that, after all, they do not have to be concerned with the consequences of their acts? Moreover, rape has not decreased, nor has incest, and I begin to suspect that neither women nor feminism have ever been taken seriously by most men. These facts are usually more spectacular in the United States, but they are evident in France as well. I must add that many films and books seem to be more hateful than ever toward women. I'm thinking of Milan Kundera's novels. The strange thing is that readers do not even seem to be aware of it. But now we can also read women's books, see women's films, go to women doctors; there are women judges, women scientists, women researchers. Even if these changes turn out to be the only improvements, our feminist struggles will have been worth it.

Follow-up Question 3: You say at a certain point that you do not want to "be catapulted into the world of the official"—while speaking about the canon and of the possible position women might occupy in the canon. How would you say it affects women to be in the canon?

—As to what will happen to the women who secure a place in what you are calling the "canon," I have no idea; nor do I know of any way to speak about it. All I know is that this term brings in resonances I dislike.

7

Jeanne Hyvrard

TRANSLATED BY PATRICIA BAUDOIN

Question 1: What does it mean to you to write at the end of the twentieth century?

—Before I read you my written response, I'd just like to say that I registered some broader concerns in your questions. Since I'm a woman who teaches economics, and am therefore interested in technical, economic, and scientific problems, I have been able, in my answers, to relocate [your primarily] literary questions within a planetary and economic process that I perceive clearly, but that those people who deal only with literature may not see. Since my work is in economics and I write for pleasure, I'm at the junction of the two fields. I think the

Excerpts from this interview, also translated by Patricia Baudoin, appeared in *Yale French Studies* (1988), vol. 75.

answers I offer take your concerns into account. I think your concerns are legitimate but that the manner in which you ask your questions reflects a time that is already, and forever, behind us.

— (Written response) I write in order to stay in touch with the sacred and with culture. To overcome the antagonism between memory and forgetfulness, eternity and time, fusion and separation. To attest to belonging to a Western civilization that nevertheless in this century crushes me. To transmit the forms and the values of the European heritage I have received. To accompany the revolution in cybernetics, in procreatics [reproductive technologies], and in geonomics.[1] To forge new tools enabling one to think the revolution and to join it. In short, to survive.

Without exaggerating anything.

— (AJ) (Conversation) Having just returned from Israel to Europe, I'm very touched by your answer.

— Well, yes, because I think that—well, how can I say this—it is totally in the, let's say, philosophical and biblical realm that I situate myself.

— (AJ) The sacred and the cybernetic. . . . Unlike many others, I, too, do not believe that there is an "elsewhere" where one can locate oneself. I think we're all in this thing, and if we are to survive, we have to . . .

— That is, the Bible does, after all, mean book. That shouldn't be forgotten. How can one write without placing oneself with regard to the Bible and the name; I don't understand.

— (AM) But still, thinking the Bible and cybernetics together. . . . It's really something. It's extraordinary.

— It's the adventure of our times. The more the branches reach upward, the longer the roots need to be for a balance to exist. And I think it's thanks to the branches and the roots that I'm not toppling over.

— (AM) You absolutely have to have both, but it's so complicated.

— No, no, it seems so natural to me. Precisely because I don't teach literature, because I have no literary degrees, because I'm not the daughter of a literary university, I'm a sort of wildwoman. I'm not even aware of the heterodoxical nature of what I represent. It affords me freedom

---

[1] Geonomics: the overall management of the earth's resources, made necessary by the disappearance of borders within an integrated world economy that little by little is replacing the international economy. [All definitions have been provided by Hvyrard.—EDS.]

because I'm not tempted by the university. I'm not tempted in economics either, although there I have an orthodox affiliation. But for literature, I'm coming in on the north side.

—(AJ) North side?

—The north side. You're not familiar with this mountain climber's term? Climbers distinguish between the northern and the southern slopes, geographically, and usually the north side is the more difficult, the wilder, because of the wind and the cold, and because there's no sun. So when one speaks of "climbing the north side," it's an expression from the climber's milieu (which my parents were a part of before the war) that means something like a bit heroic. That's how I live my life in literature: wildly.

—(AM) It's better that way, and that's visible in your text. There's a richness . . . because if you stay too close to the literature of universities, to literary criticism, you can become a bit sterile as a writer, I think.

—It's probably more difficult to be novel if you're in a university. You're trapped in forms, and you become afraid of being excluded. Me, I'm excluded as an economist. Anyway, I'm outside literature. Now, outside, I'm free. If you dealt with economics as well, you would maybe have angles of vision that we don't have.

—(AJ) Perhaps.

Question 2: Is it valid/of value to write as a woman, and is it part of your writing practice today?

—(Written response) Is it valid to write as a woman? The notion of "validity" is totally foreign to me. Since I myself partake of writing, how could I judge the relation that others have to it? The only question is whether it's true. There is no univocal response.

As far as I'm concerned, for many years[2] I did not write "as a woman" although my texts enabled me to break with the imposed model. The pressures and discrimination that I have been subjected to as a woman writer have led me to think about the cloistering of French women in the field of literature, a cultivated version of knitting. Here, they have access to other disciplines only if they respect their hierarchies, their forms, and their fashions, all of which are imposed by men. They remain in a position of subcontractors, and even then on condition that they

[2] From 1974, the beginning of my writing, to 1980, the beginning of *Canal de la Toussaint* on the beach at Dieppe, on April 7.

refrain from putting the logonomic order into question.[3] Having realized this, I had to make a choice between being satisfied with the conceded space ("write and shut up") or taking up the challenge by resorting to feminine networks to break down the dam. I tried this in *Canal de la Toussaint* by establishing philosophical tools to think through the logarchy[4] purveyed by Western males. It is indeed as a woman that I wrote *Canal de la Toussaint,* but the logarchy that is crossed is not strictly masculine, just as the forged tools are not strictly for women. New concepts like "enception" and "chaic"[5] enable us to think fusion. That is necessary in order to understand domination over so-called primitives, crazies, suicidal individuals, or several other categories, no doubt, such as alcoholics or cancer victims. Fusion is not female as such, but it has some relation to the maternal universe and to the projection one makes of it in man-to-woman relations, and more broadly logarchic/fusionary relations.[6]

—(AM) (Conversation) So, it seems to me that there you're on the same trajectory as when you were talking about planetary identity in your article, "Le Français contrelangue."[7] One has to start somewhere: you start from the fact that you are a woman, but one has to go much further, one has to refuse that definition.

—Totally. That's it exactly. The other questions expand on this even more. I think that our problems with feminism and our problems as women are all one problem. . . . Mathematicians would say they are a subset of something far broader that is happening. I don't want—and I don't think it's the right way—to cloister oneself in there.

—(AJ) Thank you for saying it.

—I think that things are happening that are twenty times more important, and that feminism, which is essential, naturally, for us, and which is even vital in my case to keep from dying, is only one element of an array of transformations that fascinates me. I love this sort of period that we're living in the midst of, where everything is toppling over. It's fantastic.

—(AJ) Yes, but with the increasing professionalization of knowl-

[3] Logonomic: relating to the mental space structured around the logos.
[4] Logarchy: power system resting on the predominance of the logos.
[5] Enception and chaic: introduced in *Canal de la Toussaint,* these are to chaos what conception and logic are to logos. Fuller discussions can be found in the philosophical dictionary *La Pensée corps.*
[6] Logarchic/fusionary: dominant and dominated in the logarchy.
[7] Appeared in the Belgian journal *Revue et corrigée* (1985), vol. 18.

edge, the ability to "look at the big picture" becomes more difficult. At that level, things aren't going well at all in the United States, especially among members of the university. . . .

—What's not going well?

—(AM) Many academic feminists realize that it's important to take all the transformations you speak of into account; and strategically, we cannot operate only as feminists to the exclusion of all our other allegiances. Yet because we haven't yet been able to fully inhabit our position as women subjects, that strategic move is extremely difficult. How can you reject an identity that you haven't yet been able to fully assume?

—Isn't that because, all in all, many American women are not very politicized?

—(AJ) At least not within the university. . . .

—As far as I could tell, in North America history hardly exists. So there is no way to recover a feminist movement in it. I make history start even before the Bible because, for example, *Mother Death* refers to a prehistoric, mythical woman, and then especially *Canal de la Toussaint* goes back to wax tablets that predate the Bible. That is, these wax tablets are the parts of Genesis that had already been cleared away when the Bible was constituted; they are called the Tablets of Mesopotamia. So I locate myself both earlier and later. In the best of all cases, even if I manage to live seventy or a hundred years, which I hope will happen, what is that life on the scale of history? Nothing. I perceive it that way and I live that out frenetically. To accompany a period completely, and to know that it is but a bright flash in eternity, that, really. . . . Now, *that* I find exalting.

—(AM) That's why you remind me of Californian women, because in California women who have no ties to university life are also looking at the past that preceded the Bible, at Greece, etc., in order to discover the goddesses and cultures that were crushed and erased.

—Yes, I think it's because of the Pacific. Something new, a Pacific civilization, is in an embryonic stage; because of Japan, because of China, because of Siberia, of Australia or New Zealand. . . . It all brings one back to this fusion. That's why thinking fusion is absolutely indispensable now. That whole area that the West has completely repressed, and that America's East Coast has marginalized even more, now has to be taken into account again to create this Pacific civilization of the twenty-first century. From now on I'm one of its members. I'm implanted in it—it seems grotesque to say so when I'm in Paris right now

—but I seem to myself to be implanted in the twenty-first-century Pacific civilization.

Question 3: Many women writing today find themselves, for the first time in history, at the center of such institutions as the university and psychoanalysis. In your opinion, will this new placement of women help them to enter the twentieth-century canon, and if so, will they be in the heart of this corpus or (still) in the footnotes?

—(Written Response) Will the rise of women in institutions help them? Everyone knows that it is not enough for one of them to be prime minister for her politics to be different from those of her male counterpart. Her "success" within logonomy[8] has only been possible because she has refused to defend [the rights of] women.

What is more worrisome, it seems to me, is the integration of women into male hierarchies on the fictive basis that "women are men like all others." The achievement of such assimilation could well lead to eviction, by those who have newly arrived, of feminine writings that attest to a sexual difference that they themselves have rejected, sometimes for having failed to take it on.

In a rather sectarian and frankly politicized France, one also has to take into account the rivalries that fuel the movement. By using local rifts, one can distinguish State feminists, liberal women, and libertarian women. It would be naïve to think that some Holy Alliance of these groups would eliminate disagreements whose stakes have nothing to do with the question of women, which is but one of the keys to social life. "All things being otherwise equal." Now, this proposition is false.

Further, the cybernetic revolution pure and simple can make the notion of literary body and canon disappear. As for the bionomics (the management of "human capital")[9] in the process of establishing itself, it could well render feminism itself obsolete. In certain respects, vis-à-vis procreatics, which also threatens men, it already is obsolete.

The question asked would have meaning only in a fixist and linear history. That is not the case. For the moment, it is impossible to predict

[8] Logonomy: mental space of the logarchy. Is not to be identified with patriarchy, nor with androcentrism, nor with phallocracy.

[9] Human capital: perception and economy of human beings that amount to considering them as a stock of spare parts that can be changed or thrown out according to profitability calculations.

the consequences of procreatic inventions. In this area, any certainty seems dangerous and perspective seems to stem more from visionary intuitions than from scientific research.

Question 4: Today, we are seeing women produce literary, philosophical, and psychoanalytical theory of recognized importance, and, parallel to this, we are also seeing a new fluidity in the borderlines among disciplines and genres of writing. Will this parallelism lead only to women being welcomed alongside men, or to a definitive blurring of these categories?

— (Written Response) Today, one can observe the arrival of women in theory and barriers breaking down between disciplines, but one cannot deduce causality from concomitance.

As far as I'm concerned, having experienced the limits of both psychoanalysis and literature has led me to work on philosophy in "Traité du désordre." [10] The confinement of French women to genres that their male counterparts consider minor can further their resorting to modes of synthetic expression that enable them to circumvent the prohibitions. I would say that then we are dealing with, and notably in my case, a culture of the clandestine.

One might think that the dam erected against women will erode in proportion to the accumulation of a body of writings that are not only feminine and feminist but also born of woman-thought, [11] its very mass making its censorship impossible. That could lead both to establishing women next to men and to the disappearance of these categories. Woman-thought is not solely meant for women; it can also be used by men. The concepts of enception and chaic may have applications in science. No doubt men already need them, although they can't manage to shape them, precisely because they are men, not in the sexual sense but in the gender sense.

As regards the fluidity of borders and the mixing of genres strictly speaking, I would like to point out that categories have always changed during the course of history. The emergence of new divisions, therefore, does not entitle us to hope. The fluidity of borders and the mixing of genres could be just a transition between two rigidities. Even if the norm changes, it could remain imperative, especially in a dogmatic

---

[10] This is the philosophical first section of *Canal de la Toussaint.*
[11] Woman-thought: set of mental tools enabling thought about problems specific to women.

France. I do not think that the categories will end up being totally mixed. Each era reorganizes its mental space. The new planetary distribution makes the emergence of new disciplines like geonomy or communications necessary. These are not definitive decompartmentalizations, but changes on the scale of fusion and separation. One might think that our era is an era of individualism and the loss of belonging-to, but during the same period of time, procreatics has been creating a common species-body by exchanging gametes, and a common televisual mental space has been constructed. The principle of the world is being displaced but its dialectic remains the same.

—(AM) (Conversation) That brings to mind another question. When one thinks about information theory or cybernetics, it is difficult, at least for the moment, to enter data without entering them in a binary system. Is that going to reinforce the Western system that is already too binary, too rigid? Or is it going to have another effect, since in a sense one can think that cybernetics will open something up?

—Cybernetics is the set of communication techniques; it's not just computer theory. The fact that information theory is stuck in a binary system is dramatically and draconianly true. But it isn't true for television. I've noticed that. For example, I teach and I try to modernize my practice with the help of video cassettes. I show students a lot of films. And, moreover, without my students, I would never have written *Canal de la Toussaint*. The notions of enception and chaic came to me from my teaching practice and from my students' reactions. Things can be communicated through images, through affect, expressions, vision, music, sounds, that are no longer binary at all. Verbal language necessarily led me to try teaching my students economic concepts, which no longer worked for them since, of course, the students are in some sense already in the twenty-first century, far more than we are. While the television was transmitting the notion of encept, all I was doing was theorizing what I noticed in them. To answer your question, therefore, for the cybernetics revolution, information theory reinforces binary thought—absolutely, that's the very principle underlying computer technology. But television and the audiovisual absolutely do not—much to the contrary. Ultimately they offer a voice to what is not binary. And I can see the difference: the concepts my students cannot understand in economics, my video cassettes transmit them as encepts, and it works!

I've been teaching for twenty years, watching my students, listening to them. And collegues say all the time, "their level is dropping; they

don't know anything"—you've heard the tune. Moreover, it's true, but that's another problem. I made the bet of saying, yes but . . .
—(AJ) Precisely. They haven't "become stupid"; there's something else going on.
—Yes. That's it. It's not possible for them to be bigger dumbshits than we were at their age! I've maintained that principle since my audiovisual experiments. I studied the question, applied myself to teaching economics, and discovered that there was another mode of communication. I wasn't transmitting concepts to them, but they were acquiring encepts and all I did was theorize them. I can't express the sort of satisfaction I experience from this intellectual adventure with these students, who are technical school students. They are not at all from the privileged classes, they are lower middle class. They are really average French folks from the heart of France. I would even say that one of the interpretive keys for *Canal de la Toussaint* could be an economics course that just doesn't gel in traditional molds and that's going to happen in a totally different mode—especially for the students. It's terrific, this sort of intellectual adventure with them. They are the ones who whispered it all to me. And if you are attentive to what your students are saying, that is, instead of flunking them and kicking them out, you say, okay, something's changed—then *you're* back in the front-row seats again.

Question 5: Given the problematic and the politics of the categories of the canon, and given the questions we've been dealing with, do you think your oeuvre wil be included in the twentieth-century canon, and if so, how will it be presented? In your opinion, what will the content of the canon be?

—(Written response) As far as I'm concerned, it would be pretentious of me to hope to figure in the classical canon. Pushed by an internal necessity, I write to keep myself alive. My moral sense orders me to witness and not to ask what our species will do with my testimony. Metaphysically, that doesn't concern me, and practically I don't worry about it. If we had to worry about the future, in addition to present difficulties, we'd never work our way out of this.

How can I know what will be said of me? The fact that my contemporaries have already managed to introduce me as a typically Caribbean writer gives humorists all sorts of green lights. But what kind of criticism would have the nerve to say, as I do: "She was a housewife who dreamt of cooking up a chocolate Bavarian cream for her big family but who was cornered, given the events that historically intervened in her life, into taking recourse in writing to emancipate herself and to rethink the world that was condemning her to death?"

Finally how could I imagine what the twentieth century canon might look like? I'm not competent in literary criticism, and in France it all has so much to do with fashion. . . .

Question 6: "Even though I'm French, 'hexagonal,' and white like all my ancestors, in everything from linguistics arguments to the Bordas Encyclopedia, *I'm introduced as a writer typically representative of Caribbean literature."*[12] *Instead of refusing this false impression, you retorted: "In my texts no identity is exploded, but a new planetary identity is anticipated." Does that transnational identity make the idea of a canon obsolete, since one of its main functions is to preserve a national culture through its language?*

—(Written Response) I'm not questioning the existence of a European culture whose homogeneity, when viewed from the Altiplano, Central Asia, or the Sahel, jumps right out at you. But I link it more to the entire continent than to national cultures that use one language as a vehicle. I'm not really convinced of any but the phantasmatic existence of a nation. At any rate that's what emerges from the diversity of provinces and social categories. History is constantly rewritten by those who win and comes to resemble (not to be critical) mythology. One can wonder then if the canon of a national culture is not itself a fantasy—in which case it could well involve the same processes in times to come.

National cultures will not necessarily be rendered obsolete by the third culture[13] currently being born. But their places, their meanings, and their value will be determined by the outcome of the struggle. One can well imagine that the constitution and the significance of the European canon will not be the same in a world dominated by Islam, the USSR, the United States, or Japan.

But one can also imagine that, in an integrated world economy, the nation fantasy might no longer be necessary and would give up its place to other ideologies born of communication and bionomics. For example, one could see a canon of fusionary culture emerge, thereby legitimating new values. The same elements would be reapportioned differently, and not only in literature. Certain authors and certain texts that have been excluded up to now might then finally be recognized.

[12] "Le Français contrelangue," *Revue et corrigée* (1985), vol. 18.
[13] "Third culture": a transnational culture transcending Western and other cultures.

8
Luce Irigaray

TRANSLATED BY MARGARET WHITFORD

Question 1: What does it mean to you to write at the end of the twentieth century?

—It means several things; these are the ones that occur to me today.

(a) I live at the end of the twentieth century and I am old enough to have learned to write.

(b) I earn my living by writing. I am a woman who is not financially dependent on a man or men, but who supports herself. I am in scientific research, and my job is to work on certain questions and to communicate the results of my work.

(c) One of the means through which thought is communicated in

Excerpts from this interview, also translated by Margaret Whitford, appeared in *Yale French Studies* (1988), vol. 75.

the late twentieth century is alphabetical writing. So I use it to communicate even though I think that it is a means that constitutes a limit on
what I have to say, particularly as a woman.

(d) Writing allows me to communicate my thought to many people
whom I do not know, who do not speak the same language I do, who
do not live in the same period I do. On these grounds, to write is to
constitute a body of work with a meaning that can be memorized and
circulated, and that may enter into history, etc. Regarding the content(s)
and form(s) of my discourse, the recourse to writing in the late twentieth century means trying to inaugurate a new cultural era: that of
sexual difference. This work seems to me necessary at this moment in
history in terms of the past, the present, and the future.

(f) After publishing *Speculum*, I was partially deprived of the means
of expressing myself orally. I had a university teaching post and it was
taken from me. Fortunately, my position as a researcher at the Centre
National de la Recherche Scientifique [CNRS][1] was not taken from me.
Fortunately, too, I write, and Minuit [Press] has continued to publish
my work. Writing, then, can represent a means of expressing oneself and
of communicating under circumstances that deprive one of one's right
to speak.

(g) Depriving someone of the right to speak can have several meanings and take several forms. It may be expressed as a conscious ban,
barring a person from teaching institutions, outlawing him or her. This
gesture may mean, at least in part: I don't understand what you are
doing, therefore I reject it, we reject it. In that case, writing is a way of
storing one's thought, keeping it available for those women and men
who, today or tomorrow, will be able to understand it. This necessity is
more readily understandable in certain areas of meaning. These include,
for different reasons, a discourse that seeks to inaugurate a new sexed/
gendered [*sexué*] culture.

*Question 2: Is it valid/of value to write as a woman, and is it part of your
writing practice today?*

—I am a woman. I write with who I am. Why would that not be
valid/of value, unless there were contempt for the value of women, or
refusal of a culture in which the sexual/gendered represented a dimension of subjectivity? But how could I be a woman on the one hand and

[1] The CNRS is a national research facility located in Paris.

write on the other? This scission or split between the one who is a woman and the one who writes can exist only for those who confine themselves to verbal reflexes, taking on the mimeticism of already constituted meaning. My whole body is sexed/gendered. My sexuality is not limited to my sexual organs and to a few sexual acts. I think that the effects of repression and above all of the lack of a sexual culture—civil and religious—are still so powerful that it is possible to make such strange statements as these: "I am a woman," and "I don't write as a woman." These declarations also conceal a secret allegiance to the cultures of men-among-themselves. Indeed, alphabetical writing is historically linked to the civil and religious codification of patriarchal powers. Not to contribute toward giving a sex/gender to language and to its written forms is to perpetuate the pseudoneutrality of the laws of traditions that privilege masculine genealogies and their codes of logic.

Question 3: Many women writing today find themselves, for the first time in history, at the center of such institutions as the university and psychoanalysis. In your opinion, will this new placement of women help them to enter the twentieth-century canon, and if so, will they be in the heart of this corpus or (still) in the footnotes?

—In the period in which we live, there are not many women in the academy. Those who are there are often confined to certain echelons in the career structure. Very few women reach the highest posts, and those who do pay a very high price, in one way or another. This reality is so true that it explains a large part of the debates concerning the names of the professions. But it is not sufficient to be in the academy to write things that make their mark on the twentieth century and won't be forgotten. Being in the academy sometimes makes it easy to spread one's thought rapidly, but that doesn't mean that it will have a significant historical impact. It's possible that many women admitted into the academy speak of a culture already past, and not of the culture that will bear the mark of the work that is going on to make the present and the future.

Where will this civilization in the process of construction express itself? Not simply in writing, of course! But if we are just talking about the written word, footnotes are sometimes the place least accessible to women, since one has to give the proper name, the title of the book, and precise references to the text—at least that's the cultural convention that I know. The contribution of certain women has already entered the body of books, but it is often assimilated without precise acknowledgment of the person who produced it.[2] Our culture has taught us to consume the body of the mother (natural and spiritual) without recognition of the debt, and, as far as the world of men is concerned, to label this appropriation with their name. Your question seems to imply that this must remain as it is. What women say would remain within the body or the notes of a text that they have not written and that does not bear their name.[3] The cultural contribution that has the greatest difficulty in gaining entry into history is the different contribution of women and men to the development of civilization. If books authored by women appeared, contributing to the elaboration of culture in a way that cannot be reduced to that of men, this would be one indication that change is really taking place. Another sign of change in the order of symbolic exchanges would be a proliferation of texts that manifest a real dialogue between women and men.

Question 4: Today we are seeing women produce literary, philosophical, and psychoanalytical theory of recognized importance, and, parallel to this, we are also seeing a new fluidity in the borderlines among disciplines and genres of writing. Will this parallelism lead only to women being welcomed alongside men, or to a definitive blurring of these categories?

—The fluidity between disciplines and between different types of writing is not great at present. The fact that branches of knowledge and new technologies are increasing in number means that the compartmentalization of knowledge is more watertight than it used to be in the past. In previous centuries, philosophers and scientists used to engage in dialogue. Nowadays, they are often strangers to each other, as their languages have become mutually incommunicable.

[2] In her response to this question, Marcelle Marini also emphasizes the extensive underquoting of women's work. This question of quotation is obviously linked to the eventual exclusion of women from the canon and institutions.

[3] We would never want to imply this. There seems to be some confusion here between the assimilation without acknowledgement of women's work in a given man's text and the process of canon formation, how a "body of work" receives official recognition. A canon does not exist until/unless it is presented and represented. Right up to the present moment, the canon has been elaborated by placing men's works at the center and displacing women's to the margins and footnotes. That would seem to be the case regardless of how many texts are written by women. What all of us are describing in different ways, nonetheless, is the continued effacement of women's works.

Among certain disciplines, such as philosophy, psychoanalysis, and literature, are there new possibilities for exchange? That is a complex question. There are attempts to move from one field to another but these attempts are not always sufficiently well-informed to be pertinent. What we are witnessing is a modification in the use of language by certain philosophers who are turning back toward the origins of their culture. Thus Nietzsche and Heidegger, but also Hegel before them, interrogated their foundations in ancient Greece, and in religion Levinas and Derrida are interrogating their relation to the texts of the Old Testament. Their gesture goes with the use of a style that comes close to that of tragedy, poetry, the Platonic dialogues, the way in which myth, parables, and liturgies are expressed. This return looks back to the moment at which male identity constituted itself as patriarchal and phallocratic. Is it that women have emerged from the privacy of the home, from silence, that has forced men to question themselves? All the philosophers I've mentioned—except Heidegger—are interested in feminine identity, and sometimes in their identity as feminine(s) or as women. Does this lead to a confusion of categories? Which ones? In the name of what? Or whom? Why? I think that what you are calling "categories" refers to the branches of knowledge, not the logical categories of discourse and truth. The installation of new logical forms and rules goes with the definition of a new subjective identity, new rules for determining meaning. That is necessary too, to enable women to situate themselves in cultural production, alongside and with men. Turning back toward the moment at which they seized sociocultural power(s), are men seeking a way to divest themselves of these powers? I hope so. Such a desire would imply that they are inviting women to share in defining truth and exercising it with them. Up to now, writing differently has not done much to transform the gender of political leaders or their civil and religious discourses.

Is it a question of patience? Is it our duty to be patient in the face of decisions made in our place and in our name? I certainly don't think we have to resort to violence, but we do need to ask ourselves how to give an identity to scientific, religious, and political discourses, and how to situate ourselves in these discourses as subjects in our own right. Literature is all well and good. But how can we persuade the world of men to rule peoples poetically, when they are interested primarily in money, in competing for power, etc.? And how can we run the world as women if we have not defined our identity, the rules of our genealogical relationships, our social, cultural, and linguistic order? For this task, psychoanalysis may be of great assistance to us, if we know how to use it in a way appropriate to our bodily and spiritual needs and desires. It can help us free ourselves from our confinement in patriarchal culture, provided that we do not allow ourselves to be defined or seduced by the theories and problems of the world of male genealogy.

Question 5: Given the problematic and the politics of the categories of the canon, and given the questions we've been dealing with, do you think your oeuvre will be included in the twentieth-century canon, and if so, how will it be presented? In your opinion, what will the content of the canon be?

—In this question, I hear a desire to anticipate and codify the future rather than to work here and now to construct it. To concern oneself in the present about the future certainly does not consist in programming it in advance but in trying to bring it into existence. That said, once a dozen or so of one's books have been in book shops and public and private libraries for fourteen years, and have been translated into several languages, they are likely to appear in the canon of the twentieth century. Unless there is a cataclysm that destroys the possibility of any canon whatsoever? Perhaps this cataclysm is part of what you refer to as "canon"? In fact, I don't understand on what grounds you speak of "the problematic and the politics of the categories of the canon." Your remarks seem to assume that all that is settled, that the future will be no more than the past, that what will define the canon of the twentieth century will not be partly decided by readers living in a time beyond this twentieth century. At the same time, you seem to be stating that there will be only *one* canon, and that it will have only *one* content. That surprises me. If there were only one, it would be unalterably programmed by the forms in which it was expressed; it would represent a language congealed at one moment in its development. But you don't seem to take into account that there is more than one language, and that they are evolving. In the case of gender/genre, for example, not all languages deal with it in the same way. What your hypothesis would come down to is the question of which language will have supremacy over the others. I don't accept the hypothetical cataclysm in all this— any more than I subscribe to the belief that there are universals, for all time and for all places, programming meaning for all women, all men, and all things.

With that clarified, your question might suggest to me the following commentary: will the future emphasize the subject or the object? communication and exchange of meaning or the ownership of possessions? To these alternatives, corresponding partly to the different expression of gender in certain Romance and Germanic languages, I would reply that I would like to see the culture of the subject to which I belong—in particular through the language that I speak—evolve in the direction of a culture of the sexed/gendered subject and not in the direction of a heedless destruction of subjectivity. From this point of view, I certainly hope that I will have a place in the cultural memory of the twentieth century and that I will contribute toward changes in the forms and contents of its discourses. For me, this goes with the hope of a future that will be more cultivated and not less cultivated than the past or the present: a future in which symbolic exchanges—including exchanges in the realm of religion, which the word "canon" brings to mind—will be freer, more just, and more elaborated than at present.

Question 6: The form your "fling with the philosophers" took in Speculum, *published in 1974, could be described as introducing a female-gendered and - embodied subjectivity into the male corpus. Is this still an indispensable strategy for women today?*

—The female body has always been present in the male corpus, not always in philosophy, it's true, although it can often be found there. I know that clearly. *Speculum* is a critique of the exclusive right of one sex to use, exchange, and represent the other. In addition, it begins to elaborate a phenomenological description by a woman—Luce Irigaray, whose name is on the book—of the self-affection and self-representation of her body. In doing this, I am implying that the female body should not remain the object of male discourse and various male arts, but that it should become central to the process of a female subjectivity experiencing and defining it/herself. Research of this kind aims at offering women a morphologic that is appropriate to their bodies. It also aims at inviting the male subject to undertake his own self-redefinition as a body, with a view to exchanges between sexed/gendered subjects. To work toward this social and cultural change is still the purpose of my work, focusing at times on one section of culture, at times on another, in order to rethink the way in which culture is constituted. I think that this dimension of research represents one of the tasks of our age, particularly following the discovery of the unconscious.

9

Sarah Kofman

TRANSLATED BY JANICE ORION

Question 1: What does it mean to you to write at the end of the twentieth century?

—What is important for me in your question is not the fact that I live in the twentieth century but that I write. I write when I am not merely translating an oral content, when I'm not merely engaged in defending certain ideas. In my writing activity, my referents—and in this respect I clearly belong to the twentieth century—are the great thinkers on writing: Blanchot, Derrida. My own psychoanalysis has also played a large part, although I wrote my first book, *The Childhood of Art*, before entering analysis. But it has allowed me to introduce both into

Excerpts from this interview, translated by Patricia Baudoin, appeared in *Yale French Studies* (1988), vol. 75.

myself and into my work a playfulness, a certain irony that is but one with writing. I turned the corner in my analysis when I ceased to talk, to tell my story in a rational and sustained fashion; when it became possible for me to talk without expecting a reply from the analyst; when I stopped trying to communicate a meaning, expecting to get one by means of frenetic demand. In short, when I became able to just speak; in other words, when I gave myself up to the play of language, that is, writing.

—(AJ) And do you think it's only in this century that people have played with language like that?

—I think that wherever writing is really at work, whatever the century, that's *how* it works. But now that we have theorized it, we can become aware of what constitutes the specificity of writing at any given time. The same is true for painting: only modern art has allowed us to understand that even Renaissance art was already an art, that is, an assemblage of the play of forms.

Question 2: Is it valid/of value to write as a woman, and is it part of your writing practice today?

—One starts from the fact that, apparently, I am, anatomically speaking, a woman, and therefore that I write as a woman. In fact, I write as a "philosopher" first and foremost. But I have demonstrated in my book on August Comte[1]—and I am not immune to this law—that even in a philosophical text, a so-called purely rational and systematic text, independent of all empirical and pathological subjectivity, and therefore of sexuality, it isn't possible to separate the text from the sexual positioning of its author. Nor can that positioning be identified with one's anatomical sex. That is, one is neither a man nor a woman: these categories are anatomical and social and refer back to the metaphysical tradition since Aristotle. The metaphysical tradition, essentially masculine, as if moved (set in motion) by a paranoid fear, has always deeply feared the confusion of the sexes (this is also to be found in Rousseau; see *Le Respect des femmes*), and therefore it attempts to separate them categorically. This separation is also achieved by the social and civil division of the sexes. When you ask me "Do you write as a woman?" I cannot accept the metaphysical formulation. With regard to this metaphysical schism, Freud's

[1] *Aberrations: Le devenir femme d'Auguste Comte.* See the appendix to this interview for a detailed discussion of this text.

introduction of an original bisexuality was already progress. But we need to go further, because each of us has multiple sexual positionings. We ought now to totally rethink the sex question beyond the hallowed categories, including the psychoanalytic ones, and talk instead, for example, of transsexuality. Now, for the moment, our society is still dependent upon these categories. Therefore it is important for a "woman" to do, as I do, theoretical work that refuses to be qualified as "feminine" and that does not accept the idea of a "specifically feminine" writing, since that would be to remain fully within metaphysics. Although that of a "woman," my writing belongs to what tradition would call masculine writing (rational, clear, philosophical, the result of nineteen years of continuous work); if I were anatomically a man, I would not have to prove that I was capable of such writing; it would seem perfectly natural. That's why my "philosophical" writings are part of my militant feminist activity. I think today it is even more necessary to show that women have this theoretical capacity than to fight for women's "specificity," within which men have always wanted to imprison women for the greatest masculine profit. We must beware, however, of concluding that a rational discourse is neuter, asexual; for I show at the same time that rational discourse also betrays a certain sexual positioning that is not necessarily to be identified with the anatomical sex. Furthermore, I am not bound to this "rational" writing as if it were my destiny. I also write other kinds of autobiographical texts in a freer writing style. They have been translated by Frances Bartkowski, and appear as "Autobiographical Writings" in [a special issue of] the journal *Sub-Stance* dedicated to anti-Semitism.[2] They have been collected in French in a Canadian journal *Trois,* along with some of my drawings.[3]

So I practice a "double strategy," showing that a "woman" (socially and anatomically) can write both what metaphysical tradition defines as "masculine" writing and what is called "feminine" writing—a strategy that ought to contribute to rearranging these categories.

Question 3: Many women writing today find themselves, for the first time in history, at the center of such institutions as the university and psychoanalysis. In your opinion, will this new placement of women help them to enter the

[2] *Sub-Stance* 49 (1986), 15(1):6–13.
[3] *Trois* (1987), vol. 3, no. 1. Published by Editions Trois, 2033 Avenue Sesson, Laval, Quebec, Canada H751X3.

twentieth-century canon, and if so, will they be in the heart of this corpus or (still) in the footnotes?

—That's my case, I'm a university professor but only a maître de conférences[4] in spite of my nineteen books—this must be kept in mind.[5] I have to say that the fact that I'm interested in women has played an important role in my philosophy department because women have long been totally excluded from these programs. And that is an enormous difference with the United States. The woman question has never come up in the preparation courses or exams for the *agrégation,*[6] that is, at the national level. And in my university, when I give a lecture on women for a seminar, or when students study the subject for a *maîtrise*[7] or for their thesis, they and I are considered less than serious. Can women who become part of the university, like myself, for example, one day change something about this situation? What matters is to determine whether there are women in the twentieth century who have done theoretical work significant enough for them to be included as authors in a curriculum or for their books to be used as a reference. On this point, I don't think that women are or have been excluded because they're women. I'm not speaking here of literature but of philosophy. The fact is that in this area few women have done work important enough or original enough to merit a place in any curriculum. That doesn't mean that I think the difference here comes from anatomy; it comes instead from the education women have received, which generally means that they are much more submissive to what they have read, more repetitive than innovative, more imitative of a master whom they need to stimulate their research.

We must wait and see if a change in education will give women greater freedom in theoretical innovation. Few women today have done original enough work in philosophy to be recognized as theoreticians. Hannah Arendt seems to have been accorded an important place in France, but at the same time it's pointed out that she was a student of Heidegger. The "great man" will always remain a man. The moment a

---

[4] A maître de conférences is roughly equivalent to an untenured associate professor.

[5] This year, the Université de Paris I—Pantheon—Sorbonne once again refused to promote me to professor. The "scandalous injustice" of this refusal led to a unanimous protest on the part of all the famous contemporary philosophers and the entire French press. [—Kofman's note.]

[6] Competitive exams taken to become a secondary school teacher.

[7] A research degree roughly equivalent to a master's degree.

woman seems to acquire intellectual autonomy, there are always well-intentioned men ready to reduce her to a simple disciple, the underling of a recognized master. In my own case, I worked in total isolation until 1969. The first text I published was on Sartre in 1962.[8] Then I worked alone on Nietzsche and Freud and published my first texts on these two authors before having either read or met Derrida. My later reading of Derrida allowed me to generalize the type of reading I had done in isolation on these two authors. At that time there was a fascination on my part that introduced a certain mimeticism into my writing, which I think I have done away with now. So I have never been a "disciple" of Derrida in the proper sense of the word; our real encounter was marked by a collaboration on a book series, "La Philosophie en effet," coedited by Jacques Derrida, myself, Jean-Luc Nancy, and Philippe Lacoue-LaBarthe—and we are all four very different, over and above our profound community of ideas. But assimilation being easy, particularly where a woman is concerned, one must sometimes clarify certain things.

Question 4: Today we are seeing women produce literary, philosophical, and psychoanalytic theory of recognized importance, and, parallel to this, we are also seeing a new fluidity in the borderlines among disciplines and genres of writing. Will this parallelism lead only to women being welcomed alongside men, or to a definitive blurring of these categories?

—From a philosophical point of view, I think it's extremely important, but originally the two problems were not necessarily parallel. It is to Nietzsche that we owe the idea that philosophy and literature are not inherently heterogeneous to each other. If it is true that a philosophical system can no longer, since Nietzsche, be evaluated from the standpoint of its truth, then philosophy becomes, like literature, a particular writing symptomatic of a certain type of drive that it affirms. This blurring of the boundaries between philosophy and literature is part and parcel of the putting under erasure of all metaphysical oppositions, including, among others, the feminine and the masculine. But perhaps this latter is not just one opposition among others. Nietzsche was particularly well situated, because of his sexual positioning, to effect this erasure of opposites. Speaking of himself, he says in effect that he is his own double, (see *Ecce Homo*), that is, he possesses within himself a double

---

[8] "Le Problème moral dans une philosophie de l'absurde," *Revue de l'Enseignement philosophique*, October–November, 1963.

system of evaluations that comes from his mother on one side and from his father on the other. I don't think what "women" produce, as such, can lead to a scrambling of the categories. Rather, it is important that both men and women be able to produce in the areas usually reserved for one or the other sex, and in this way to blur the boundaries. For example, I write an overwhelming number of philosophical texts in the manner described as masculine, but I also write psychoanalytical and autobiographical texts that are closer to literature.

As regards the psychoanalytical production of women, here too, it seems to me, all possible originality in the area is repressed. Lacan dominates in the Freudian school: this school has enormous editorial power; its numerous journals systematically eliminate reporting of work that is not strictly Lacanian or else criticize it because Lacan is not quoted. Only one of my books on psychoanalysis has been reviewed by *L'Ane—Un métier impossible*—only to be censured as "non-Lacanian."[9] On the other hand, Lacan in person publicly recognized in his seminars the originality and importance of my work; for example, speaking of my *Quatre romans analytiques,* he said it was "entirely her own," and he telephoned me after the publication of each of my books—all the while remaining surprised that I did not go to his seminar and was not a "Lacanian." As for the other schools, either they swear only by Freud who is untouchable, or else they tend to be offended that anyone who is not an analyst (which is my case) could write on Freud: to both comprehend and criticize him, to be both for and against Freud—that is the ambivalence of my position. I think that in these circles I am excluded not for being a woman, but rather for being a philosopher—as if I laid claim to knowing psychoanalysis better than the psychoanalysts. On the whole, the non-Lacanians certainly read my work but don't take it into account in their journals or in their work.

In any case, among the psychoanalysts I don't see any female writing of significance. Melanie Klein herself, in spite of the important innovations she has introduced, remains derivative of Freud and his concepts; she remains derivative of the categories and oppositions of metaphysics. A whole detailed study would have to be made of this. But at any rate she has made a name for herself in this area. I don't see many others to mention. In France, all the women at all known in this area are philoso-

---

[9] *L'Ane: Le Magazine Freudien* is the journal of the French Freudian school of psycho-analysis. Jean-Pierre Klotz's review of Kofman's book was entitled "Jeu de constructions: L'analyste policier," *L'Ane* (1983), 10:27.

phers as well: me, Monique Schneider, Monique David-Ménard, for example; as for Kristeva, she came to psychoanalysis very late.[10] Catherine Clément is likewise a philosopher, as is Luce Irigaray. Still, psychoanalysis, as well as philosophy, is a field in which creativity and originality should be able to manifest themselves more than elsewhere because these two disciplines are enterprises of lucidity and probity and take a stand against any principle of authority. At least in theory, if not in fact.

Question 5: Given the problematic and the politics of the categories of the canon, and given the questions we've been dealing with, do you think your oeuvre will be included in the twentieth-century canon, and if so, how will it be presented? In your opinion, what will the content of the canon be?

—It's quite difficult (and rather pretentious) for a writer to say "my work will be represented." And what is a work? I'm in *Who's Who*. So there are traces, and my books are traces. In addition, the feminist movement has been such that a woman's work cannot be erased. And the people who publish *Who's Who,* far from excluding women, since there are few famous ones, tend to put them all in. They will figure as women but perhaps not with all the nuances I include in this term. As for the business of the canon, the canon implies the idea of a norm in our literary history. But given the blurring of the boundaries, it is no longer possible to write pure literary history. It would be very retrograde to do so. And in this new kind of literary history it will not be possible to do without a chapter on women. To know how my "work" will be presented is difficult to foretell. For it to be presented "appropriately," the categories would have to change; among others, those of Literary Genre (which is not independent of genre/gender as sexual category). In *Autobiogriffures,*[11] my book on Hoffman's *Kater Murr, the Educated Cat,* I pointed out what editorial problems are provoked by any unusual writing, for instance that of a cat that tears and rips to shreds all received categories: any free "bastard" book, written by at least two hands, is in this day and age unclassifiable. That's what is happening right now with most of my books. *The Enigma of Woman* is classified in the United

---

[10] Schneider's most recent book is *La Parole et l'inceste: De l'enclos linguistique à la liturgie psychanalytique* (Paris: Aubier Montaigne, 1980). David-Ménard's book *Hysteria from Freud to Lacan: Body and Language in Psychoanalysis* (Ithaca, N.Y.: Cornell University Press, 1989) was translated by Catherine Porter, with a foreword by Ned Lukacher.

[11] One chapter of *Autobiogriffures,* translated by Winnie Woodhull, appeared as "No Longer Full-Fledged: Autobiogriffies," in *Sub-Stance* 29 (1980), 9(4):3–22.

States as Women's Studies. In fact it could also be classified as psycho-analysis or philosophy. My book on Nerval[12] is classified in France as literature, but it could also be classified as psychoanalysis. It's the same for my recent *Conversions*, which concerns *The Merchant of Venice* but is also a critical rereading of Freud's theme of "the three caskets." In the same vein, how can one classify *Paroles suffoquées?*—as literary criticism, politics, or autobiography?

Generally speaking, my books are found scattered all over the book-stores—except in those places where I am recognized, although I am a woman, as having enough of a reputation that everything is classified under the rubric "Kofman"—which settles without settling the question of genre/gender.

Question 6: As a philosopher and a Derridean, how would you go about discussing the notion of the canon?

—It is amusing to see, first, that while you seem to me to be trying to question metaphysical categories and oppositions, in this last question you are reintroducing a simple category: philosophy. Second, and in addition, while your questionnaire seemed to me to want to stress the originality of feminine work, you classified me right away as Derridean and therefore subordinate to a male philosopher.

—(AJ) It was a sort of trap, but not meant to be wicked.

—I do want to keep the title of philosopher, but in quotation marks, because I think the specificity of philosophy is rigorous conceptual thinking, and I affirm and claim that. On the other hand, I am troubled by your qualifier "Derridean," not because I want to hide my strong ties to Derrida—a real encounter—but because when I'm asked to think about the notion of the canon, that excludes classifying me within a genre. If I think, I can only think by myself. If I think "as a Derridean," just then I'm not thinking anymore. Moreover, would there be an a priori way of thinking about the notion that would be Derridean? And if yes, why not ask Jacques Derrida about it rather than me? Doesn't the formulation of your question imply that there is a Derridean canon, although Derrida wants to displace all the canons, and, in addition, that there is a Derridean canon for talking about the canon? In that case, your question makes no sense at all. I'm willing to answer the question, but only insofar as I am a person who engages in reflection. Perhaps

---

[12] *Nerval: Le Charme de la répétition. Lecture de Sylvie.*

Derrida would answer much the same, since we have often "met" each other, since we both think, I believe, rigorously, seriously, and we "deconstruct." For my part, I'm not borrowing that word from Derrida, who borrowed it from Heidegger, but from Nietzsche. The way you posed your last question destroys all the progressiveness of the other questions. My answer would be that it's not possible to do a serious job of thinking in five minutes; that one must be prudent. Perhaps you'll tell me that too is a Derridean answer?

Appendix to Question 2, note 1

Aberrations, le devenir femme d'Auguste Comte [*Aberrations: The Becoming-Woman of Auguste Comte*] makes it possible to resolve a philosophical problem concerning Comte that has led to much debate: the relationship between his first works, *The Course in Positivist Philosophy*, essentially "scientific," and the last ones, *System of Positivist Politics* [*politique*]—that is, those of the religion of humanity. In the first, woman occupies a subordinate position, is declared incapable of attaining the positivist age. The positivist age is the only age of the mind valorized by Comte, and only white, masculine, civilized man is apt to reach it. Comte described this age, which represents the norm, in a word as "the age of virility." (The other two ages, according to Comte, are pathological; these are the theological and metaphysical ages—at best, woman can attain the latter.)

In Comte's last works, however, woman is glorified and deified. The difference between the two works is explained by a change in Comte's sexual positioning, which passes from a paranoid positioning to a melancholic one where he embodies the image of the beloved and dead woman, Clotilde de Vaux. He identifies with her, and thus permits himself to assume within and outside himself the femininity he had hitherto rejected.

10

Julia Kristeva

TRANSLATED BY KATHERINE ANN JENSEN

Question 1: What does it mean to you to write at the end of the twentieth century?

—It means trying to be the most personal I can be by eluding all forms of pressure, whether that's from groups, the media, public opinion, or ideology.

—(AM) And what's the implication of this personal writing?

—I'm not sure, but it's a way to preserve a margin of surprise and of the unknown.

—(AJ) And is the effect of the unknown important for you?

—Yes, because contrary to how it seems, I think we're seeing a kind

Excerpts from this interview, translated by Anne M. Menke, appeared in *Yale French Studies* (1988), vol. 75.

of standardization of mentalities, of information, and of education. It's difficult to preserve individual voices, personal voices inside this standardization.

—(AJ) Which helps to explain the boredom that seems to be around?

—Absolutely. The personal is really a guarantee of freedom.

—(AM) Does what you're calling "speaking in a personal voice" have anything to do with the concept of the individual as it was constructed at a given historical moment, or is it something else?

—It's probably something else. That is, the notion of the individual is historically dated and supposes different ideological "sedimentations," but this notion of the individual also changes according to the places in which it's used. Obviously, to say "individual" in Moscow means something different from what it means to say it in the United States; it doesn't have the same value. But nonetheless I keep the word's connotations of liberty and rebelliousness. Perhaps we could keep this function for it when speaking of the twentieth century.

Question 2: Is it valid/of value to write as a woman, and is it part of your writing today?

—Yes, for me it's really a necessity, but I have the feeling that it depends on what I was saying in the last question, on the need to write in my personal name. This seems to me to protect against the risks involved in writing "as a woman," for that can end up being a kind of uniform: writing as all women write. So, I think that the necessity of writing as a woman can be maintained under the condition that this be subordinated to the necessity of writing in one's own name. Otherwise there is the risk of making writing uniform.

—(AM) In what you've written about poetry, you talk about the semiotic versus the symbolic.[1] The semiotic is closer to the body and can be communicated in language through rhythms, for example. Does the personal effect you were speaking about come from the body, and if so, is it important in this sense to write as a woman? That is, does the female body have different rhythms and sensations than the male? Should sexuality enter into this personal effect on account of the rhythms of writing?

—Sexuality is different; it can be expressed on different levels, on the level of style or in the recognition of some sexual thematic. It can also

---

[1] *Revolution in Poetic Language.*

be on the cognitive level. I'm not at all one of those women who believes that, when one is a woman, one must express oneself in a subterranean, elliptical, or rhythmic language. That can be a solution, but it's not the only one. We can simply change the objects of thought. The terrain of thought is not necessarily male, in my opinion, and women can do something right now by presenting new objects of thought.

Question 3: Many women writing today find themselves, for the first time in history, at the center of institutions, such as the university or psychoanalysis. In your opinion, will this new placement of women help them to enter the twentieth-century canon, and if so will they be at the heart of this corpus or (still) in the footnotes?

—I think there are two sides to the problem. Obviously, it's an important gain for women to be in the institution, whether that's the university or psychoanalysis, and we must rejoice at this. This must be consolidated, this placement must be made more significant, and women need to be in more decision-making positions. But that doesn't mean that once this has been achieved, the battle is won. I believe one has to remain constantly vigilant. At least that's been my approach. One can't fall asleep, can't close even one eye. One has to be in a constant state of wakefulness and struggle. Otherwise, whether one is in the university or in psychoanalysis, even in apparently important positions, one's personal work won't be noticed or appreciated. I wonder, though, if this is the case only for women. I think that men too, if they fall asleep at their chairman's job, will be finished. I think that for all individuals, though perhaps especially for a woman because of all the resistance, gains cannot be considered definitive. Important gains have to be consolidated, and that's where all the work begins. One must remain in a permanent state of vigilance and combat.

—(AJ) Let's say that a woman does manage to incorporate this personal effect into the work she does inside the academic institution. We know that ideology and the institution are masculine. Given that, do you think this personal effect will be recognized, or is it going to disappear again? That is, I'm trying to see whether the fact of being inside the institution . . .

—Should I say, guarantees recognition?

—(AJ) Yes, guarantees recognition. Because I don't find that to be the case.

—I think that we're in a completely uncertain situation, because you can say neither that you must be absolutely on the outside in order to be an individual and personal and to continue research, nor that you have to be inside in order to continue research and to transmit it. I think it's a question of an individual fighting spirit—almost animal-like—for someone to remain vigilant while being on the inside. That might also be the case for those on the outside who manage to make their marginality known yet not get buried in a kind of permanent demand for marginality. For me, there's no guarantee in either direction, and I think you have to emphasize that nothing's won in advance and no situation is comfortable. Women have to understand that the battle will go on forever. But this is something that the tradition of woman—the woman-mother, the homemaker, and the woman-object—could never accept. For there are benefits to marginality, to being outside history: you can rest, you can do nothing, you have some small pleasures—which aren't simply secondary but can be extremely important. Now that women have entered the institution, there's also a heavy emphasis on combative and virile qualities that can quickly get blocked and result in women acting like bosses. And at that point, one loses the open structure that is as necessary for personal life, for personal happiness—I was even going to say for personal pleasure—as it is for creation. So, the necessary ideal is a kind of balance between the inside and the outside. But that depends on a permanent vigilance and a constant working on oneself.

Question 4: Today we are seeing women produce literary, philosophical, and psychoanalytical theory of recognized importance, and parallel to this, we are seeing a new fluidity in the borderlines among disciplines and genres of writing. Will this parallelism lead only to women being welcomed alongside men, or to a definitive blurring of these categories?

—What struck me in your question and what's presently in debate is the issue of the blurring of sexual difference. We would seem to be moving toward a future that effaces sexual difference, in parallel perhaps with other differences. It would seem that humanity must prepare itself for the fact that men could be women and women men. That's a fairly troubling problem to which there are two solutions. First, let's say that this really is going to happen, and that in the twenty-first century there will be no difference between the sexes. There will be a kind of perpetual androgyny even to the extent that—as certain fictions say—men will give birth, and from that point on, the difference of reproduction, which up to that point had been women's realm, will disappear.

I think that if this happens, if we are witnessing a blurring of sexual difference—and why not consider that hypothesis—then two phenomena will accompany this fact. The first is that we're going to witness the end of a certain kind of desire and sexual pleasure. For, after all, if you level out difference, given that it's difference that's desirable and provokes sexual pleasure, you could see a kind of sexual anesthesia, and this in an incubator society where the question of reproduction will be posed by way of machines and bioscientific methods in order for the species to continue. That's extremely troubling first for the individual's psychic life whose leveling off rules out desire and pleasure and, second, for the individual's creative possibilities. What can that individual invent that's new, surprising, or evolving? By moving toward this sexual homeostasis, won't we see some sort of symbolic homeostasis and therefore very little creation? Or, then again—since the kind of societies and psychic life we've known up until now haven't tolerated this homeostasis—won't new differences be invented? But in that case, won't they also be very problematic? For example, in certain marginal societies, we already see victimizing attitudes created within androgynous couples, as well as extremely violent sadomasochistic practices that can go so far as to libidinalize death. On the other hand, other differences might be emphasized, making them extremely heterogeneous and therefore capable of attracting desire as well as a desire for death. These could be racial differences, for example. An extreme version would be that while there'd be no difference between men and women, we'd hear instead, "Arabs are filth; I hate them and I'll kill them."

I think this possibility exists; it's already quite visible in certain age and social groups. For example, at adolescence, or menopause or andropause, when the individual is in a state of agitation, this kind of ideology or attempt to regulate difference and psychic life can seem very appealing. Apart from that, there are periods when perversion seems self-evident and can be legalized. Perversion becomes the social law. Having said that, I actually think society is going to defend itself against this because on the one hand, repression works against these zones of paroxystic pleasures and on the other, there are a number of rationalizations being elaborated now that will slow down this kind of behavior. But I think we will see a reformulation of difference.

I imagine the end of this century—since we really are talking about science fiction—and what will come afterward as a life of difference but in other forms. That is, ones that recognize in a more marked way than at present the bisexuality of each sex, not that the feminine won't be dominant in the female and the masculine in the male, but there will be more recognition of women's right to power and affirmation, etc., and of men's possibilities for passivity and all sorts of behaviors that are coded as feminine, like tenderness, interest in children, all that. So there will be a redistribution of this kind, but while maintaining differences.

So much for the question of the sexes. As for fluidity among disciplines. . . . I'm particularly interested right now by the possible or impossible encounter between neuroscience and psychoanalysis, two realms that have been irreconcilable up until now. With research in its current state, it's hard, really, to see, for example, the bridge between treatment with different antidepressants and psychoanalytic treatment. Yet all the work of certain researchers is moving toward creating models in neuroscience on the one hand and in psychoanalysis on the other that can, if not communicate, at least ask questions reciprocally. Each can ask interesting questions of the other science. Well, that's where we are for the moment, while recognizing, nonetheless, the enormous gap between biochemical treatment and psychic representation. And the abyss between cells on the one hand and representation on the other remains, for the moment, unbridgeable.

—(AJ) Do you find that women's presence in this . . .

—. . . this kind of dialogue?

—(AJ) Yes, does their presence help blur the categories in question? Is there a historical or ideological reason why women entering this debate would encourage this dialogue?

—Well, the work I'm familiar with in this area isn't necessarily female or male. For the moment, I don't see a particular contribution [by women]. But it's possible that insofar as women are especially interested in the psychic aspect of things or, in other realms, in bodily functions—for example, the relationship between menstruation and psychic life—they might be inclined to ask overlapping questions. But that's just a hypothesis. In practice, in the group in which I work on these matters, there are two women and the rest are men. I don't think that men, because they're men, are cut off from this kind of issue.

—(AJ) This difficulty of crossing boundaries may be more evident in American universities, for example in Women's Studies where there is a demand for interdisciplinary work. There are always men around saying,

"No, you can't ask those kinds of questions because they're about literature, or psychology, and we cannot blur, we cannot mix these things
up."

—Perhaps it's like this overall on the university level, but is the same
true in research groups? Right now, I'm reading a book by Morton
Reiser called *Mind, Brain, Body: Toward a Convergence of Psychoanalysis
and Neurobiology*.[2] He's someone who asks these kinds of questions
about psychoanalytic-neurobiological relationships. I find he's too re-
ductive and so I don't agree with him, but at least he's asking questions
that bridge disciplines. He cites work by some biologists, one of whom
is a woman. On the basis of biology, this woman is asking questions
about the relationship between social conditioning and learning and cell
modification.[3] These factors aren't necessarily psychological—because
we're talking about animals—but are external factors of behavior, society, and conditioning that influence the cell. So there is an example of a
woman whose interests overlap. Perhaps what we need to question here
is precisely the institution. The university institution is actually quite
conservative, but research groups are something different.

—(AM) I think, rather, that it's because historically we see these two
things at the same time—women in institutions and the blurring of
boundaries between disciplines—that we relate them. Is there really a
link between them? Or do we find one now when, for the first time,
many women are in the institution and in research groups? Maybe they
don't have anything to do with one another.

—(AJ) Perhaps it's a coincidence?

—The framework is important, though. For example, as you say,
society is masculine. But it has created frameworks where contamination
is possible. At the university, we tend to say, "Don't touch, everyone
remain normal, we're conservative, but even so, we'll let ourselves have
a small research group where anything is possible and where there will
be mixtures and blending; afterward, we'll see." But on the overall
university level, that won't really come about for another fifty years.

[2] New York: Basic Books, 1984.
[3] The woman in question is Patricia Goldman-Rakic. See P. S. Goldman and P. T.
Rakic, "Impact of the Outside World Upon the Developing Primate Brain," in a special
issue of the *Bulletin of the Menninger Clinic* (January 1979), 43(1):20–28; and Patricia S.
Goldman-Rakic, Ami Isseroff, Michael L. Schwartz, and Nellie M. Bugbee, "The Neuro-
biology of Cognitive Development," in Marshall M. Haith and Joseph J. Campos, eds.,
Infancy and Developmental Psychobiology. Vol. 2 of *Handbook of Child Psychology* (New York:
John Wiley and Sons, 1983), pp. 281–344.

—(AM) If it's that soon.

—And the human sciences[4] are even more conservative; the emphasis now is on neuroscience and possibly on psychology. That raises a lot of problems in any event. Many neurobiologists say, "All that psychoanalysis stuff is crap. Soon we will discover pills that will get rid of all mental illnesses; so we don't need to bother with the psychic aspect." Then there are psychoanalysts who are completely closed to any relation with neurobiology, and sometimes they're right, because there can be all sorts of abuses leading people to believe that a pill can get rid of your problems, which isn't true. But I think we can find interesting bridges.

Question 5: Given the problematic and the politics of the categories of the canon, and given the questions we've been dealing with here, do you think your oeuvre will be included in the twentieth-century canon, and if so, how will it be presented? In your opinion, what will be the content of the canon?

—Well I was just thinking of a play on words here. One has the canon and the gunpowder in the canon. One day there will be no more canon, only powder, nothing in fact but a screen of gunsmoke [*de la poudre aux yeux*]. What I'm trying to say is that it seems to me that the question you're asking is really about education and the transmission of information. I see this transmission as if by a TV with fifty to a hundred stations, each different, transmitting very different information—although they cancel each other out—since one often has the impression they all participate in the same ideology or, in any case, in something held in common and not easily discernible but that is perhaps a form of resistance to anything surprising or to anything that could undermine the norm. In any event, it's my impression that soon there won't be a canon, at least not in the current sense of the word, given this plurality of information that the media have already started to transmit and that the schools and universities work against. When you see what's being taught in the universities and then, on the other hand, what people read and what movies they see, what music they listen to, there's often no correlation. So sometimes you say to yourself, thank goodness for the university, because a certain classical culture is maintained. But conversely, it's not clear that this classical culture is maintained such that it's

[4] In French, the human sciences refer to a combination of the social sciences and humanities where there is a specific focus on "the human," e.g., anthropology, psychology, linguistics, literature, etc.

integrated within modernity. At times, classical culture is maintained in such a way that it's completely rejected and unassimilable in the modern world, and so one emphasizes even more its expulsion through this kind of [university] transmission. So, we're going to see a sort of sabotaging of formal education and university information by the plurality of communication; and in that framework, the canon will be exploded, reduced to powder—it will be pulverized and pluralized. For example, there are already no longer any master thinkers.

The example of France, a centralized, Jacobin country, is instructive from this standpoint because up until five or six years ago, the canon was heavily imposing; there were five or six ranking members that everyone repeated/imitated or tried to align themselves with. But now, we see all this work being neutralized, like on a TV where nothing makes any sense. At this point, then, the issue for me is not about knowing whether I'm going to be maintained in an institutional canon, which in some universities will be transmitted as but a vestige of the past, a kind of relic, whereas people aren't at all interested in all that, [for they live] in a culture where everything possible is done to blur the canon or make it impossible to transmit. The question is to know whether one can ask interesting questions, or pose problems that interest people in the twentieth century. It's a question of the whole problematic of adaptation to evolution, and at the same time, of nonconformity to fashion, which is a giant and tricky slalom. This supposes both the possibility of being able to listen and a self-accountability where one tries to impose what one believes to be a personal truth. From then on, what may arise as an interesting practice is not a canon but [a way of posing] problems that can respond to the crises people live from day to day.

—(AJ) So, even if people continue to teach this canon within the university, even if French high schools continue to teach *Lagarde et Michard,* and so on, in your view, all this has died, it's not anything to fight against?

—I think that in the form it's taught, it really is dead. There's also the other side of the problem: how do we react to the leveling out and anesthetizing of thought that this "multichannel communication"[5] produces? In such a case, there might, in fact, be a way to show that Racine and Homer are readable today and that even a kid who watches Zorro

---

5 In English in the interview.

can think so too. But then, you have to find ways to make this reading correspond to current tastes.

— (AJ)   And the dinosaurs will disappear by themselves?

— Or else just stay the way they are, like a sort of . . .

— (AJ)   vestige . . .

— of a dead culture. I've recently read a thesis on cultural survival that puts these things quite clearly. The man who wrote it took street names and translations as signs of the canon. Well, who names streets? The municipality, the establishment. If you name a street Bernanos, you think Bernanos is in the canon. But when a guy passes Bernanos street, he doesn't have any idea who that is. It's an empty name, it contains no information. Or Jussieu. Who knows who he was? He was some scientist, but even the majority of our students in humanities here at Jussieu don't know that. It's the name of a metro stop. A canon, if you like. But does that really make sense as a means for a culture to transmit itself? On the other hand, if you look at what's going on in translations, there's a certain kind of translation that's done by pressure groups—publishing houses obviously have lobbyists with their own tastes and ideologies, etc. But given the mass-media status of publishing as well, there's an enormous number of things that get translated and that aren't coded. Detective stories or other things that aren't considered valuable are more readily translated than Balzac. Antonin Artaud or other important writers who are considered to have marked culture are rarely translated. So there's a dilution which shows that, outside transmissions canonized by pressure groups, outside classical culture and the establishment, there's a culture of desire, almost a cathartic culture, one of expenditure, of pleasures, which doesn't become a new canon but a new corporation [capable of] exploitation.

Question 6: In the diversity of your work, one always finds the epistemological problems that have been posed throughout time examined from a contemporary perspective. This perspective is a knowingly critical one, and since it is also that of a psychoanalyst, it must necessarily take sexual difference into account. How is it possible to work in that way without at least appearing to repeat on a theoretical level the historical gesture of organizing knowledge by relegating women-subjects and their texts to the background?

— I don't happen to agree with the position that because the gesture that organizes knowledge is based on effacing sexual difference in the

name of an absolute or neutral subject, women should refuse that gesture. I think that there are different manifestations of culture, and
knowledge is one of them. Women must take their place inside the
cultural field by trying to discover objects of thought or knowledge that
men haven't. In doing this, then, do women respond as women? No
doubt they do, if one considers that we are always constituted bisexually
and that a woman who makes the historical gesture of organizing knowledge her own gesture is exhibiting her phallic component. I don't see
why women shouldn't exhibit that component. However, once they do
exhibit it, from the moment they create new objects of knowledge, they
also reveal their specificity, which is not phallic, but which has to do, for
example, with their sensitivity to the mother-child bond, which is something that men can't necessarily delimit. Or another example is women's
interest in the modulations of language that don't come from the language of everyday communication but that recall archaic situations.

So I would keep this of way of operating and consider it valuable and
interesting. I also think men can find analogous objects of knowledge
through their bisexuality; women don't have a monopoly on this. But I
believe that to insist on sexual difference doesn't prevent thinking or
even demanding both permutations, and that work done by a man can
also be done by a woman. Otherwise, we regionalize culture and consider one aspect as female, another as male, and in that way, we castrate
the essential polyvalence of subjects. Nonetheless, I would like to insist
again that within this organizing gesture, the tonality a woman would
bring—in the way she presents a new object, or in the way she treats it
—is totally particular. We're not going to keep a woman from playing
Bach because Bach was a man.

—(AJ) I completely agree with you within the context of working on
our own historical moment. But women working on other historical
periods have had to confront the fact that most of what's called phallocentric thought—the thought we have inherited from the fathers, this
entirely historical philosophy—must be completely questioned because
it was created only by men. This is a real problem for feminist critics
who work on past texts: how not to repeat the historical gesture that
has effaced the texts that somehow didn't fit in?

—What do they have to do if they want to rehabilitate these texts?
Possibly, they will change the standards, but these women will remain
within the framework of conceptual thought. So, they'll remain within
the gestures of Western knowledge, but they will say, "There used to be

criteria X and Y, but I'm going to invent a criterion Z that hasn't been considered by men or by those who evaluate texts in men's name, and I'm going to consider that such a woman, who was thought of as obscure in her time, has qualities." But by adopting this perspective, they're still operating with Aristotle's categories, with criteria of thought based on good and less good, within an existing rationality. They're not placing themselves outside epistemology.

11

Eugénie Lemoine-Luccioni

TRANSLATED BY LAUREN DOYLE-MCCOMBS

Paris, May 18, 1986

DEAR COLLEAGUES,

In response to your letter [describing your project and inviting me to participate in it], here are a few thoughts.

The destitution[1] of the imaginary phallus is perhaps our society's most prominent fact, even if the phallus has kept all its power in the political and economic arenas. We should note, at least, that the phallus has renounced outward appearances and apparatus: kings have become bourgeois and heads of state debonair, and the biggest capitalists tend

Excerpts from this interview, translated by Patricia Baudoin, appeared in *Yale French Studies* (1988), vol. 75.

[1] "Evacuation" and "impoverishment" also seemed appropriate, but I elected to keep "destitution" here. —TRANS.

to be anonymous. Let's just say that power no longer declares itself openly.

Yet this destitution is the fact of psychoanalysis, as it is of other social elements. Freud proposed the rock of castration as the end point of analysis for men as well as for women—although it is surely an impossible end. Lacan went so far as to declare that the analyst who could not accept putting himself in the feminine position would have little chance of being an analyst.

For future psychoanalyst-writers, whether they are men or women, the traditional vocation of the *masculine* creator and genius (as messianic and sovereign incarnation of the divine word) is thus doomed to failure from the outset. [That outmoded tradition considered writers] masculine, not feminine, regardless of their sex.

This is still our tradition (in France), even if Louise Labé or Madame de Lafayette, and today, Marguerite Yourcenar or Marguerite Duras, has taken her place alongside *les plus grands* (strictly in the masculine!): the greatest are men.

As for the destitution of the phallus, with which I began because of its unsuspected revolutionary power, far from weakening men's arrogance [*la superbe des hommes*], it's primary effect has been to give heads of newspapers and publishing houses, as well as our masculine colleagues already in place in intimidating institutions, another weapon against women who find it hard to write and publish. Certainly even a woman of equal merit can get killed out there.

That is not true in analytic circles. And so Melanie Klein figures at the head of an international school. What does this phenomenon mean?

I gave the beginnings of an explanation in my first lines. It may be objected that in spite of the principle of the necessary destitution of the phallus, Jacques Lacan seems to have despised women because he wrote that "woman does not exist."

Yes, but we must read Lacan's entire text, which also says that one woman after the other does exist. Doubtless each woman has to invent herself, but there is nothing humble about this destiny.

Jacques Lacan's disdain extended, in fact, to all production (and to anything claiming to present itself as such); even his own production did not escape being an *objet petit a*[2] of his sarcasm. Yet for Lacan, every

---

[2] As Alan Sheridan explains in his translator's note to the English edition of Lacan's *Ecrits:* "The '*a*' in question stands for '*autre*' (other), the concept having been developed out of the Freudian 'object' and Lacan's own exploitation of 'otherness.' The '*petit a*' (small 'a') differentiates the object from (while relating to it) the '*Autre*' or '*grand Autre*' (the

theory had to be written down, whether the author was a man or a woman.

The equality of treatment of the sexes does not imply the abolition of difference, of course. So what does it imply?

I will respond to this last question personally, and for two reasons. The first is that I find it repugnant to take part in any philosophical or anthropological research that might tend to specify a feminine genius or nature. That type of research leads to nothing but impasses. Men and women change, whereas that sort of research postulates essences which are immediately given the lie by what the research reveals, I would even say by what it *produces*—and the changes have never been more dizzying than they are today. Finally, worrying about equality contradicts the postulate of difference, in fact if not by law; women's revindication of radical difference seems inextricably linked to a passionate search for equality. But it is also true, as I have said, that the world of empowered men continues to aggravate this passion because of the fear men have of women. As we well know, that fear has its roots elsewhere than in sound reason.

My decision to respond personally is founded on another, far more forceful necessity: I started my life as a writer by writing short stories, with a very clear feeling that as a woman I was writing women's stories, even if the storyteller was most often called "Michel." Those little stories, short and not much to the public taste, very noncommercial, had quite a respectable critical reception in the literary world, though they had no impact at all on the larger public. Discouraged by life's difficulties and my relative lack of success, I threw myself into more lucrative activities, such as translations or reading manuscripts, and less absorbing ones, such as literary criticism. That was less risky as well for my own equilibrium . . . until the day, actually quite recent, when I encountered psychoanalysis and Jacques Lacan. After a few years of apprenticeship (for I was a complete novice), I began to write works of so-called psychoanalytic theory. I have never gone back to short stories, even though the desire to often returns. It's a lost gift, like dancing.

My books of analytical theory brought to an abrupt end my personal, "confidential" writing. But I have the distinct feeling of having been carried along by Jacques Lacan and his theory. Have I lost myself in doing so?

Yet my first work, *The Dividing of Women's Lot,* was a woman's book.

capitalized 'Other')." Jacques Lacan, *Ecrits: A Selection,* trans. Alan Sheridan (New York: Norton, 1977), p. xi.

No one has suggested otherwise. In my latest book, *Psychanalyse pour la vie quotidienne*, I reveal how, as a writer-analyst and as a woman, I consider myself one of the links in the transmission of psychoanalysis.

This phenomenon of transmission—paradoxical in that psychoanalysis requires neither a university-style pedagogy nor an initiatory transmission, while any claim to mastery of it is denounced—is done from within analysis itself, in dialysis [*la dialyse*] (the name I have given to supervised analysis), groups [*cartels*], and each school's own seminars. Transmission in psychoanalysis comes up against Oedipus like any other phenomenon of transmission or act of generation, and thus contains rape, resistance, identification, murder, and childbirth.

Lacan has left us with a theory of transference: through transference, the emerging subject disengages itself from repetition, which appears like a diseased form of this transference. Lacan himself, owing to a similar transference, did not renounce Freud. He proceeds from Freud, but for that, he is no less Jacques Lacan; you cannot say, after all, that Jacques Lacan resembles Freud. Each of Lacan's students thus proceeds from him, though none resembles him. If the student is a woman, she remains a woman.

For this reason I can say that I have invented nothing regarding Freudian theory or Lacanian theory (which are two different things): they taught me everything. I can also say that I have continued to write in my theoretical works just what I was already writing in my literary texts.

In fact, the signifiers are the same: the rendezvous, the step, the face, the event, the voice, and the circle, all organizing my discourse here and there. As for my style, it has remained the same: brief, allusive, and rhythmic, perhaps hardly more discursive, as it happens.

My style has nothing to do with the intentional complication, the gongorism[3] or baroquism of Jacques Lacan. Moreover, I have continued to participate in literary activities; I belong to both the Friends of George Bataille and the Friends of Zola [literary organizations]. Chapters given over to writers make up a great part of my work, less by imitation of the interest Jacques Lacan and Freud had in great works than to keep alive an old passion.

---

[3] "Gongorism" is a pejorative term deriving from the style of the Spanish poet Gongora (1561–1627). The *Petit Robert 1* describes it as preciosity of style, or abuse of images or metaphors.

I wanted to show you what is feminine [*le "la"*] about my position as woman and writer. And I would be happy to meet face to face with either of you.

It goes without saying that this first reaction will not prejudice in any way an eventual written or oral text.

I hope that by my response I have shown that I associate myself very willingly with your research.

I hope to see you soon.

EUGÉNIE LEMOINE-LUCCIONI

INTERVIEW

Question 1: What does it mean to you to write at the end of the twentieth century?

—To write at the end of the twentieth century? It's not the end of the century, is it?

—(AJ) Yes, almost.

—Yes, that's true. It means absolutely nothing, if you'll excuse me, because I can't see myself writing in any other century; though it's true that I'm writing toward the end of the twentieth century . . . you saw my hesitation, didn't you? It's just that I began writing in the middle of the century, in the forties—even earlier, writing is such a permanent function with me. But yes, writing for others, for a public, happened only in the middle of the century. If certain changes came about, that's not as a result of the turn of the century. It's rather as a result of my encounters, as I have explained [in the above letter]. I think that if I had continued to write literary texts, they would have become dated. That is, I belong to a literary generation that is defined differently. But it is true too that if I had kept on, I would have been obliged to change along with everyone else. Was it this change that I found difficult? I don't think so, because the texts that I was writing in the fifties were part of the avant-garde. So I think that I would have continued with the avant-garde. But I stopped, and when I started again, it was no longer possible to write as I had before the interruption, it wouldn't have been acceptable. This doesn't worry me—I don't think my current texts have more or less value, it's just that they are more responsive to a reading public.

—(AJ) But your theoretical writings *have* had an important impact at the end of the twentieth century. How does this affect you?

—The impact doesn't have much reality for me; I don't live in circles where one might see any effect or sign of it. No one recognizes me in the street, except those from psychoanalytic circles. Being a writer doesn't change your status in the psychoanalytic field. We don't accord the same importance to a work as other fields of knowledge or art do. An analytic work has value, if at all, only because of the interventions or echoes that it facilitates among readers on the couches and chairs of analysts or in study groups. I remain cut off from the larger public, which I may have influenced here and there, especially in university circles. A few exceptions aside, very little gets back to me.

—(AM) Do you think that theoretical writing is less marked by time than fictional writing?

—No, really, I don't think so at all. If I make reference to Jacques Lacan rather than to myself—it's certainly true that he's very much of our century, and of a certain time period. I don't see how anyone could have written like him—even if you were to search out his ancestors, Mallarmé, for example, and others—no one could have written like him in another time period.

—(AM) I was referring to your statement that your fictional writing would have been dated, that you would have been obliged to change how you wrote had you continued to write literature. That gave me the impression that the passage of time did not pose a problem for you in your theoretical writing.

—No! It's because when I gave up writing short stories I also lost the tools that had enabled me to write them. And if I have commented on such a rupture, it is for many reasons, all of which I can group together under the rubric of powerlessness. Let's just say that I didn't hold up. Later, it was hard for me to begin again from scratch in that realm. So I wrote and translated articles. I pulled myself out of my own poetic universe, and from there I entered into the analytic realm. I have remained in it, and my writing has taken off from there. You know, we can't rewrite history once things have happened, and they have happened; afterward the conditions are no longer the same. What you write at the age of twenty, especially if you're a poet, which I am a little, you don't ever write again. You can't imagine what you would have written had you continued; it's not possible. It is true, though, that there has been a break in my writing.

Question 2: Is it valid/of value to write as a woman, and is it part of your writing practice today?

—Yes, most definitely. That is, I don't know if it's valid or of value, but it certainly is a part of my writing practice. The stakes are extremely important, and this importance has to do with the place of women in Lacanian theory. For Lacan, if one can permit oneself to sum things up like this, woman would be man's symptom in that she designates the place where there is no longer anything more to be said. Obviously here we have man who no longer has anything more to say about the emptiness he finds there. So woman is man's symptom, his unconscious, if you will, or even his sense of the real—although the unconscious is not to be confused with the real. It can be said in any case that woman is the limit of what man can think of to say. Here I'm giving you the phallic perspective, man's perspective. So must woman keep quiet? About herself as the unconscious? Of course not, because in this respect, there are not men *and* women. There is a phallic function in women as well, and in that respect, woman speaks and is not merely a hole. What I always maintain is that there aren't two humanities; there aren't two races. We don't have, on the one side, the unconscious, which would be women who cannot speak for themselves, and about which one can say nothing, and, on the other side, men—that's absurd. What's true is that this dissymmetry puts women in a divided position that I explained in *The Dividing of Woman's Lot,* that is, in a divided position that doubles the division of the subject. As we know, the subject is divided. The division that is proper to women doubles the radical division of the subject.

—(AM) So, even if you write as a woman, you are making your masculine side speak?

—The phallus is neither a man nor a woman.

—(AM) I'm referring to what you said in your letter. First you talk about the failure of the vocation of the masculine genius and creator, and that the genius is considered masculine regardless of the sex of the author. But then you say the greatest writers are men. I'm not sure I understand what you mean: is it only the masculine that creates?

—I'm saying the opposite. If women like Louise Labé have taken their place as women, one can't simply say they have a masculine genius. The masculine tradition whereby women write like men has been defeated. The differentiation between masculine and feminine styles doesn't exactly coincide with the differentiation between the sexes. Women can write and speak because, as I've said, they have a phallic function. They can decide whether or not to assume it. But if women do assume their phallic function, if they do write and speak, they do it as women. When men write and speak, they do it as men. But the position of the writer, like that of the artist, feminizes men; it just so happens that it virilizes women. To speak only of women, the fact of writing puts them in a paradoxical position; it has been said that the difficulty women experience in speaking and writing is peculiar to them. It is a particular form of castration that affects speaking and writing. Women do not feel the threat of castration of their sexual organ since they do not have the organ subject to castration; but perhaps for just that reason, since they are phallic all the same, women are threatened by the castration of what they have that is the most phallic—speech.

—(AJ) Just one last thing: how do you think men live with the fact that women are speaking and writing more and more today?

—They find it hard to live with, and for good reason. Certainly in the heterosexual couple, and even in the homosexual one, there is a kind of love that Freud was correct in describing as profoundly ambivalent, that is, where love and hate go hand in hand. Therefore a man feels threatened when a woman exists on her own. She regains her autonomy: if she is autonomous, if she no longer needs a man, then another equation within the couple, which is always in disequilibrium, must be found. In any case, Lacan said, "There is no relation between the sexes." He doesn't mean that there is no sexual relationship, but that it is impossible to equate the sexes, that there is no sexual equation. In Spanish there is only one word for "relationship" [rapport] and "relation" [relation], so you see how complicated it is.

—(AJ) It is complicated in English as well, so there have been many misreadings of Lacan.

—There are any number of possible and imaginable relations, but there is no relationship, that is, we can't establish an equation of complementarity or of equality where one-fifth plus one-fifth equals one, or even one plus one equals two. . . . It's not possible, is it? There's no sense of completeness. So in any case the equilibrium is unstable; and this unstable equilibrium is further threatened by one or the other [sex]. There are two reasons for this: as Freud observed, human institutions— and publishing is an institution in itself—are homosexual; since men dominate these homosexual institutions, such as the army, they view women's arrival in them unfavorably, and this is for sexual rather than ideological reasons. I don't think it's a question of there not being enough room; it's that the men are uncomfortable. There are homosexuals who can't stand to see a woman approach them, and on the other hand, homosexuals who adore women. But there are so many who fear women enormously, aren't there? It's a phobia. So we understand that they don't want to be bothered, since they are already so comfortable with each other. This is perhaps why publishers like Editions Des femmes were created. Perhaps those women are homosexuals. I don't know if they are or not, but they are comfortable among themselves. I think it's true that men don't like to see women enter their world. It's true for the couple and for institutions. But we need not draw any conclusions from this.

That is, it wasn't any better before; the supremacy of men in these institutions was not fair either. I have experienced it myself. I was a member of the editorial board of *Esprit,* which was an extraordinarily open and sympathetic journal, with worthy people who were feminists before that was fashionable and therefore very open to women. But I remember that at the first meetings of *Esprit,* the women knitted ostentatiously. I have always felt that they were entirely welcome only if they proclaimed their femininity. So there is always a point at which you cease to put up with it. I say this about *Esprit,* but I could say the same, *a fortiori,* about any cultural institution—except, perhaps, about analytic circles. I think that in analytic circles there isn't prejudice of any kind, even unconsciously. I haven't experienced prejudice at all. Is this why I felt good about it right from the start? It's quite possible.

—(AJ) But I think that you're not the only one.

—Oh yes, after all, the first feminist movements were born in analytic circles: the psychoanalysis of women, psychoanalysis and feminism. These movements are one of the consequences of psychoanalysis, even if Lacan himself never imagined such a thing: the proof is that the Dissolution [of his school] was carried out, in part, against feminist analysts—for theoretical reasons. Thus feminist analysts who claimed to have based their work on Lacan went too far. That doesn't change the fact that analysis has had an impact on feminism.

Question 3: This brings us to our third question, which is, in fact, about psychoanalysis. Many women writing today find themselves, for the first time

in history, at the center of such institutions as the university and psychoanaly-
sis. In your opinion, will this new placement of women help them to enter the
twentieth-century canon, and if so, will they be in the heart of this corpus or
(still) in the footnotes?

—It's hard to foresee what will happen to women; but I think that they have transformed themselves to such an extent (as have men) that they will have gotten beyond these problematics. That's how I feel.

—(AM) For example, you can say that Melanie Klein is at the very top of her profession in the world, in psychoanalysis. . . .

—But she has always been there, and that has not changed even today. She is there as an analyst; she has perhaps not occupied the place she deserves in other institutions—was that your question?

—(AM) But she is well known, even outside psychoanalysis.

—Of course, but she hasn't been made cabinet minister for all that.

—(AM) No, no, that's not it.

—You see, what I mean is that women have always had, even in Freud's time, an extremely important place in spite of the fact that it was a man who invented psychoanalysis—Freud—and that there is another man, in France at least, who redefined it—Lacan. But that doesn't matter: women have, with no difficulty whatsoever, occupied whatever place they wanted in the analytic field.

—(AJ) Perhaps the next question will make this clearer, because if it's true that it works this way in psychoanalysis, it isn't at all evident that it happens so easily in other disciplines.

—No, that's why I said that it doesn't mean that doors will be opened to them in other institutions: I wouldn't know anything about them.

Question 4: Today we are seeing women produce literary, philosophical, and
psychoanalytical theory of recognized importance, and, parallel to this, we are
also seeing a new fluidity in the borderlines among disciplines and genres of
writing. Will this parallelism lead only to women being welcomed alongside
men, or to a definitive blurring of these categories?

—That's why I said that I don't know what women will be, nor what men will be either, at that point in time. The problem is that the borders are shifting: therefore, they are in flux between the sexes as well. That does not mean that our difference shouldn't be maintained, but perhaps it should be a mobile difference. Anything that was fixed, established, and subject to legislation on all levels—moral, intellectual—has started to move. Sex is shifting too. That is, one can see many aberrations, in the etymological sense of the term, on one side and on the other, but these aberrations do not elicit a reaction from anyone. Perhaps the site of differentiation—I prefer to speak of differentiation rather than difference—will be mobile. Difference will choose its arena. This does not mean that ours will turn into a society entirely monstrous by comparison with what we know, but it is true that we can imagine many, many profound transformations. Our society could get to the point where engendering is suppressed, and why not? That goes far beyond any of the problems raised here, however.

—(AJ) But for example, in the same line of thought, sometimes as one shuttles between France and the United States, one goes through periods of anxiety about analytic work and the place it will or will not have in the future, given all the blurring of borders between disciplines. For example, I have the impression that *Lagarde et Michard* will continue on into the twenty-first century, that one will read canonized twentieth-century texts, and that psychoanalytical texts will not be among them. They will say that the canon is a literary thing that has nothing to do with psychoanalysis, while so much of what has been written, currently and for a number of years now, has everything to do with psychoanalysis. I wonder if psychoanalysis itself will be erased from other disciplines and their monuments, or if it is psychoanalysis that will open up *Lagarde et Michard* and other "monuments."

—There are many questions in the question you're asking me; I'm afraid my response will be a little confusing, so excuse me. On the one hand, there is the future of psychoanalysis, to which I respond in my book *Psychanalyse pour la vie quotidienne*. It is useless to wonder whether psychoanalysis will disappear or if it is bound to disappear. I don't see why it shouldn't, since after all, it was born at a given moment and I don't see why it would exist eternally just as we know it now. Everything is always replaced by something else, as psychoanalysis will be. There's no reason to suppose that we have found this thing, that it has established itself, and that the *Lagarde et Michard* of the twenty-first century should account for it as having installed itself definitively in the collegiate canon, except out of respect for history. Second, there is, after all, an element in psychoanalysis that makes us resist it, and if we resist it so little that it becomes material for a textbook, I wonder to what extent it will be psychoanalysis. There are, therefore, two distinct questions: the perpetuation of canons and the penetration of psychoanalysis into one of Lacan's Four Discourses—into University Discourse, which is not the Analyst's Discourse. Furthermore, and in spite of Freud and Lacan, psychoanalysis has yet to become a part of philosophy texts, much less a part of literary studies!

—(AJ) Just the same, in the United States, there are many works produced today, anthologies and others, where there is a mixture of philosophy, literature, and psychoanalysis.

—We're returning there to the question of borders.

—(AJ) While in France, the borders remain. . . .

—Not really. In daily literary and philosophical life, Freud and Lacan are everywhere: among the literary, the sociologists, the anthropologists, mathematicians, everyone.

—(AJ) Do you find that women theoreticians whose work you know tend to mix disciplines more than men, or . . .

—Perhaps, but no more than Freud or Lacan!

Question 5: We've gotten to the question that no one likes, and to which no one responds: Given the problematic and the politics of the categories of the canon, and given the questions we've been dealing with, do you think your oeuvre will be included in the twentieth-century canon, and if so, how will it be presented? In your opinion, what will the content of the canon be?

—To some extent I have already responded to this by saying that a canon cannot be foreseen, it becomes evident after the fact, it is a state of affairs; otherwise, what would it be? On the other hand, will I personally be a part of the canon? Listen—and this is not false modesty —I don't accord a sure value to what I do on the level of theoretical inventiveness, for example. Let me share with you all my thoughts on this: I don't think women are given to theoretical invention. For example, I don't think it's pure chance that Freud was a man, that Lacan was a man, that Einstein was a man. I also don't think, as many women do, that after a few centuries of feminist revolution, women will become capable of theoretical invention. This isn't modesty, because theory has lost its former, dominating position. Moreover, I think women are capable of other things; what we write, men do not. Perhaps it is the very notion of theory or of canon that is changing. So you can't say that there is a new canon or that it can be defined. That's the trouble, except that we can always refer to the moment when, in the *Symposium*, Socrates lets Diotima speak—not that I want to say that I am Diotima.

—(AJ) And who would be Socrates?!

—Yet Socrates, at one point in the *Symposium*—and this has more to do with these questions and is more current than one might think—lets Diotima speak because he no longer has anything to say. I would recommend this to you for your conclusion, if you wish: Lacan adds, "He lets the woman that is in him speak." So you see, that goes beyond anything we might say. Perhaps the canon will find itself changed by it.

Question 6: We come now to our last question, which we formulated after having read some of your books: as an analyst and as a, quote, "disciple" of . . .

—I'd put quotation marks around "analyst" myself!

—(AJ) All right, around both! *As a "psychoanalyst" and a "disciple of Lacan," with lots of quotation marks, how do you interpret our project on the canon?*

—I don't interpret it at all, it isn't a matter to be interpreted. You're trying, I think, to define something. Just a moment ago, I expressed the distrust I feel personally toward definitions, but I don't interpret your own desire to classify and define, or even to foresee. Is there some uneasiness in this project? Probably, since you are necessarily intellectuals, and women, from what I can see. So you probably are uneasy, but I couldn't interpret your project myself.

—(AM) But does the fact that women are working on the canon, and asking questions like: "Will we women have a place in the canon?" not seem to you to be a symptom of something?

—Yes, probably, since you mention it. Yes, this must certainly be true. That's why you're asking me, I, who have never wondered if I would have a place in the twenty-first century! But probably you're wondering about this. First, you're younger than I, which means, of course, that you're interested in having your place at the beginning of the twenty-first century; while as for me, it has been some time since my place in eternity has been assured. But, this said, the preoccupation with having a place proves your uneasiness. It is probably quite legitimate. I would be all the more uneasy about the place I would have in the twenty-first century if I were a man, but a man in the human sense, you know. You may say that I see everything in negative terms, but humanity has such a destructive force that—and this is very Freudian, and it is in exactly this sense that I am very Freudian—I would not be surprised if humanity committed suicide.

—(AJ) No, neither would I. That has come out in our interviews with many of these remarkable women: something . . . I would hesitate to call it pessimism . . . along with a recognition of the fact that humanity is capable of killing itself.

—We've known this since Freud . . . since the Greeks, but it was Freud who said it, wasn't it?

—(AJ) But now it is *possible*.

—Yes, yes, now it is possible. Do women have a particular reaction, do they always want to save? Doubtless they always want to save. Yes, it's very possible that it is woman who doesn't want it to die. But I speak thus by intuition, and for myself. We're no longer talking about Freud's death wish, as you well know. Because wanting to conserve, to save, is in fact a function of narcissism, and at that point we are blurring the theoretical basis of Freudianism to take up what is perhaps purely a reaction in women. What I mean is that women participate just as much in this destruction, but that in another way, maybe they experience a burst of narcissistic desire to save and conserve that men, in any case as they are described to us, don't come by spontaneously. Because here too we're simplifying a lot; it's a problem of representation. It's still true, however, that the most dangerous inventions are men's inventions. But neither can you say that women are not just as dangerous on other levels, because if men are so afraid of them, it must be for good reason!

—(AJ) Yes, there must be something to it. It's true, I have often wondered: what are men so afraid of? On the basis of what we have learned from Freud, can we ask why woman is so terrifying?

—Is it not because of death? Woman is the carrier of death. If beyond that she wants to save us or have us live or have us be born or continue life, this too is true, but we can't say it in any clear or simple way.

—(AJ) Nor in any categorical way!

12
Marcelle Marini

TRANSLATED BY MARY-KAY MILLER

Question 1: What does it mean to you to write at the end of the twentieth century?

—That's the most perplexing question for me, because I don't know what my status as a writer is: it's true that I write critical discourse, but a critical discourse that is not always—not often—academic, that does not respect the academic canons. Rather, I write within a genre that you would call the essay, or else I write articles, which are not filled with references and constructed according to the rules, with the obligatory theoretical vocabulary. As a result I don't quite know what my place is, but I do know which place is not mine—that of a [fiction] writer,

Excerpts from this interview, translated by Anne M. Menke, appeared in *Yale French Studies* (1988), vol. 75.

because I can write only from a secondary position. Often, writers—notably women—have asked me, as did Marguerite Duras, for example, "But why don't you write 'directly'?" as we say here, that is, in relation to experience, or to the world. I think I would answer that it must somehow frighten me. When I write like that, what I write is bad. It's as if there were a screen; whereas if it's a question of someone else's text, this text on the contrary is not at all opaque, it conveys experience to me. So I need to pass through symbolization, via someone else's writing, through work that is already literary, in order to be free once again to write. Therefore, mine is a somewhat illegitimate status. You will tell me that that's the case of all writers: that you always write in a tradition (since that's the question being asked today)—but for [fiction] writers, the tradition is secondary, it's in the background, whereas I need to put it in the foreground.

Once I have put someone else's text in the foreground, it seems to me that I enter a much more open space, and I feel more at liberty to write. Therefore, I know very well that I do not occupy the particular place of a writer, but I don't know which place I do occupy; that is, what does it mean to write? I do write . . . the fact that I'm in this protected place perhaps keeps me from contemplating the problems of . . . how shall I say it . . . of knowing if what I write will survive me or not. There's a whole series of questions, which are very difficult, that I often hear from people who write, and which are ultimately unfamiliar to me.

—(AJ) But do you think that *your* status—because that's really the question—as someone who writes at the end of the twentieth century, from this place, or these places that you see yourself occupying with regard to writing, is specific to the twentieth century? In other words, do you have the impression of writing at the end of the twentieth century?

—Yes, because I believe that I'm writing, after all, within a critical tradition. The essay form has been an important literary form in France since at least the nineteenth century; it became more developed at the beginning of the twentieth century. The essay has always been a form that we can't define, a style in which writing is inseparable from reading. That's why I think that for women, right now, it's an important form to explore, and actually to inhabit. But it's also true that it is part of a general movement, because whether it's a question of philosophy, literature, or psychoanalysis, or at present any number of fields—a question of politics, also—it seems to me that the essay form is, I wouldn't say the dominant form, but rather the chosen one, even for people who initially wrote from within a system. It is a much freer form, I think, and it is a form that remains marginal to any totalizing system. And perhaps this condition of being a slightly marginal form of writing is what is most interesting. If I look around me, I notice that men as well as women, and even people who have produced either scholarly papers or very structured, theoretical works, with rigorous argumentation, sooner or later move to the essay. There's the example of Derrida, of course, but there's also the example of Julia Kristeva, which is quite striking. Since we're concerned with women here, it is interesting to see the evolution of the form in which Kristeva has written, which, in my opinion, has accompanied a transformation of her position, and of what she is communicating. She no longer conveys her message in the same way. And when you look at scholarly papers being written, you can see clearly that people are tending to withdraw: either they tend to revert to primary, fundamental, theoretical definitions—which appear as very strong foundations upon which they once again build a system—or on the other hand, they are beginning to consider things in a different way, in essay form. Now there, I think, is an interesting evolution; but then you both know French literature, criticism, and theory well: currently the essay is an area of freedom and invention for everyone, don't you think? Which of course doesn't mean that it is recognized institutionally.

Question 2: Is it valid/of value to write as a woman, and is it part of your writing practice today?

—Yes . . . but I share all the anxieties and the perplexities surrounding that question. I think that at the moment when you are writing, when you are truly immersed in writing, things can vary greatly. Fortunately, you cannot always be conscious of your gender! And I think that it's crucial for women to reach a point where, indeed, gender specificity can fade away, and where they can enter a realm where what they say . . . where their experience *is not just there to "play woman" [faire femme] but to communicate their thoughts, I would say, to everyone.* There's a moment when indeterminacy is essential. I think that this also comes into play when you read, and once again, thankfully so. But, at the same time, there is always a moment, either when reading or when writing, a moment—that seems to spring up involuntarily—when it is definitely your sexual identity that asserts itself. And I can give very concrete

examples; you need only think of Marcel Proust or Michel Leiris . . .
consider autobiographies written by men or women. There's a moment,
all of a sudden, when a memory, or writing, or something comes from
sexuality, but truly from sexuality in the strict sense of the term—at the
same time, though, in the general sense, that is, a sexuality based in
actions. . . .

—(AJ) In experiences?

—In experiences—"sensual" is also too weak a term, but let's just say
extremely physical experiences—ones that concern the sexual body. You
notice, at that point, that something of a very different nature comes
into play, and sometimes it can carry over into the rhythm of the
sentence, or leave other such traces, but all connected to the fact that
what asserts itself then is an experience—one that definitely comes from
the fact that sexuality is not without differentiation. It is not constantly
without differentiation, and it constructs itself as life progresses, I think.
That is, I still believe that sexuality constructs itself, favoring one side or
the other; but for now, one cannot define it. We don't know how to
define feminine sexuality, nor masculine sexuality, and of course, these
sexualities are plural. But even so, there is a moment when you feel sure
that each man/woman inscribes him/herself in the world in a certain
fashion. For me, certain pages of Proust and of Leiris are a part of—
rightly or wrongly—my great revelations about masculine sexuality (or
sensitivity) as other. Their work thus acquires a moving singularity.

—(AM) I wanted to ask if one could introduce a "feminine" rhythm
into essays. If it is in the rhythm, in part, that this sexuality of writing
lies, can that be transferred to essays? Is it more difficult there than in
poetry, for example?

—I would say that it's different—it's possible, but it would not take
the same form. In fact, you're not aware of doing it; that is, if you truly
enter into writing in an essay, there are moments when you're in writing,
truly, you don't know what you're writing. I mean that it is no longer a
question of gender or genre: you grapple with something that is emerging through symbolization, without knowing from which angle you're
approaching it, and at that particular point I think there's a mode of
writing that may also vary according to whether a woman or a man is
writing. However, there are moments when you're on the verge of
something, you sense a change in register or rhythm. I don't believe that
this can be catalogued or theorized or inventoried, that's all. That's the
incapability we face, and perhaps it's good to be incapable of saying:

"That's feminine, that's masculine, and that's general, it's neuter." Rather, there's something more unusual that appears—a rhythm that a man could very well feel while reading, because it is going to enrich his own rhythms, and why not? I believe strongly in multiple identifications, and I believe that ideology and finally, education—the entire construction of the imaginary in childhood—causes us to place ourselves in one specific role or another, and causes us to reject as feminine—or, with some feminists, as masculine—a certain number of practices of writing, or of vocabulary, or of rhythm, because you feel that it belongs to the other sex. But I think that someone who really enters into writing welcomes all that, unknowingly (as opposed to with a sense of mastery or of manipulation). Identification plays a large role, and by that I mean identification with certain ways of phrasing, certain methods of approach—sometimes, quite simply, with an image that comes to us.

—(AJ) Let's talk a bit about your own experience of writing as a woman on a more conscious level. In two of your books that I have read, there is nevertheless a clearly conscious intention to write as a woman. In your book on Duras, it's everywhere, it jumps off the page; and even in your book on Lacan, if it isn't explicitly stated, it's there; after all, it is a book on Lacan written by a woman.[1] That, for me, is fundamental.

—I would say that on a conscious level, there are several aspects to consider, and this is the point I wanted to come to. First, there is writing as a woman, that is, assuming being a woman writer in society. In France, that's a real gesture, it's an act that says: "I write, in this instance critical books—but I do it as a woman. In other words, that does not erase the fact that I'm a woman in society." For me that is essential, because it's an act that is often refused, after all. It is often toned down, because you think that you will be better accepted by saying "Well no, I don't write as a woman but in the universal arena." You do this without perceiving that you thus enter into the dominant arena and that therefore, from then on, there are modes of discourse that will no longer appear in your writing. If you enter this arena, which you believe to be the arena of the universal, you discover that, on the contrary, it is narrower.

I'm taking a position here vis-à-vis an act that must be endlessly repeated, usually beginning from some founding experience. For ex-

---

[1] *Territoires du féminin: Avec Marguerite Duras* and *Lacan*.

ample, I remember when I first felt compelled to take action. I had begun to write on Barbey d'Aurevilly, and I said to myself, "I must write." I then asked some friends who wanted me to do a lecture: "Ask me to write an article, if not I'll never write; I have to throw myself into it." So I did write that article. It ended up being a psychoanalytic reading of the text *Les Diaboliques* (whose perspective is definitely masculine even if women figure in it).[2] Suddenly I said to myself, "Where am I?" Now, there was a character in the text who showed clearly that she was "standing aside." In the margins of one story, in an epigraph, there's a short dialogue by a woman who utters a sentence signaling her withdrawal, which says "But those are your illusions, your stories," and ultimately "I am not there." That is, in general, what she says. And that's in a nineteenth-century man's text; it's very interesting. All of a sudden, that created for me a kind of collusion, and I wrote a sentence, a single sentence, at the end of this article: "It is probably not insignificant that it is a woman who protests against these stories built on the negation of her sex, and who claims to be outside the circle of fascination."

At the time, my male colleagues immediately said to me: "You're a feminist." That sentence alone sufficed to label me. Some of them were very sympathetic and said to me "My, my, you're daring" because what I said was obviously a little provocative for the time (although I didn't say "these are stories for gentlemen" in response to the habitual refrain: "These are women's stories"). What was I doing, given my sex, in this story? I wasn't really there.

From that time on, I've noticed how psychoanalytical reading works too well, because the theory and the literary texts, or the particular case histories . . . all work so well that you are completely trapped. It's a system of mirrors where the two kinds of texts engender each other within a masculine framework, and you can't get away from it. But if you begin to place a woman's text at the center of this, then uh oh! look out for the ruins of theory!

That's what happened when I worked on Duras—it was really an exultation. I think it was a quest on my part. Is it possible to write without putting aside the fact of being a woman, and what does that mean, because in fact, does one know what it means "to be a woman"? The question then comes up at that particular moment, at every level, at the same time, and it actually can be very conscious. And I think that it's very important.

[2] Barbey d'Aurevilly, *Les Diaboliques*, ed. Michel Crouzet (Paris: Imprimerie Nationale, 1989). *The She-devils*, Ernest Boyd, trans. (London: Dedalus, 1986).

I have also worked on the question of "the neuter" in Nathalie Sarraute (I haven't yet published this). I love the voyages that I take through her work: I discover things that are classified from an ideological point of view, like the stereotypes of the feminine; and yet she manages to undo them, to erase the differences between them, and to universalize starting from stereotypes that would appear gender specific. Sarraute returns stereotypes to the community (for example, "men too are talkative and passive"), and she does it very well through the play of pronouns, without seeming to try. There is also the fact that she is looking for zones "before" sexual difference; that is, much more troubled zones, where one no longer knows what it is to be a man or a woman. It's fascinating, this changeability. There are moments when a lack of differentiation is very useful. And when I think of Lacan, it's the same thing: with his work, one could not simply posit difference in the usual terms: women readers can be divided among themselves over his work, as are men; he touched upon a completely different dimension, a dimension of ethics, for example.

—(AJ) You have written a book on an illustrious woman and an illustrious man. Were they very different writing experiences for you?

—It's important to point out that their texts are written in very different registers. If I had also written a book on a male writer. . . . I can't really make a comparison. With Lacan, I was interested in venturing into analytical theory because it overlaps with the realm of the imaginary, and because there is a whole reemphasis on narcissism, sexuality, and intersubjectivity in Lacan about which it is important to speak. Right now I'm working on both men's and women's works and I find it difficult and fascinating because finally you cannot insist either on the oppositions or on the complementarities.

—(AJ) Categorization becomes impossible.

—Indeed.

Question 3: Many women writing today find themselves, for the first time in history, at the center of such institutions as the university and psychoanalysis. In your opinion, will this new placement of women help them to enter the twentieth-century canon, and if so, will they be in the heart of this corpus or (still) in the footnotes?

—Are you talking here only about theory? Or are you also talking about (women) writers?

—(AJ) Both.

—I think that my answer is more or less the same: I think that you cannot give an answer. While on some days I'm optimistic, because I see the new generations becoming active, at other times I'm not at all optimistic, because I say to myself that it would take very little for us women to sink back into oblivion. After all, we know how much the mentality of any given country can change quite rapidly. I don't think that women will be able to enter the twentieth-century canons unless women participate in the elaboration of these canons; in other words, unless women are finally allowed to participate in the elaboration of these canons. There are, however, two things that could interfere with this. First, you can marginalize women, in other words, you can relegate women to one side . . . "women's theories" . . . the ghetto. Indeed, this is always the problem of the opposition between specificity and the norm. Or the other way is for women to make advances, be it in literature or in theory. But then these advances are taken up in some man's discourse. What will finally become known will be the text of the man who takes these ideas for his own use, who reorganizes them in his own thought or reconsiders them on his own ground—and that, in my opinion, is the most dangerous thing. In fact, I fear that's what we are now witnessing to some degree. That is, what men are saying about the feminine in men is what they have taken from women. And while there's nothing really to reproach them for in this—it is normal that they receive from women—they also take this feminine discovery as their own, and afterward they identify women with themselves, and women's work is reintegrated into *their* system.

So men nourish themselves without acknowledging the debt. And since today we're still operating within a system of symbolic debt, of acknowledgment of debt, appropriating women's work is dangerous if there isn't this acknowledgment of the debt. That's especially true since the one who appears innovative might not have been the first to have thought of something. Provided he is a man (because he has appropriated it), everyone accepts the feminine better, because it is presented in a familiar form, linked to more familiar, more accepted elements. Well, in this case, it is the man's work that has a good chance of being accepted, while the other work (by the woman) will appear minor or will be forgotten.

The workings of the collective memory are complex: we have seen that in the past, and it can recur. Currently women are a strong presence in literature, they are increasingly present in psychoanalysis, they are entering the realm of philosophy, all this because the canons have shifted, because women are displacing the canons, and because the canons have shifted enough so that women can have a place in them. It's always during a period of theoretical crisis, of crisis in writing practices but also of crisis of the imaginary, of theories, certainties, institutions, and economic and social practices (because today there is a crisis of certainties, a crisis of models)—it's always during a period of crisis that women have their chance. It's obvious that we are in this type of period now. But we have known throughout history, especially in literature—there it is quite clear—that very well-known women, who enjoyed an extraordinary success and were quite famous, were nonetheless buried thirty years later. Nothing guarantees anything for us—for example, I don't feel confident enough to say that in fifty years you will not be able to return Marguerite Duras to the rank of a minor writer just because the canons will have been reconstructed differently. Nor am I at all sure that in psychoanalysis, philosophy, or politics anything has been definitively acquired just because there's a political field and discourse that women are in the process of transforming. At present we are engaged in mixed discourses, and so an exchange is being made, but it isn't certain that later women will be acknowledged to the same degree. Women can very well fall back into the trap of history, they can be left along the way in the construction of tradition, of what makes up collective memory.

The only guarantee that I can see would be to ensure a succession of generations of women—I'm going to say "feminist women" but certainly feminists in a different way. For we're going to have to work differently, we're beginning now to work differently, and that is our only chance of remaining close to the young women who come after us; that is, we must deal more with the exchange between the sexes. I think that women are self-assured enough today to attempt a transmission among women *without* a radical exclusion of men.

—(AJ) Is anything happening along these lines in France? For it's being said in the United States that our generations have neglected their daughters. In first- and second-year university courses, for example, when you listen to many of the young women students who are entering the university, it could be said that they are not feminists; they seem to have little or no gender—let alone race or class—consciousness. They tell themselves that it's completely normal for them to be at Harvard, for example; all that is normal, and "has always been that way." There is, especially in the United States, a widespread and quite unbelievable

erasure of memory, a playing down of history in the era of mass media
—to such an extent that many of these young women tend to react to
feminist teachers by asking "But what is feminism?"

—(AM) There's even a lack of reaction. Not that they are antifeminist, they just do not understand why we are feminists.

—It's the same here. But I think it's necessary to take into account
their reaction; it is necessary first to recognize that for the time being
they are not entering the same world, and that they're going to need a
certain amount of time. Since they're not encountering the same obstacles we did, they're not going to react and become conscious at the same
point and when faced with the same situations we did. But certain things
will happen to them in life.

—(AM) So it will happen to them later!

—(AJ) Yes, that's what I am sometimes driven to say: "Wait five
years, you'll see!"

—Not all of them, of course. But nevertheless there is an inevitable
period of euphoria for young women, and I think that they are right to
claim that—and besides, it's important. It gives them strength. Either
young women will continue our struggles because what we were demanding seems to them to be normal, a "natural desire," or they themselves will encounter some obstacles along the way and they will invent
their own struggles. I'm not in favor of permanent militancy; women
must, according to the situation in which they find themselves, according to their experience, be able to move from one situation to another.
It's very important that a woman at least have the experience of working
in a mixed, male and female, environment, assuming all its rights for
herself. It's important for a woman to carry on even a very structured
discourse in the institution, thinking that she is fully identified with it—
of course, she doesn't know it consciously, but that's it: she is one of
them, "one of the masters." After all, that can be an important apprenticeship even if there's always a danger. It's wonderful to fully assume
your place in society. Some of my students who are thirty, thirty-two
years old, tell me that they were like that at twenty, twenty-two, or
twenty-five. And that later, things changed for them. Then they tell the
story of the moment of their first awareness—and it is different.

Neither can you forget that for my generation there was—it's already
history—the same euphoria: I don't know what happened in the United
States, but for us, at the end of the war, there were two factors, the vote
and employment. Women had won the right to vote, and as they had

only just gotten it, it was experienced as an acknowledgment: we were full-fledged citizens, we experienced something like equality. Gone were the dark days. . . . Very few of us saw later (in the fifties and sixties) how superficial it had all been, and took up a discourse that was labeled feminist; we remained isolated, there was no women's movement. Why? Because there was plenty of employment. Employers were looking for people. Women had jobs they had never had before, and therefore they had the feeling both of being useful to society and also of being in an important position. And as a result, women did not question themselves about what they were teaching, for example, or about what they were doing when they were lawyers. Law was Law, Literature was Literature, and they had truly made the transition.

I think sometimes that Beauvoir stated it well—she was from another generation though, a generation of exceptional women—after the war, there was a generation, several generations actually, that broke into fields like philosophy fairly easily. It is not by chance that the "second wave" feminist movement came into being in response to a very particular moment: the moment when it became obvious [to the male establishment] that an imbalance between the number of men versus women educated had already existed for awhile. It was in the early seventies, for example, that one saw the appearance of tracts—[written] because there were more and more women doctors: there were as many and maybe a few more female students in medicine than male students, and when the time came for the selection process some extremely violent tracts against women emerged, written by male students. When I read Virginia Woolf, it struck me as being somewhat of a repetition of the same history and story: the dissemination of extremely violent pamphlets—something you can do when you're a medical student, with a crudeness you can imagine—because there were "too many women" in medicine. There's always that terror, as soon as a field contains 30 or 40 percent women, just as for foreigners and immigrants, there's the notion of a "threshold of tolerance." At 30 percent, one considers the profession to be "feminized," that it's the victim of parasites, that it has been invaded.

—(AJ) That's what is happening in the humanities right now in the United States.

—And we might well take a few steps backward because of that . . . and therefore young women will become conscious in another way. I think that in our field, this is recurring just now. But in France we no longer even have this problem because the university has not recruited [professors] for a very long time; that is, feminist literary critics, for example, are few in number in France, a handful really. There are quite a few researchers, but they're not employed in the academic institutions: they write their dissertations and afterward . . .

—(AJ) How many feminist critics are there in France who refer to themselves as "feminist literary critics"? Very few, right?

—Yes, I don't know if I can think of ten—because most of the literary people moved toward sociology and history when they declared themselves feminists. But the truly literary people are isolated both in the movement and in the academic institution. It's a difficult position. So in terms of those declaring themselves truly feminist, there are between five and ten, maybe?

—(AM) I read an article in the *Wall Street Journal*, written by some man who is perturbed by the rise in theoretical, psychoanalytic, and especially feminist criticism in American universities. He is ridiculously paranoid. . . .

—(AJ) A journalist?

—(AM) No, I think he teaches. The *Wall Street Journal* gave almost an entire page to this man so that he could denounce feminists, Derrideans, post-structuralists. . . .

—(AJ) It's true that in America we've all been lumped together.

—(AM) Everything that has come out of France and Germany. . . .

—Here in France the problem is that the present generation is not molding the generation to come. There's a generation of women missing. So we're attempting to remedy it through meetings and groups, but that is clearly insufficient. As for male students, there's also a lack, because certain male students are also very interested in all this, but they won't get university posts either, especially given the dominant ideology. I know less about the effects in secondary schools; some groups study these questions, but France is a small country, and in crisis. We have created, under Mitterand, a real Research Center at the Centre National de la Recherche Scientifique [CNRS], but it's a precarious and provisional one, and we're not at all certain that everything will not be buried once again. Obviously, literary life has a place, but literature already has such a small place in the CNRS and in the Women's Movement. So what remains for us is the publishing world. In my opinion, I think that you must work in both areas, especially in France: in institutional areas and in the Women's Movement, but the task is too great.

—(AJ) Especially when there are so few positions to be had in the university.

—There are really very few of us: one cannot manage to run around looking for funding, teach, and work at the CNRS all at the same time. We're overwhelmed, and we can't manage to . . . I don't know, perhaps we must try to succeed in doing something in the area of publishing—that's what we're trying to do through these research teams made up of women who are in the academic institution. These are groups that enable other women who are not part of the institution to participate in the research. If there are enough women in the institution, the group can be created—providing these women accept it politically. So then other women become involved, and they're all brought together in a common place, they work together: perhaps there's a chance here, which is why I have participated fully in it, because of this problem of generations, and of exchange and publication.

—(AJ) It's very important.

—It's very important, but in France it's fairly difficult. For example, the journal *Les Cahiers du GRIF* is now open to men; it contains men's texts. Even before that, there were fairly democratic journals in which women had important roles, and in which, therefore, there was a variety of articles—journals in which feminist articles appeared alongside other articles, which distributes them better. Instead of having special feminist issues, or feminist journals, now we would really like it if—by osmosis—our journals could be read by everyone, that is to say, that there be different viewpoints, etc. and . . . do you understand? It's another tactic, but not everyone is in agreement. . . .

—(AM) I think it's a very good idea to open up . . .

—It's actually a strategy, but it nevertheless implies a conception not only of feminism but of women, of their place in society, a conception of politics that not all feminists agree on. . . .

Question 4: Today we are seeing women produce literary, philosophical, and psychoanalytical theory of recognized importance, and, parallel to this, we are also seeing a new fluidity in the borderlines among disciplines and genres of writing. Will this parallelism lead only to women being welcomed alongside men, or to a definitive blurring of these categories?

—This question is very similar to the last one, and I have already partially responded to it, since I had them both in mind. It seems difficult to make projections: you hope for—I think that you must hope, that's my personal belief—the blurring of these boundaries, and I would say also the blurring of places of enunciation, which means that identity, the representations that one fashions of sexual identity, can be transformed as well. They will not be denied, they will not be erased, but they will, I hope, be different.

—(AJ) But do you think that the presence of women in academic institutions will help to blur these boundaries, or that our presence has already helped to do that?

—Oh, I'm persuaded that this has helped to blur the boundaries, but it's completely dialectical in my opinion. That's what I was saying: when there are crises, the models change. There are political crises—"the crisis of the university" is an example. If you think about philosophy in France at this time, it comes from within the university but not from without; it is closely tied to the university, the great philosophers are in the university, in different posts, but I consider the university to include all research centers. These are truly what one could call intellectuals. We cannot say now, as we could in other eras, that the university is only maintaining its role of transmission, and a transmission mainly of the past, while others outside the university create the thought or the literature that is *currently* emerging. In this respect, I think there's already been a preliminary blurring of categories in France that has happened primarily since the war, since the Liberation. And that's why it is a period that greatly interests me. You see people who are at once teachers, writers, and journalists. Sometimes they leave, or they become politically active—these are very porous environments. For philosophy, that has been important. Psychoanalysis is different, but psychoanalysis, nevertheless, eventually became part of the university, something that it had long resisted. It causes problems, but nonetheless it's a sign. That's why I say that things are really happening, in different ways, that I think that in this period of crisis women can seize opportunities. Of course, there was a time when women were beginning to enter somewhat further into literary areas in the university. But today there are still only a very few of us. I learned recently that finally, out of all the tenured professors in France, only 2 percent are women.

—(AM) Two percent!

—Mainly because in the scientific and medical realms, law, etc., there are practically none. (Someone gave me this figure, so I cannot confirm it: but there are sociological studies in progress.) It is true that many women are lecturers and not professors, and that's certainly a problem, but not the most important one—mainly because there are universities where the distinction between professor and lecturer matters less since the administration is democratic, and no one imposes his/her curriculum on the others. There's a relative equality and relative autonomy of individuals, and a sharing of tasks. So women have, after all, benefited from this. Of course, being a lecturer, as I am, is burdensome—politically and from a union perspective, this has been discussed often—since one is doing the same work as other people while being paid much less. That said, perhaps politically, for the future, we're managing to put something new in place. In any case, it's always in that particular instance of crisis that women manage to speak and to create. So I believe that by doing this, they participate in the movement. I think that they participate in the movement through their different modes of writing, for example. It's fine that some women show that they write according to canons that are still traditional, and that other women, on the contrary, are involved in the blurring of boundaries. I don't think it would be good to wish that all women do the same thing—I think that they must be everywhere, and always interesting. It can be good discipline to enter, at a given moment, a very structured, traditional universe that had been closed to us and to master its ins and outs. Of course, the fact of inequality within the institution still remains.

Question 5: Given the problematic and the politics of the categories of the canon, and given the questions we've been dealing with, do you think your oeuvre will be included in the twentieth-century canon, and if so, how will it be presented? In your opinion, what will the content of the canon be?

—On that I'm pessimistic. For example, I wrote an article on feminist criticism that is out in the United States now, in the book *Women in Culture and Politics.*[3] I responded in the article to both the preceding question and to this one; I reflected on the spirit of the discipline. I can answer only for my narrow field: literary criticism, for me, does not exist, it isn't really a scientific field, it's a field of research, reflection, and writing. It's a crossroads traversed by all kinds of other discourses, and it seems to me that literary criticism works with all kinds of other discourses, and that one must continue to proceed in this direction. That

[3] "Feminism and Literary Criticism: Reflections on the Disciplinary Approach," Carol Barko, trans., in Judith Friedlander, Blanche Wiesen Cook, Alice Kessler-Harris, and Carroll Smith-Rosenberg, eds., *Women in Culture and Politics: A Century of Change* (Bloomington: Indiana University Press, 1986), pp. 144–63.

is, it isn't a discipline in the scientific sense of the term, nor in the way Foucault meant it, with procedures that can be repeated. Naturally, a certain number of procedures are repeated, are transmitted, and why not? But they all involve erudition, the establishment of texts, things like that. As for reading, interpretation, and everything that constitutes the field of literary criticism, which is after all quite vast, I think it's a site of the abolition of boundaries, which is unique to our era. We must remember that there has always been a, shall we say, cultivated literary criticism, one that worked with literary discourse simultaneously with scientific discourse or with the evolving discourses in the social sciences. Even Tainian criticism functioned in that way. But in recent times—since the entire field of human sciences was created, each of these sciences with its own type of discourse, its own type of procedure—I think that, for about the last twenty years, it is "literary criticism" that has been combining these discourses. I think all of us, but especially we women, should continue this effort in a more calculated manner. Criticism must put the contradictions between fields to work; it must refuse to be a separate discipline but rather remain an area of confrontation and meeting, an area of tension. That affects vocabulary and it affects the method of writing. That's why I personally don't like to write so-called "academic" articles; if I have to, I will, but it doesn't interest me. But the new kind of writing we're doing comes across . . . less well, because it's difficult to get it across—it requires way too much effort for the small circulation it would have. We must be very clear: we're in a market system; therefore what you would do for a very well-known writer, you are not going to do for a minor writer, and even less for a critic if she or he does not respect the traditional canons. So this somewhat complex writing will be put aside, and from this comes I think a certain marginalization.

Similarly, regarding quotation, I think that there are other obstacles for women: at least in France, women are quoted infrequently. Perhaps in general we function less according to quotation here than in the United States, but women are certainly quoted much less frequently. Even feminists, even women who do research quote other women less frequently; even if they have read these other women, they quote only those who are very well known. I have had female students to whom I have said, "But after all, in your thesis, your idea comes from such and such a woman's text." "Oh, you know it?" I said, "Yes, you were lucky not to have defended your master's thesis with me, because it would have gone very badly; not quoting her is, after all, scandalous; this idea forms the essence of your thesis. . . ."

—(AJ) It wasn't cited even in a thesis?

—In preparation for a master's thesis, on the part of someone who wanted to write her thesis with me—naturally I didn't agree to direct her thesis. And I asked her "why?" Because I wanted to understand. So she came to my seminar and she responded, "I thought that was the way it was done in the university, and that if the woman writer wasn't widely known and she was a feminist, it wasn't necessary to quote her." So I said that you have to quote all the people with whom you think. And I opened my eyes, and I realized the number of times my ideas and formulas are used without quoting me; it's almost systematic. There is a kind of forgetting, an effacing of women, even by women (although more generally by men), including women who work on women: sometimes you'll find the text in the bibliography, but it does not appear in the book.

—(AM) But that's unthinkable!

—I find it tremendously shocking. I feel like writing an article on it, because now I have enough examples.

—(AJ) The men, I understand, it's less surprising, but the women . . .

—From men, it's shocking, and in fact, even more so. I'm not saying that everyone proceeds like that, but it happens frequently enough to disturb me. Actually, when you consider that literary criticism is not a discipline, when you avoid thinking of it as a method of formulation and realize that it actually has no concepts (in the truly philosophical sense of the term). . . . It has notions but does it really have specific concepts? It works with concepts, but can it create for itself universal concepts, for all literary criticism, which would be truly philosophical, theoretical concepts? So if you think this way about literary criticism, you tend to escape the system of quotation; which is to say that you don't have the obligatory sentence that states: now, such and such an author is, the style is, the stylistic is . . . and therefore you make the transmission of other's ideas much more difficult because the easy solution is always to find one pithy phrase somewhere rather than to cite a thought process. If you put all the work into the process, and much less into the conceptualization, you lose. But if you use formulas that are easy to retain, it creates the *effect* of truth, the effect of generality, and it can be used in all the scholarly papers of France and Navarre. Again, with the essay, you remain somewhat marginal to the academic and scholastic fields, because the whole tradition in France is the academic tradition of the scholarly paper—where one finds a phrase that will show up in three different papers.

—(AJ) Many feminists working on "the French canon" try to keep the *Lagarde et Michard* in mind, because it is after all one of the major textbooks, "the canon" of the literary tradition in France. We ourselves asked the question, half seriously, half jokingly: will the important texts written in the twentieth century by women, in the area of literary criticism, but also in the area of psychoanalysis and other areas, become part of this *Lagarde and Michard* canon, or be abandoned?

—I can answer this question, since the *Lagarde et Michard* on the second half of the twentieth century has just come out. It contains some Sarraute, some Duras, a certain number of contemporary women writers. I remember that the people who were putting together this book wrote me a note to tell me "and even your book will be cited," which proved that including me was not an obvious thing to do but rather was "progressive." This said, I did a study once on the *Lagarde et Michard,* concerning Nathalie Sarraute, for a course. What remains in the *Lagarde et Michard* is the whole French system: the whole system of filiation, masters of thought, symbolic filiation, paternity, hierarchy, hierarchy within a generation, hierarchy of genres within one period as well, the notion of a school of thought, groups that make up a school (there must be a leader), etc. That's typical of their entry on the Nouveau Roman, since they designated Robbe-Grillet [as leader]. Therefore we have the Nouveau Roman as category, a chart of dates, beginning with the first work of Robbe-Grillet. Sarraute was indeed mentioned there at the same time, but because she had also published something the same year, whereas what she had published beforehand does not appear. Now Sarraute sees herself as having been part of the avant-garde, as having invented all that before the war. Her first critical articles were written long before those of Robbe-Grillet. They appeared in *Les Temps Modernes*—she says that *she* was the pioneer.[4] Of course she can say that, but it has absolutely no effect as far as tradition is concerned. She is there, in the *Lagarde et Michard,* but she's there as a woman in a male school—there are several men and one woman, with Robbe-Grillet as the leader.

4 See the following articles by Sarraute in *Les Temps Modernes:* "Portrait d'un inconnu: Fragment" (1946), 1(4):601–24; "Paul Valéry et l'enfant d'éléphant" (1947), 2(16):610–37; "L'Ere du soupçon" (1950), 5(52):1417–28, and "Marterau" (1953), 8(90):1665–91.

In this regard, one also wonders about Claude Simon: how Robbe-Grillet can be seen as "the leader" of Claude Simon, I don't know. You could say that Robbe-Grillet wrote the theoretical texts, but it's not true. Nathalie Sarraute wrote the first important theoretical texts of the Nouveau Roman. Now that is revealing, and when I tell that to my students, it is perceived as due to my feminism, in other words as a "revindication." So the students laugh, they're annoyed, they think that I'm exaggerating, that I'm being picky; and yet, I believe that there, I have come upon a fact, I'm not dealing in intuitions. . . . I have come upon a verifiable fact. . . .

—(AM) I don't know if you know this, but Sarraute categorically refused to participate in this project.

—I think that here in France, women writers, once they have achieved a certain level of recognition, think that they are writers and not women-writers. First there's the whole image of the literary woman, the "poetess," the female novelist that can be pejorative here. The same is true with the expression "woman doctor" [*doctoresse*]; women prefer to be called doctor, rather than "woman doctor," because "woman doctor" has been a belittling expression. We really have to fight to return these words to the margins of language . . . these and others, in order to find a way to "feminize" language without being pejorative. I also think that this is related to what I was saying at the beginning of our interview. I mean the fact that it's true that when you write, the question of your gender is not the object of the writing, and that, on the contrary, you simply navigate from one frontier to the other. In other words, Sarraute partakes of a much larger realm. You have only to read her first critical articles: she wrote about Proust—and about Virginia Woolf at a time when no one in France spoke of her. She spoke of Ivy Compton-Burnett when no one in France knew her; it is only now, with the women's movement, that Compton-Burnett is translated a lot. Nathalie Sarraute has contributed to making women writers known, but she is one of the rare ones to do so. I think that she gets annoyed [at requests like yours] because she thinks that when she writes, she does not write as a woman; that is, she does not choose subjects that are clearly "women's subjects" —that's a kind of labeling she fights against. There's another thing: she must think that, after all, in her social position, she is a woman who writes (which is another realm) and that as such, she runs the risk, as do other women, of finding herself on the "dusty shelves of libraries" that Virginia Woolf talks about. And this is very important indeed.

For example, for the national competitive exams here, we actually had a lot of difficulty placing women's texts on the list. One year there was [a text by] Duras and it was a real scandal. I was on the exam committee that year and it was really quite amazing. We had meetings, and the men kept saying "But we don't understand Duras at all; how are we going to teach her work to the students? How are they going to be able to prepare the exam on *The Ravishing of Lol V. Stein?*" They probably swore to themselves never to do that again—and so put Duras on the reading list for only one year. I had gone to this place only for feminist reasons and so I left it very quickly, but the women who continued to participate in this preparation of exams wanted to maintain the tradition of a woman's text. Well, they did not win their case. They had proposed George Sand or Nathalie Sarraute. George Sand? Too easy. Nathalie Sarraute? Too difficult! Women, then, are either too much or too little: therefore, for many different reasons, they run the risk of not being taught. I dare say that they cannot be commented upon or become part of the collective memory, of the tradition.

—(AJ) Why is putting one woman on the reading list so frightening? Is it because it touches the collective memory?

—Yes, that's what I think.

—(AM) Is it because it's something so official? One cannot accept that women . . .

—Women are the private, men are the social: one admits them a bit into the social, as women, but only in a certain way and place. For instance, notably in France, one sees that we have not succeeded, contrary to what has been said, in unsettling the patronymic, because although children now have the right to bear the name of both parents, that's not what will appear in official records. Therefore, I don't consider it to be a victory. In life one always does what one wants: if both names don't appear in the official records we can consider the patronymic as still dominant, and there is no other solution. Using both names facilitates daily life when people are divorced, etc., but we haven't disturbed the patronymic system. Naming is a problem of the same order. That is, I think there is still—this is a little hasty, but I think that there's something to it—the idea that creation and procreation are divided between the sexes and that one must not confuse them. I have worked on language as related to production and reproduction. It's a question of social hierarchy, a hierarchy of values in order to protect, on the symbolic level, something much stronger, which is that the power of creation is located on the side of the masculine sex, including even the creation of children. There is anguish for men when they are faced with the possibility of women producing children at the same time as they produce books or other kinds of socially legitimate activities. I think that in this area a profound anguish exists, so profound that it does not even express itself, or is ashamed to express itself, because once it is said it's a little . . . One reveals one's vulnerability, and so it is uncomfortable, but it still plays a part. For example, the anguish that it will make boys "effeminate" to identify with a woman, and especially a woman who writes. Women writers must therefore remain clandestine. All these stereotypes linger on.

Question 6: You are already trying, from inside the French university system, to change the canon concretely, by teaching through a feminist optic literature written by women. You are well placed, therefore, to speak to us of the reaction of the institution in the face of such a procedure.

—(AJ) Discreetly, of course!

—Oh, it doesn't bother me to do it. I won't cite names indiscreetly. . . . When I decided to write a book on Marguerite Duras, a book that I wanted to write truly outside institutional constraints, I made a choice. That is, I did not complete a dissertation, I wrote a book that I published directly with a publishing house; which means that I turned toward another institution, and I did it on my own, outside my own institution. Strategically, or rather tactically, that was not a very good idea, because it led to my not getting a doctorate; but for me writing the Duras book was fundamental. There, you see, one touches upon the really important problem, the price to be paid. I think that we will manage to make progress only if we accept paying a certain price. I knew at that point that if I were to say to my thesis director, "I want to write a book on Duras," he was immediately going to say to me, "Yes, but you must . . ." I was going to lose a large part of my freedom because, no matter what, I was going to have to adhere to a minimum of academic conventions, and for this particular book I didn't want to do that. Therefore, I marginalized myself, relatively speaking—although I wasn't taking a great risk because I held an appointed post. (I do not recommend this tactic at all to students or to those who are waiting to be appointed.) And then there's the other practice many women engage in, which is to respect the academic conventions and to participate in feminist literature and feminist criticism after their dissertation, once they have rendered unto Caesar the things that are Caesar's. That's also a strategy that appears effective to me, provided that it doesn't take too long. The reactions to my strategy, then, were varied. They were varied because there was a lot of unrest in the university at that time; it was right in the middle of a crisis. I have the good fortune of being at Paris-VII, which is a very flexible university, where I can say, practically, that the fact of being a lecturer is not at all bothersome for me because I choose my own curriculum, I do what I feel like doing, I do advanced seminars. I am sustained by the fact that many students come to my courses, from other universities and from abroad. That makes a contribution to the university; the university has something to gain from it. I would say that an attitude of tolerance exists because everyone has something to gain from it. So, you have to know how to negotiate, for if the flow of students were to dry up, the powers that be would say: "What does that have to do with us?"

That doesn't prevent a perpetual interrogation, discreet or indiscreet, or an ironic comment on "that feminist seminar." And sometimes it's respect. It fluctuates, but the most difficult moment—the crisis—took place around the male students who were coming to my courses. In our classes there are people of all ages, students, people who have returned to school, highly motivated people and some fairly argumentative and politicized male students who are capable of intervening strongly on their own behalf. And in certain of my male colleagues' classes, my male students began to question what was being said. It was at that point that my male colleagues came to me and said: "But what are you doing to our men?" In sum: "They belong to us. Take the girls if you wish, but leave us our boys." And so I said "For whom do you take your boys if you think that it is my discourse that makes them like that? I think that they're quite capable of thinking for themselves—it's the whole of society that's seeking change, you must go along with it." And that incident created some real hostility toward me—which doesn't have any real institutional influence, since I'm not applying for a professor's post. There I think I would have difficulty.

So, there are a certain number of things that I call "the price to be paid." There are things that you have to know how to accept. You cannot be feminist and constantly complain: I really believe that. As a feminist, you're in combat—I am not going to call it a sacrifice, but you're in the position of making a political choice where there's a price.

It's like the union people, or anything that one does when one is involved in politics. A price must be paid: the least difficult one possible —I'm not at all a martyr. For example, at one point I was invited to give some lectures. There was a course in a university that lasted a full year on the image of the woman in the nineteenth- and twentieth-century novel. The women professors had really struggled to have two women authors put on the syllabus(!)—one of them being Marguerite Duras. So they asked me to do three series of three-hour lectures, or something like that, on Duras. I did my three series of lectures, but the male professor did not come to them, because he said "Marguerite Duras is not a writer." That was in 1980, or around that time, let's say '79. He didn't come, fine, but I was never paid. They had worked it out. . . . I called several times . . . but they had worked it out among themselves to wait until the course was finished, and then to say "Oh no, there's been a mistake."

—(AJ) That's so outrageous!

—Well, I was furious, because I think that I should have fought more, but that would have put the women who had invited me in a difficult position. I just didn't have the necessary presence of mind to . . . Now I wouldn't do it, I would go in search of my money. I was wrong in not doing that. But you see just how far it can go. Similarly, when it was a question of getting my doctorate on the basis of the work I had done. . . . Many men, in fact, encouraged me to petition for my doctorate, and in truth, if they reestablish the state doctorate, I will apply for it on the basis of my work. At that time, however, I had seen Jean-Pierre Richard, who absolutely wanted me to apply for a doctorate. He invited me to the Sorbonne (he was no longer at the University of Paris VIII), and he said to me, "Why didn't you come sooner? Even the book on Duras could have served as a dissertation." I told him "I don't regret it," and that back then, I didn't have the presence of mind, and . . . Then he said to me, "But if you write 100 pages for me, with the rest of your books . . . I think that I'll be able to . . . It only takes two people at the Sorbonne, and for the rest, we'll choose the people carefully. I think that I could get together a jury, but since I had such a terrible time helping Michael Butor, I don't want this to recur with you, so I'm going to make some inquiries." One week later he called me and said: "I was stupefied: psychoanalysis is 'outmoded'; as for Lacan and Lacanian criticism, 'it was annoying, but its time has passed' " (and he had looked for the most neutral people, the least conspicuous people).

But feminism! " 'It's over.' " He said to me, "I'm very sorry, I'm ashamed, but it isn't possible at this time." Well, there you have it.

I constantly meet students who say to me, "I don't have anyone to direct my dissertation," or "I cannot do my dissertation, they're making it difficult for me. . . . " There are very few of us women. And there are some very open men—sometimes they're more open than certain women, but not yet numerous enough, especially in twentieth-century studies. There are few twentieth-century specialists—there are underlings, and with them it is, after all, hard enough, so that a feminist reading . . . But even so, it's changing, because there are men who accept it very well, but they *accept* it, that's all. I think that it's tolerated because it works. Literary scholars are threatened in a university such as ours, where there are many scientists; so if you publish a lot, if you attract a lot of people from France and abroad . . . For example, if you create new exchanges with the United States . . . my feminist seminar would no longer exist if I had not opened up an intellectual exchange between the United States, other European countries, and France—it's that simple. And so now, as a matter of fact, as far as Paris VII is concerned, as far as the administration is concerned, my feminist seminar is working, because of international relations. From the moment that there are international relations, or students from the *grandes écoles,* or a number of women students, there are political opportunities in the eyes of the administration. But that doesn't mean that the administration recognizes that intellectually or politically this feminist work has value or relevance. They consider it a project, perhaps a useless project. Do they find it pertinent? I think that if you took a poll, few people would respond that feminist work is pertinent. Because (it's ironic) it always comes back to the way in which one judges feminism in general in France—as does Duras, as a matter of fact, when she speaks of it as a "party," as if there were a structured feminist party! When you think of the anarchy in which we in the movement find ourselves—almost in anarchistic individualism—and yet we are accused of forming a party, almost like the Communist Party— it's flabbergasting! But things still function like this in the collective imaginary, without any link to reality. Feminism is still seen as a war machine, or as a simplistic idea, not as a different method of approach, or finally as a practice of tolerance to alterity.

—(AM) Is it because people don't read feminist work?

—No, the works are not read. Or, yes, they're read by some men: the very free and marginal ones or those who are very sincere but constrained by institutions; they read our work in private, write to us in private, and that's all.

—(AJ) Unfortunately, that's also the case in the United States. Things can become quite intolerable, really, because much of the really important and innovative theoretical work done by women just isn't read by men.

—Men very rarely read even literary texts written by women, or if they read them, it's in order to relax. They enjoy these texts, but they don't write much on them.

13

Michèle Montrelay

TRANSLATED BY CARRIE NOLAND

Question 1: What does it mean to you to write at the end of the twentieth century?

—It means: (1) researching, making a contribution through my work, so that the part of the human being known since the nineteenth century as the "unconscious" can be understood more and more rigorously, in terms of its "laws," its structure, its dynamic, etc. It also means: (2) witnessing. A physicist does not have to prove the existence of matter (except perhaps to himself!). A biologist does not have to convince anyone that a cell is a reality, nor a historian that Louis XIV or Julius Caesar were in fact real human beings. However, it always seems as if

Excerpts from this interview, translated by Patricia Baudoin, appeared in *Yale French Studies* (1988) vol. 75.

the existence of the object of my discipline, while acknowledged theoretically, has to be proved again and again. The unconscious is the object of censorship and repression—that is its essence. This can be verified not only on an individual basis but on cultural and social levels as well. People acknowledge that the unconscious exists, but they don't really believe in it. For instance, philosophy leaves it completely out of the picture; currently there is no philosophical enterprise—with the exception of Michel Henry's—that takes the reciprocal relations between the unconscious and the conscious into account. Another example is the censorship of psychoanalysis practiced by the media. Publications that claim to represent French culture and its latest innovations, such as *Le Monde* and *Le Nouvel Observateur*, never cite psychoanalysis except to satirize it, mock it, testify to its decadence or uselessness, or to drive home the ridicule of specific psychoanalysts. Certainly some of the latter are mediocre practitioners of their profession. But does this justify the consistent refusal on the part of these publications to take the existence of the unconscious seriously? *Le Monde* has never devoted one of its weekly science columns to the unconscious, whereas it regularly provides space for psychiatry. And psychiatry just as regularly takes advantage of the opportunity to deprecate psychoanalysis or to announce its demise. *Le Monde* never, however, invites one of the practitioners of psychoanalysis to defend their position and point of view.

What do I make of the favor Jacques Lacan enjoyed, you might ask? Well, you have to understand that this favor only lasted a few years—at the end of his life—and that it was a fashion, one of those snobbish crazes so particular to French intellectuals. But I always sensed in the popularity of Lacan a way—perhaps more subtle than the others—of censuring the unconscious as an object of scientific research worthy of the name.

Now, that object does indeed exist. Freud saw that the unconscious possesses its own laws and structures, but even he did not have the last word on it. Others came after him, and still more will follow. What I mean by this is that, like other sciences, ours can exist only on the condition that it enlarge, specify, and refine over time its models and modes of experimentation. I'm trying to contribute to this process.

The work of psychoanalysis is also a political battle, one that is rather obscure because it ignores fashion and the mass media, but one that is, in my opinion, absolutely essential. I am profoundly convinced that in our civilization, psychoanalysis, as theory and as treatment, is one of the highest, most valuable, and most symbolic forms of human freedom. The psychoanalytic practice simultaneously recognizes the existence of violence, of homicidal desire in every man, and yet wagers that he will not remain that way, that he will transform himself as soon as a space is opened up in which he can speak of this violence to another. In this regard, the stakes of freedom are fantastically high. Totalitarian states understand the implications of such a wager, judging from the extent to which psychoanalysis has been the object of persecution within their borders. Our journalists—who invariably think of themselves as being on the "left" out of some kind of snobbery—would do well to reconsider their ridicule of psychoanalysis. In my opinion, to say that "psychoanalysis is finished" is to participate in the most sinister kind of repression.

These are some of the reasons why I write, but there is also a more personal one: I love language, I love the French language, and words themselves, with their sonorities and rhythms. Grammar and syntax take hold of me, they fascinate and enchant me. Sometimes I spend several days on the same sentence, crossing and uncrossing the logical threads of words until I've got it just right, until "it" [ça] comes out and detaches itself from me. This labor of writing is a luxury, one for which my patients and my large family hardly leave me time, but which nevertheless I shall not renounce.

Question 2: Is it valid/of value to write as a woman, and is it part of your writing practice today?

—I never say to myself: "I am writing as a woman, I am going to get this message across better than a man, or not as well." What is important, I repeat, is the unconscious, the feminine unconscious, or the masculine unconscious, which is the one that concerns me at the moment. The important thing is to continue to seek, discover, and articulate—to make myself heard by at least a few people.

However, I should note, after the fact, that I certainly would not have written the texts I can now reread, if I'd been a man. That's for sure!

"Writing as a woman" can also mean: writing to express and to defend points of view, truths, and rights that are particular to women. It can mean: to be a feminist writer. But I never was one. I wrote the text "Inquiry into femininity"[1] during the years 1967 and 1968. That subject was no more important to me than those I treated before and after it. In some ways, history and the events that took place around 1970 are what made of it a pioneering, precursor text.

Since I have always been a little mistrustful of feminism, I tried at that point to be particularly clear, and the French feminists were not deceived. They did not count me as one of their own (or at the least, only very provisionally).

Currently, it is not the text I just cited that is the most important one for me, but rather other texts, such as "Le Saut du loup," "Folding and Unfolding," "Le Double statut flottant et fragmentaire de l'inconscient."[2] It seems to me that I offer some truly new hypotheses in these works—it just so happens that they deal more with male sexuality. And that's logical: men don't perceive what is specifically masculine in their sexual and affective behavior. They want less to know themselves than to act. They have little liking for thinking about themselves, which is another way in which they are different from us.

Question 3: Many women writing today find themselves, for the first time in history, at the center of such institutions as the university and psychoanalysis. In your opinion, will this new placement of women help them to enter the twentieth-century canon, and if so, will they be in the heart of this corpus or (still) in the footnotes?

—This new status permits women to acquire credibility, notoriety, and a workplace more easily. Regarding the canon, history will decide. What values in the next few centuries will determine that this woman, and not another, is to be placed in the canon? I cannot tell you that, but I'm inclined to think that women will find themselves there thanks to values that are foreign to institutions. These women will be included because they will be recognized either as brilliant writers or as pioneers and precursors.

[1] "Inquiry into Femininity," trans. Parveen Adams, appeared in Toril Moi, ed., *French Feminist Thought: A Reader* (New York: Basil Blackwell, 1987), pp. 227–49.

[2] "Le Saut du loup" appeared in *L'Ombre et le nom;* "Folding and Unfolding" in *Psychoanalytic Inquiry;* and "Le Double statut flottant et fragmentaire de l'inconscient" in Michel Cazenave, ed., *Colloques de Tsukuba: Sciences et Symboles* (Paris: Albin Michel, 1986).

Question 4: Today we are seeing women produce literary, philosophical, and psychoanalytical theory of recognized importance, and, parallel to this, we are also seeing a new fluidity in the border lines among disciplines and genres of writing. Will this parallelism lead only to women being welcomed alongside men, or to a definitive blurring of these categories?

—Paradoxically, I find that at the moment my work is better appreciated in interdisciplinary circles than among psychoanalysts, especially French psychoanalysts. I don't attribute that to my gender but rather to the fact that in these interdisciplinary circles, each individual is less threatened, more at ease. Questions of propriety and jealousy lose their immediacy, and do so regardless of gender.

Question 5: Given the problematic and the politics of the categories of the canon, and given the questions we've been dealing with, do you think your oeuvre will be included in the twentieth-century canon, and if so, how will it be presented? In your opinion, what will the content of the canon be?

—I don't know how to reply to your question, because I never think about it. But since you have prompted me to do so, this is what I've come up with: I would like for it to be said of my way of thinking that while being a woman's—I mean while being gendered feminine—it was rigorous and bold. Perhaps I should be more precise while we're on the subject. When I speak of a feminine-gendered thought process, I imagine that this style of thinking would not go in for the kind of conceptualizing that is proper to men, the thing that makes it possible for them to recognize one another, to take pleasure in the use of certain passwords. The intellectual exercise of all that "university discourse" bores me. I can do it as well as anyone else, but it's a waste of my time. True rigor and logic must pass through places where subjectivity, imagination, and the writer's own values and anguish are put into play. That's what interests me, but for the moment I'm far from having realized this project in the form of a finished oeuvre.

Strange and paradoxical as it may seem, this personal and lively way of writing, what I've been trying to evoke by calling it "feminine," this discourse that is as little restrained [*corsetée*] by the intellectual as possible, can often be acquired and used by men, by the few inspired men of each generation. On the whole, I would say that there is no inspired man who does not express his femininity. For example, the great philosophers, such as Descartes, Spinoza, and Heidegger, were able to allow the feminine as well as the masculine power of creation to infuse their styles. Similarly, Racine, Balzac, Flaubert, Proust, and others wrote with another part of themselves, with what eludes everyday life—what is, therefore, the unconscious part, the part that, as Jung recognized, is feminine.

On the other hand, the feminine is so present in a woman, so engaged in the everyday, so familiar, that she lacks this mystery, this inspired dimension that is proper to the feminine, whereas a male writer allows it—without volition—to pass through him. Women who are made (psychically) like men, the truest of true homosexuals (and who, by the way, can discuss admirably motherhood, sexual pleasure, etc.), these women are, from the start, much more gifted than other women at writing a great work, one that time will memorialize. At this point there are two or three of these women in French literature who will last. But since I'm not one of them, I have to make an even greater effort to create the kind of work I would like, work that is scientific, imaginative, and practical, all at the same time.

Question 6: In your work L'Ombre et le nom, *you explore the relationships between primary imagination and the feminine. You speak of this feminine in terms that one could qualify as traditional, such as the "shadow," [ombre], the "nonrepresentable," the "outside," [dehors], etc. Far from criticizing such a metaphoric description of femininity, you confer value on it by designating it as an essential supporting element of culture, a support that must not be endangered. What do we risk if, in spite of everything, women move out of the shadow to touch the male corpus of the canon?*

—All women will not move out of the shadow; only some will. Perhaps, during the course of this new generation, more will be able to. But allow me to come back to some of your formulations. It isn't because more men than women have a place in the "canon" that it remains masculine. What enters the canon is what lasts, therefore what matters, artistically and scientifically, what is a *work* in the strong sense of the word. And all human work worthy of that name is what reconciles and reunites—each time in its own way—the masculine and the feminine. I don't think a very gendered work, one excessively colored by virility or femininity, will ever make it into the canon. All great works are bisexual, resulting from the most extreme tension between these two poles.

Besides, the sense of the word "shadow" that you use is not exactly my own. I speak in my book not of the shadow a body casts and projects before itself, but of the shadow as conceived by Hofmannsthal in stories like "The Woman Without a Shadow," where, for instance, "shadow" means that possibility a female body presents of making itself into a screen for light and representation. The body is there; it conveys a truth that it contains, without, however, being aware of it.

Follow-up Question: Could you explain to us why you mistrust feminism?

—To mistrust is not to reject, but rather to not trust completely, to say to oneself: be careful! If being a feminist means seeing to it that the condition of women and their rights are increasingly respected, then, far from feeling reluctant, I adhere without hesitation to this project. However, certain methods of serving this cause I do mistrust. Why? Because they're not realistic. Certain ways of being a feminist are, in the long term, dangerous. We run the risk of having these feminisms turn against us women, to the extent that they are dependent upon a feminist theoretical base that seems to me to be in large part false. Feminist theory (at least, what I know of it) affirms that male/female relationships have to be seen in terms of power: men love power so much that they refuse to share it. It is true that this refusal exists, that wherever important business is transacted, wherever people are plotting, writing contracts, making decisions in the heat of passion—in sum, in all the "hot spots"—a priori women are not welcome. But feminist theory is mistaken regarding the reason for this exclusion. Possessiveness, which feminist theory attributes to men, is a very feminine trait. It is we women who need to possess in order to reassure ourselves, to protect either ourselves or others. Men have less of a need to possess than to play, and specifically to play in a group, with partners carried away by a passion they all share.

Play [*le jeu*] rules the world. Play is everywhere, even where things seem to be most serious. The power that makes you hold your breath in a stadium, that inspires a crowd at a race track or poker players gathered all night around a card table, that's the power we think of when we talk about the kind of fascination play exercises. But here I'm talking about extreme cases, stereotypical images that intensify and dramatize the thrill of the game. They make us forget that in a less obvious way, this pleasure is an indispensable part of everyday life. Naturally the more banal forms of play vary from country to country. I suppose hunting—on foot, with a rifle—isn't as popular in the United States as it is here. In France hundreds of thousands of men await the opening of hunting season at the end of every summer, totally fixated on this dreamed-of moment, feverishly making a million and one preparations. Not to mention the political and athletic jousting that is ardently followed on television.

But the best playing field—and I think it's the same in the United States as in all industrialized countries—is the professional workplace, because what is essential in order to succeed there is this gratuitous pleasure you take in overcoming obstacles, wrestling with the unknown, outplaying the adversary, even laughing with him. There is no discussion in business, however implacable, that does not partake of the tacit rules of a game, rules that confirm a kind of complicity among the players. As you know, without this no agreement can be reached.

There are many playing fields, including the arena of thought. And no one really talks about it, nor accords to this phenomenon the considerable importance it has in reality. To explain this lack of interest, we have to look at the difference between men and women. In the case of men, the pleasure of the game is so necessary, so spontaneous, it is such a profound component of both work and leisure, that to think about it would have the effect of checking its free rein. In the case of women, it is just as difficult to perceive its importance, but for the opposite reason; it's that this phenomenon has not been experienced and profoundly acknowledged as such. You will say: but women play, and in all sorts of ways! Women can show themselves to be clever and able players, more gifted than even their male partners! I agree with you completely on that point. But—there's a big "but"—they play for reasons other than the gratuitous pleasure of the game. They play because of desires that for them count much more than the game itself: love, the need to possess I was speaking about earlier, eroticism, seduction. In short, women play games, but without being particularly concerned with what, for men, is the foundation of the game, namely, gratuitous pleasure. Don't think that I'm telling you that men are better than women, that they're more generous. Not at all: they're no more angels than we are, they can be very partial when playing; in their endeavors, money and power play a considerable role, just as you say. But what you do not emphasize enough is that the power and the money are there as stakes of the game; they function as the bid or the winnings, increasing the pleasure of risk-taking, of going for broke. And a moment comes when even the most greedy of men, the biggest cheater of them all, starts to play for the sake of playing, forgetting his own interests, accepting that finally everything, even the impossible, even failure, could be the outcome. Thus, it isn't that players as individuals are disinterested, but rather that the pleasure of the game, which is far stronger than they are, makes them forget themselves.

When we see men playing together, we often regard them with a kind of amused compassion: they are children, we think to ourselves, their amusements aren't really serious. And we don't understand that this "not really serious" aspect of the game—its masculine dimension of gratuitous play—is the key, the very foundation of social power, from which women are excluded. Why? because the game is not what interests women the most; because women are not "real" players; they lack that sense of free play that is, in essence, the spirit of the game.

Perhaps certain feminists have come up with the same analysis I am elaborating here. I would be interested in meeting them and finding out what practical conclusions they have drawn from their analysis, how it has helped them to determine what actions to take.

Now, to be realistic, we have to go even a bit further. We have to recognize the way in which we women are excluded. Certain men—the really ferocious misogynists—exclude us deliberately. But the most common form of exclusion, and consequently that from which we suffer the most, does not come about in this way. The most common form of exclusion is the result of an anonymous yet organized collective. If we take seriously the idea that power is always instigated, articulated, and distributed in a kind of playing field, then this collective must be conceived of accordingly. We should state the problem in the following way: it is the playing field itself that is excluding us, more than any particular man or men; men are really just the subjects, the pawns, of the game. The next step would be to specify exactly what this playing field consists of, taking the word "playing field" not simply as the designation of a circumscribed space, an area, but as the sphere specific to the masculine game itself. We'd have to try to comprehend its raison d'être—something I won't try to do here and now. The book I'm writing on masculine sexuality begins with a discourse on play similar to the one I've just been giving you.[3] This discourse begs for further

3 The book, entitled L'Appareillage, is forthcoming.

elaboration, but rest assured, I'm not going to take it any further today!

Well, maybe just one more brief comment. This sphere can be thought of as an organism that possesses its own laws, organs, economy, and libido. Like a living body, it has its own system of expulsion. And we—women who aren't "real" players—we are the foreign bodies ejected by this organism, we are like organs that are supposed to be grafted onto the organism, but that it can't help but reject. That's how we're shut out —as if spontaneously, out of neither good nor bad will.

I believe that all the women who share a little piece of the power pie with men, those who are out on the playing field, and who thus work most effectively for the feminist cause, these women have sized up the game and the masculine pleasure that is part of it, and have discovered, whether consciously or unconsciously, how to come to terms with it. How? You'll have to ask them.

14

Christiane Rochefort

TRANSLATED BY CARRIE NOLAND

Question 1: What does it mean to you to write at the end of the twentieth century?

—How can I answer that question when I don't even understand what you're asking me? What does it mean to me to live now? Well, it means, here I am, living in the twentieth century! How do you expect me to know what it would mean to live at any other time? In any other century? That's the only thing I know, what can I say? So it means that —well, I've lived through a couple of important historical moments, some in my childhood, which I still remember, and then some really good moments, like in the sixties. Now we're in an extremely frighten-

Excerpts from this interview with Alice Jardine, translated by Anne M. Menke, appeared in *Yale French Studies* (1988), vol. 75.

ing, a really terrifying period: the eighties. So, what does that mean to me? I'm pretty up on history and current events. I'm like a sponge that soaks up whatever's going on around me, so I have to deal with whatever goes on in the century I'm in. I'm afraid I don't know how else to answer your question.

Question 2: Is it valid/of value to write as a woman, and is it part of your writing practice today?

—A lot of stupid things have been written about "writing as a woman," especially in reference to biology. You can't determine what biological differences are; they're so overlaid with culture that it's absolutely impossible to get a clear picture of them. And it's stupid to try, so I'm not going to talk about biology. Besides, I'm not sure I believe in biological differences. People do have different experiences, of course, but writing as a woman is like writing as a black, or writing as a coal miner, a samurai, an Indian Buddhist, or the head of some huge corporation. Each person has certain material to work with that isn't exactly the same as the material of the person next door. That's what writing as a woman means to me: I have a certain material to work with. But that doesn't mean that there's a specificity to the *writing*. I could just as easily have given you the response you got from Sarraute: "I'm not a woman writer; I'm a writer."

—(AJ) It's interesting that you say that.

—I'm a writer. And so okay, let's see. . . . My material is . . . well . . . there is an experience peculiar to being a woman, just as there's one peculiar to being a coal miner.

—(AJ) And how has that experience crossed over into your writing? I ask that because there are many women who responded—and I mean that in the strongest sense of the word—to your works, to your books. Take *Les Stances à Sophie,* for example: that book has a lot to say to me, as a woman.

—Yes, take something like *Les Stances à Sophie,* which deals with a classical marriage, quite a typical one really. It's a blueprint, that book, a kind of blueprint of what one encounters in a typical marriage. And what happens in this book most directly resembles my own personal experience: I actually had that kind of marriage. I mean, okay, things are different, everything has changed, but that's the kind of marriage I had. It's part of my life experience as a woman.

—(AJ) That's exactly what I was getting at.

—Because men can't *have* the experience of being a married woman.

—(AJ) But, at least in theory, if "all is culture," then it should be possible.

—But it *is* possible. That's where I agree with Shakespeare: if one is a creator, then one is both sexes at the same time. I have to be able to write about the experience of a dog, or of a cat (but then we're talking about nuances!). A writer should be able to write about . . . You know, I wrote a story about two young men who fall in love with each other, who feel passionately attracted toward each other. Do you think that has anything to do with me? Two boys? And if you asked me why I chose two boys, I couldn't answer you. It's because I use whatever material I come across. I had this idea of a young boy who leaves home, who has a traumatic experience, and who realizes that his father is crazy. Well, almost crazy. He's not really crazy; the poor guy is really just like everybody else, but you know, he's in a world of crazy people and that's how it begins . . . that's how it is . . . so here I've got this boy: what's going to happen to him? He screws around with women, with girls really, and then suddenly, to his own surprise, to his horror, he feels passionately drawn to a young man, a student he didn't respond to at first, but then they get sexually involved. And what was I supposed to do? Talk about experience! What was I going to do? When I realized where things had gotten to . . . And I had tried to avoid it, there was something in me that didn't want to deal with all that stuff—but no luck. . . . They were in bed together . . . they were involved. So that was that. They had fallen into each other's arms! I said to myself: "What am I doing here? What's going to happen next? How am I going to get out of this? What am I getting mixed up in?" And then everybody's going to say: "What are you meddling in?" Especially the homosexuals, they're going to jump all over me. Oh well, there I was. . . . I had done it. . . . I had invented the whole thing. I had identified myself thoroughly with their experience. Afterward, to give you the whole story, I showed the scene to two homosexual friends of mine, honest guys, nice, cynical, charming, witty. . . . I said to them: "Listen, I'd like to know if I've said a bunch of crap. Tell me if I've put in things that are totally silly or unbelievable." So they read it and they said: "But how did you know this? How?"

—(AJ) That's pretty impressive.

—"How did you know?" But they found something that didn't seem realistic; I won't tell you exactly what it was because it's very, very sexual, very dirty. I said to them: "Listen, I think you're the ones who've got it wrong." And they thought about it and then said: "Good God, who knows? We should give it a try!" So there's my answer to what "personal experience" is all about.

—(AJ) You mentioned that you "identified" with the experience of the two boys. Do you mean that when you write you have a tendency to identify with the characters in your novels?

—Well, if you take a look at my novels, *Le Repos du guerrier,* for example, I didn't identify at all with the woman who narrates in the first person. Everyone assumed I was her, but that's not me at all. *Le Repos du guerrier* was my first novel. As subject matter I took the germ of a story that kept running through my head, a story about the ravages of love on poets. . . .

—(AJ) Quite a subject!

—Well, you know . . . a story about that kind of thing . . . I started to write off the cuff using the pronoun "he," and then I realized that it wasn't working. So I took the character who knew the least about what was going on, the most intellectually limited character, who really didn't understand a thing, and that was this woman—sorry, may all women who hear this forgive me, but it can happen. This woman didn't understand a thing, she was completely out of it. When I began using this woman to tell the story, I said to myself: "That's it! I'm finally writing." *Not* because I had chosen the woman, but because I had chosen the character who was the most marginal, the most limited, the one whose vision was the most circumscribed. Then I knew that I had begun to write. Still, it's clear that the character who speaks for me in the novel is the man.

—(AJ) Is that true for most of your novels?

—No, but it is for that one.

—(AJ) It changes? It depends . . .

—Yes. The next novel is about a little girl from a big family who grows up in a housing project, which isn't my case at all. I'm an only child. Did I live in a housing project when I was young? No, never. So you see, the only material I took from my own experience was that for a short time I actually did live—or let's say tried to live—in a huge apartment complex when I was a sculptor. Someone gave me a studio there so I tried to live in it. I couldn't, but I gathered some information while I was there. And that's all. Other than that, I don't really identify with the little girl in the story. I use my imagination instead.

—(AJ) I find your response very interesting, but I wonder . . .

—So there's no real identification going on except in *Les Stances à Sophie,* but writing it was also a sacrificial experience.

—(AJ) Really? In what way?

—I believed that marriage was completely old-fashioned, that nobody thought about it anymore. But, to my surprise, plenty of my friends were getting married. All around me people were getting married! "They're *still* doing that?" I said. I was pretty naïve, I guess; I thought we were living in the modern world; I realized, "No, not on your life!" Women are still stuck in the same place! Men are stuck in the same place! How awful!

So, to make a long story short, I took off from there to write about marriage. I thought, "Okay, so, we can still write about that stuff." Then I gave myself over to writing a description of marriage. To do that I used my brief—thank God—experience. That's true, I did make use of it. . . .

What happened after *Les Stances à Sophie?* I don't know anymore. In any case, from then on I did not write from personal experience. The next novel takes place during the eleventh century. It's about children. You know, I have a way with children. I know how to get along with them, how to behave with them. I like that. I enjoy them.

To sum it up then, writing as a woman is not valid for me.

—(AJ) But it's still a part of your practice.

—Writing as a woman is no more valid for me than writing as a man, or as a chimpanzee. If you take the example of the chimpanzees who know how to use a typewriter . . . well, you know, theirs is a specific experience like any other. It's specific to the individual case, I mean. Women don't all have the same experience either. What is all this nonsense?

—(AJ) But, as you well know, there are a lot of women in the United States, in Women's Studies and elsewhere—there are also feminists like me, men and women (and more and more men)—who read novels either in order to look more closely at representations of women characters, or in order to analyze linguistically the textual differences between works by women and works by men. According to what you've just said, it's a kind of work that. . . .

—Let them enjoy themselves with my style. I hope they get a kick out of it. Let them look for specific stylistic features linked to my being a woman, but these specific features would indicate some kind of biological specificity, and I just don't believe in one.

—(AJ) Sure, that's right. But . . .

—Naturally the experience of child-bearing—an experience I haven't had, by the way—is specific to women. I guess that makes me a man.

—(AJ) Oh, come on. . . .

—Well, what do you want me to say? That's the way it is if you're talking about biology. . . . I'm not different from men in this way. I'm just not, case closed. If one wants to look for biological differences, I find that extremely reactionary.

—(AJ) No. *Not* biological, but cultural differences.

—Oh, well, that . . . cultural differences. . . . Naturally there's tons of those. Of course.

—(AJ) It's true that there was a tendency to look for "the biological difference," and the two, biological and cultural, are often confused.

—Especially in France. In the United States too?

—(AJ) Yes.

Question 3: Many women writing today find themselves, for the first time in history, at the center of such institutions as the university and psychoanalysis. In your opinion, will this new placement of women help them to enter the twentieth-century canon, and if so, will they be in the heart of this corpus or (still) in the footnotes?

—That's a complicated question.

—(AJ) Yes, rather.

—Wait a minute. What canon? You mean posterity? Being in literary histories?

—(AJ) Yes, in literary histories.

—In books studied in school?

—(AJ) Survival.

—The canon in that sense is constituted first of all by cooptation. There's a good chance that the people who are already in the canon will simply coopt others who are already in the canon. What I'm saying is that it doesn't mean anything. This canon, it isn't . . . there are people, men and women, who aren't in the canon and who are very worthwhile writers, don't you think?

—(AJ) Absolutely.

—Right. But still, historically, there are a lot more worthwhile women who didn't make it into the canon because no one paid any attention to them.

—(AJ) Yes.

—There's a considerable number of them. Before, especially. Today that situation is being repaired because there's an old boy's network and now there's an old girl's network to boot. Things are beginning to even out, but within that old-boy, old-girl network. Women will be excluded less often because of that sort of thing.

—(AJ) Do you think things have changed to that extent?

—There probably won't be as many women who disappear completely.

—(AJ) Yes, someone did describe this era as that of *les femmes en relais*, as the moment for women to carry the torch. . . . Which means that these days there are more women in institutions like the university system, more women in publishing, etc., even if they don't usually have the same power as men, at least not in the United States. We get to a certain point and then we're . . .

—But still, since women are doing the work, they have a certain power to affect things.

—(AJ) Yes, that's true. They're going to keep alive a certain number of texts by women. That's the theory, in any case. I have no idea whether in practice . . .

—You know, we're talking about a kind of rite of passage here. Personally, I refuse to privilege texts by women; I privilege good texts. That's what this is really all about, isn't it? I think this equalizing business is a good thing. That's more or less going to be the case in publishing, one of the areas where there's been the most progress, but I would emphasize that that's for the simple reason that publishers can make more money if they publish women's books too. It has nothing to do with being more liberal—in fact, they aren't; but they realize that women's books make money. So, of course, they've been reading manuscripts by women as well as by men for quite a while now. In France, women are being published more frequently, not just since Sagan, but Françoise Sagan definitely advanced women in the publishing world more than Simone de Beauvoir did . . . and there are many others. Things are pretty good right now, so that to get your foot in the door . . . But actually, it'll still be the same thing: there's always little Mafias, networking in the universities, whether we're talking about men or women. And women will have more of a tendency to discover other women than will men. But women will also discover men, I'm sure. It's still a little lopsided, but the problem of women's posterity is going to be taken care of; they're going to be known as a matter of course from now on. Complete disappearance is a thing of the past.

There were some really serious omissions in the past—there are going to be people who will see to it that those books are sought out and discovered. For the most part, women will be doing it, of course. And that's okay. I read some unknown works that were fabulous.

—(AJ) There's a lot of research of that kind going on in the United States.

—And that research has to be done, that's for sure. You've got to do research, but in order to equalize things, not to privilege one sex over another. Unrecognized quality has to be recognized. That's the level on which it interests me personally.

—(AJ) I'd like to push you just a little further. You said "a good text," and you talked about "quality." What is "quality"? And who determines what it is? There are a lot of feminist critics in the United States who are trying to look again at this question of "quality" because a text can be considered "good" by some people but not by others. So how does one decide?

—Listen, there's the obvious and then there's the subtle, right? Now, there's no denying that during the first wave of enthusiasm over women's writing, a lot of women started writing and they wrote no matter what in no matter what way. Not really no matter what—it isn't as if their ideas were always bad—but in no matter what way. There was so much pitiful stuff written, and here too there was a period during which everyone had to expectorate their miseries, you know what I mean? And this literature of experience was abominable. Actually, I was going to use a more vulgar word: they literally spit up this stuff; it was truly dreadful, because everyone wanted to talk about themselves . . . which was not lacking in interest, if you will, but when it's not writing, when it's not art, then it's nothing. The effect is lost.

—(AJ) But . . .

—So there was a whole lot of mediocre stuff that came out at a given moment, whether in France or in the United States or in Germany or wherever; a bunch of things that simply weren't any good appeared and were destined to disappear. But that's the obvious stuff; that stuff will disappear on its own. As for the nuances, the small differences in quality. . . . It's clear that at a certain point we're just talking about a matter of taste.

—(AJ) And about ideology.

—For men also, you know, some distinctions are made and some aren't. But my God! the mass of bad literature by men that's coming out in France these days! How do we come to terms with that? When I see how certain books are such a hit and the guy is always on television whenever we turn around, I'm ready to jump out of my skin! I know it's shit . . . and then there are the others who don't know it's shit. There's nothing universal about taste.

—(AJ) That's exactly why I reacted to the word "good."

—There are people who get caught up in the media, who believe all that media hype, and then there are others who don't . . . What can you do? . . . But still, you can't set up an absolute standard of what's good and what isn't good. I have my standards; there's a couple of us here who share approximately the same standards. But even among ourselves, we're very demanding. I have three or four friends who are like that: very demanding, even with one another. One of them said to me once: "Hey, read this, it's fantastic." I read it; I said: "Listen, are you out of your mind or what?" You see? You can't determine an absolute standard in art.

And I'm not even sure that it's time that determines an absolute standard. Some things will survive that aren't worth the paper they're written on.

—(AJ) So for you, the fact that until very recently it was men who decided what was good and what wasn't, that didn't have any effect on women?

—Actually, I've noticed that among critics, in France at any rate—I can't speak for the United States—the women are just about as sexist as the men.

—(AJ) Yes, that's sometimes the case.

—Once they've got a job working for a newspaper they hang onto that job for dear life and just follow the crowd. And if the truth were known, in professional circles there are a lot of people who go along with the status quo, and I mean people who have achieved a certain position, men and women. There are really very few critics of any quality these days. I can't tell you what's going on in the United States. As for critics here in France, they're beginning to calm down now about all that, but there was a period that lasted until just recently when male critics didn't read women's books the same way as they read books by men. And sometimes female critics had the same bias. I know some female critics who really *hate* women, believe it or not, and that's even worse!

—(AJ) I've noticed that too.

—That kind of thing is still around. It might go away as time passes, I can't tell. But bad critics will always be bad. And it's true that they read men's books and women's books differently; it's one of the things we in France have really suffered from. If you wanted women's books, you'd find them in the "knitting section," stuff like that. They threw all the women together. I remember finding myself in the company of Simone de Beauvoir and Françoise Sagan, which is no dishonor, if you ask me.

—(AJ) Not at all!

—Yes, but why did they throw us all together? There's nothing similar about our work, but they threw us together.

—(AJ) In the United States, there's a continuing argument about that; for example, there's a book called *The Norton Anthology* that more or less establishes the canon for literature written in English, because it's used for university teaching. Literature in English—all in one package —just like that. It's a pretty hefty volume! So two women came along, two feminist critics, and they put together one of these big books just on literature in English by women. Everyone was screaming about it; there were women who said: "But you're doing exactly what men have always done to women: you throw them all together and publish a big book, but this time *against* the canon." Then others, mostly men, said: "But that's not good literature! Norton shouldn't have published it." So people were shouting on all sides. I was more or less in favor of the project just because it made so many people from so many different perspectives shout and get hysterical.

—If *The Norton Anthology of Women* published work of lesser quality than *The Norton Anthology of Men,* then no, they shouldn't do that. But if it's of the same quality, then you should put them all together.

—(AJ) But who decides? That's the problem!

—Oh well, the editor decides, of course! No, but seriously, when I say "of quality" and "good," I mean that it's either well written or it isn't. "Well written"? I have a concept of what good writing is that has to do with the concept of distance, the concept of internal structure. These aren't completely vague concepts; after all, you have to keep an eye on things.

Question 4: Today we are seeing women produce literary, philosophical, and psychoanalytical theory of recognized importance, and . . .

—I can already answer that; to begin with, we're seeing far too much literary theory being written today, considering literary theory isn't at all important. The last thing I find important is theory, whether it's literary, philosophical, or psychoanalytical. Most of the time it's just nonsense. First there was the terrible period when literature was theoretically analyzed by using autobiography and biography. Now we're in the terrible period when literature is being analyzed by using—what?

—(AJ) Post-structuralism?

—Right, that's it. All that is just a succession of terrible periods with theories that don't mean a thing. And by that, I mean that these people don't know what it means to write. They haven't done it!

—(AJ) Are there people who write on literature that you do like?

—I don't think so. I avoid reading that stuff. But I do have a friend in Israel who is an excellent analyst. She analyzes the social and historical situation of the author and then she analyzes the style, the rationale for the style, and the internal structures. That can be done, but for a specific book, one specific work by one specific author. General theories—what should be done and what shouldn't be done—all the *Tel Quel* theory, for example—in my opinion it should be put in the trash can. No question about it. It's wrong. Straight into the trash can because it's wrong. I'm not saying that people aren't capable of writing good theory, but only a very few can do it. You have to really be on the inside. There are a couple of people who truly love literature, like . . . well, there's Marthe Robert. But I find that she tends too much toward the psychoanalytic. Much too much.

—(AJ) She *is* a true lover of literature.

—Well, there are literature lovers who have the right to speak about the books they love. In that case, they can look at how the book is constructed. But to know how it's constructed, you have to ask the author most of the time anyway. Because that's still the person who knows best.

—(AJ) I like that expression, "literature lover," because literary criticism . . .

—They're what was called "amateurs" in the seventeenth or eighteenth century.

—(AJ) Exactly.

—The "amateurs." Now the word "amateur" seems feeble, so we say "lover." The big fans of literature, who can sometimes make mistakes, you know, have at least tried to understand from the inside. They haven't tried to validate their own way of thinking, which is what the theorists do when they use the book just as a crutch to prop up their own ideas. Personally, I have to be more explicit about things—why I like reading Faulkner, for example. I had an experience with Faulkner: I used to adore Faulkner—well, not adore—I read a lot of Faulkner, I was fascinated by him. Just after reading Faulkner I started writing. Unfortunately, I started writing Faulkners! They were absolutely abominable. Really horrific. Just bad stuff. Luckily, I realized what I was doing. . . . So I threw them out. And then soon after I heard Raymond Queneau say that he had been tremendously influenced by the Americans, especially by Faulkner. So I said to myself: "Hey, that's like me. I was also influenced by the Americans." Not by a single French author, except maybe Queneau. Anyway, soon after that I started to reread Faulkner, thinking, "Let's see what we find." Oh my God! First of all, it was badly translated, I didn't read Faulkner in English, and what I had thought was well translated earlier on I now found racist and puritanical. The point is, I had simply evolved a little. Now I didn't even find the story interesting. "What is he trying to tell me? What did I see in it before? How could I have been inspired by this stuff?" Oh well, it *is* structured . . . and basically, without really having understood it at the time, I had felt that it was good writing because it was structured, and it got me away from the blah-blah-blah that I was so used to in my own country.

In his writing there's a kind of spiral that encircles the hero and presses in on him, corners him; it's really quite extraordinary. That's what works in him. I can sometimes make things explicit like that, but without saying that that's the only thing that works. Don't get me wrong: that's how *I* felt, you see? That's an experience I had because I had read him a long time ago and then I picked him up again. That's when I realized why it had had an effect on me.

—(AJ) Given all this, and getting back to our question, what do you think about the fact that today women are writing more and more, and at the same time . . .

—Theory or writing?

—(AJ) Both.

—Okay.

—(AJ) . . . and at the same time we're seeing a new fluidity between disciplines and between literary genres; that is, even in the university we're beginning to see that you can't just say anymore that this is philosophy and that is history, and so on. We're beginning to draw things together in new ways in order to ask new questions. People are trying to do interdisciplinary work. Instead of saying, "I'm a historian, I only do history," we say, "No, I want to work on women's history but I also want to be an archaeologist."

—However, literature has remained outside all that you just mentioned. Literature is a separate entity, except when every now and then a philosopher comes along who knows how to write. That happens sometimes, as with Nietzsche, for example.

—(AJ) Right, there you go.

—That changes everything.

—(AJ) Yes, but it's rare.

—It's very rare, and by the way, that's when he becomes a good philosopher; because there's only one true form of expression that uses words and that's writing, not theory or ideology. . . . Ideology, for me, is nothing but the dross. It's refuse.

It's a good idea to be interdisciplinary, whether the subject being studied is women or elephants. It's great to look into absolutely everything when you're studying a subject. Sure.

For instance, one time I got into a confrontation with some sociologists over large housing projects and their effect on the mentality of the people who live in them, and I started talking about the way the brain works. Their mouths fell open. I said to them, "You don't know about that, huh? The thalamus? You didn't study the structure of the brain to be a sociologist, huh? That's a shame. You should know how the brain functions too." I didn't say the entire body, although that's not a bad idea, is it? Studying the body is fundamental for all kinds of work. I'm completely for interdisciplinary work like that.

—(AJ) What we're trying to get at is, isn't it possible that there's a parallel between these two facts: on the one hand women are writing, or at least publishing, a lot more, and, on the other, the frontiers between disciplines are being blurred and people are trying to be more interdisciplinary?

It's a positive conjuncture, for the most part, even if it can also be negative at times. But the conjuncture of these two facts might be welcoming to women, even if there's a risk that the fundamental structures won't be changed.

—But why talk about blurring category distinctions? I'm not so sure it blurs them.

—(AJ) Maybe that's not the right word.

—On the contrary, I think it should clarify them. In any case, I don't see the blurring of categories in interdisciplinary work. What's for sure is that it's about time people were interdisciplinary; classifying things is a result of the nineteenth century, of that rational century, so I don't see what women have to do with it. Everyone needs to do it.

Question 5: Given what we've been saying about the problematic and the politics of the categories of the canon—namely, the previous exclusion of women—and given the questions we've addressed here, do you think your oeuvre—this is a wicked question—but do you think your oeuvre will figure in the canon of the twentieth century, and if so, how will it be presented? In your opinion, what will the content of the canon be?

—That is a wicked question, a very wicked one; it's impossible to answer! I really don't know! But I can tell you that I'm already being taught in grade school.

—(AJ) In grade school? Already?

—Yes, I'm in the textbooks.

—(AJ) So you're already in the high schools too?

—I'm already in the high schools. I don't know if I'll go any higher than that, though. I believe I'm the victim of a certain kind of ostracism.

—(AJ) Ostracism?

—I mean, a kind of rejection ... how can I say it? Not racism, because it's not collective.

—(AJ) What kind of rejection?

—It's not easy to classify me because I'm a straight-shooter, I don't fit in, I can't be assimilated. I'm not part of the consensus. So to the extent that the words "canon" and "consensus" can be confused—and they can be, the line between them can get smudged—my work doesn't stand much chance of being included. I belong more to the *poètes maudits*, the marginal nonconformist writers. Well, I'm exaggerating a bit. But that's more or less the category I'd fall into. The idea people have of me in terms of the canon isn't real positive. I piss people off. And troublemakers aren't exactly sought after, are they?

—(AJ) And in terms of survival? The survival of your work? The fact that your work might disappear doesn't worry you?

—To tell you the truth, I really couldn't care less. I did have something happen to me once, though. A friend of mine told me about this friend of hers who was half crazy. This guy had been sent to fight in the Algerian War even though he was of Berber descent. He deserted from the army and lost his mind. At some point, when he got to a small village, someone lent him one of my books, *Les Petits enfants du siècle*. It gave him back his courage and calmed him down. He was cured by it; it had a marvelous effect on him, and afterward he felt better. When I heard that I said to myself, "Wait a minute, I'm not down there! He's 4,000 kilometers away!" It had been a long time since I had written that book; both in time and geography I was miles away. But when I heard that, I said, "God, now I can die happy."

It was something that pleased me so much. My work kept on when I was no longer writing it, when I was no longer there, in my absence, you see, as if I were already dead. And yet it still had an effect on someone. It's true that I'm not in the canon, but I was pleased anyway. I was very moved by that story. I said to myself, "I don't even have to be there. It's wonderful." But things don't happen in literary histories or in literary anthologies; they happen in real life. And so if things like that happen, I'm happy. You can say to yourself, "It's great! I don't even need to be *there!*"

—(AJ) That's a beautiful story—and a wonderful answer!

—Now *that* is immortality. I've rarely been so moved. It's not that I seek that out, it's not that I want it that badly, and, by the way, it's not being in the canon—it's people, it's readers. Because on one level there's the canon and on the other, there's readers. So maybe I'm not well regarded as far as the canon goes, but that can't last long, anyway.

—(AJ) That's true: things can change.

—Absolutely. Things can change. In terms of my readers, I've had fantastic feedback. Really fantastic, and I'm really happy about the feedback. Readers aren't looking for theory, or for fashions, or for all sorts of difficulties that aren't there. Readers pick up a book, they're all alone at home, usually at night. They're in bed or in an armchair and they're alone with their book and they get all wrapped up in it . . . with no intermediaries. They plunge into it . . . directly. Or they aren't interested and they put it down, or else they hate it and they write you insulting letters. But sometimes it does them good, they're happy, they find something in it for themselves. Like I find in my reading. What I want to know is whether the theoreticians and the writers of literary anthologies read books all by themselves at home at night.

—(AJ) Some of them do!

—Yes, well, there must be some literature lovers among them.

—(AJ) Usually that's why one becomes a critic.

Question 6: Now, people don't usually have a smile on their faces when they're reading a book that is supposed to be feminist, but they do when reading Les Stances à Sophie, *for example. Will this funny kind of marriage between criticism of masculine society and feminine-style humor help a body of work such as your own be included in the canon or will it act as an obstacle to inclusion?*

—I just answered more or less the same question.

—(AJ) In a way, yes.

—It's an obstacle because not everyone has a sense of humor.

—(AJ) That's for sure.

—I can assure you, some people weren't exactly tickled by *Les Stances à Sophie*.

—(AJ) Oh, really?

—My God, they were furious! Absolutely furious! I had a literary godfather, he's dead now—may he rest in peace—who made a scene in public over that book. Since I was his literary goddaughter—incidentally, he was more convinced of it than I was—he said to me, "How could you; I nurtured you at my breast, you viper!" Ho boy, he really wrote me off! But I was happy about it.

—(AJ) Was it principally men who reacted that way?

—Oh, sure, especially after *Les Stances à Sophie*, because they were the target. It was directed against them.

—(AJ) And they knew it.

—The women in the book were absolutely adorable; it was very unfair. The women were utterly charming and delightful but the men . . . was there a single nice man? Yes, I think she finds one in Italy. Anyway, there were some nice guys but the husband and the husband's best friend were two typical macho jerks. So not all the readers found that funny; that was certainly an obstacle. More than anything, it's the people who serve as go-betweens, the media people, the people who serve on literary juries. They wouldn't have given me a prize for all the world. Those people constitute the primary obstacle, whereas they're supposed to serve as a liaison between the book and the public. And since it's normally these people who make the canon. . . . I don't even know if I'm in the *History of French Literature* by Mister so-and-so; I really haven't the slightest idea. And if I am, then what's written about me is favorable.

—(AJ) The underlying question is really "Are feminism and a sense of humor compatible?"

—Why yes, of course, my kind at least. But I'm not sure. Perhaps on the one hand but not on the other, you know what I mean? But it's always the same thing: it's the individual that ultimately matters more than the collective in these things.

It isn't because I'm a woman that this kind of thing happens to me. It's because I'm a human being. It's because that's how I am.

You know, there's even a kind of privilege given to women in certain fields, like high-powered academics. It's better to have the advanced degrees than not to have them, wouldn't you say? A degree gets respect! But I came out of nowhere. You see, there's a question of class here, also.

—(AJ) Absolutely.

—You mustn't think it's just a question of gender. There's a certain class, the class that has the degrees, a good education, a professor's chair, disciples, students, a whole . . .

—(AJ) . . . structure.

—. . . an establishment, a status. . . . That stuff's intimidating; without status you're less intimidating to start with. And if on top of that you make trouble, if you have anarchistic ideas, then oh boy. . . . So there's the maligned aspect, the class aspect, and the individual aspect.

—(AJ) Yes.

—And then there's maybe the woman aspect. On that score, I'm spoiled!

—(AJ) I was just about to say that a few years ago I participated in a panel discussion on "Feminism, Women Writers, and Humor." We all tried to find three or four examples of twentieth-century fiction in French that were both sensitive to the representation of women in fiction and contained humorous passages. And you know what? Besides *Les Stances à Sophie* we couldn't find a single other book published in France and written by a woman that was really funny and where there was also evidence of a feminist sensibility.

—I guess it's pretty rare then.

—(AJ) It's rare.

—On the other hand, it's been said many times that oppression normally gives rise to a sense of humor. But maybe it has to get to an extreme point before you can laugh about it. I remember that in the beginning of the Women's Movement there were about fifteen of us in the same group and a couple of us said, "We're not going to have a demonstration unless it's funny." There can be no revolution or change without a sense of humor. If it's humorless, it's meaningless. You can be sure there's something wrong if it's never funny. But when the leftists, the Maoists, the different Bolshevik groups, people like that, stepped in, it was always completely humorless. We'd say, "If it's humorless, it's botched; it's worthless." Of course, we didn't win; humor never does. The truth is, humor is a minority, too. It's so rare. I don't know if it's oppression or else an entire culture of wailing, complaining, pain, misfortune, and misery that makes women tend to bemoan their fate, to go around wailing; whereas men in other oppressed groups, blacks, for example, they're sometimes funny. But there's this whole culture of wailing that makes humor off-limits. I recently read some books on incest; they were completely scientific, dreadful, from some Association, etc. I said, "There's no way I'm going to get involved with this stuff because there's nothing funny in it." "What! You want to joke about it?" That's right. I want to be able to joke about it, and if I didn't manage to joke about incest in my last book, then . . .[1]

—(AJ) Touching the sacred subject!

—The book's going to make waves; it won't be appreciated. Still, there are things I can't joke about, such as Hitler's concentration camps, Nazism, things like that. Hitler isn't funny. In that particular case I just can't find anything to laugh about. I admit it, I just can't. Maybe that's my mistake, but I just can't. But it's only stuff like that. I don't know if I could joke about the extinction of whales. . . . I don't know. . . . But if I wrote books on them, they'd probably be funny anyway.

I've allowed myself to do some pretty outrageous things. But not too often. But hey, I try to. . . . but you know, I'm very cynical. Cynicism is the source of my humor. It's a kind of lucidity. We don't know all the sources of a sense of humor; it's very mysterious. But all I know is that understanding is necessary for a sense of humor. And also, I'm completely convinced that this wailing style, all this seriousness, it's totally ridiculous and ineffectual. That's not what's going to change the world.

[1] *La Porte du fond* (Paris: Grasset, 1988).

15

Monique Wittig

Question 1: What does it mean to you to write at the end of the twentieth century?

—If I were to answer this question from the point of view of literary history, I would remind us that our century has taught us, more than once, what the revolution of the novel is about. I am thinking of Stein, Proust, Joyce, Dos Passos, Faulkner, Woolf, Sarraute, etc. These are the giants of our century. I always keep them in mind, for they taught us that form is meaning. They taught us to tear off limb by limb a new literary reality from the literary landscape of the time. The accent on form is what is new to this century. And a writer's work today is on form. But to invent a form that is new and raw is difficult. We aren't

This interview, conducted in English, appeared in *Yale French Studies* (1988), vol. 75.

here to make pretty things. We might ask who is writing the new American experimental novel today? Is it not our work as writers to experiment so as to fight the canon, to break it down? A writer never works in (or to be in) the canon. All the above writers were fighting the canon.

Question 2: Is it valid/of value to write as a woman, and is it part of your writing practice today?[1]

Question 3: Many women writing today find themselves, for the first time in history, at the center of such institutions as the university and psychoanalysis. In your opinion, will this new placement of women help them to enter the twentieth-century canon, and if so, will they be in the heart of this corpus or (still) in the footnotes?

—To say that writers have been excluded from the canon because they are women not only seems to me inexact, but the very idea proceeds from a trend toward theories of victimization. There are few great writers in any century. Each time there was one, not only was she welcome within the canon, but she was acclaimed, applauded, and praised in her time—sometimes *especially* because she was a woman. I'm thinking of Sand and Colette. I do not think that real innovators have been passed by. In the university, we ruin the purpose of what we do if we make a special category for women—especially when teaching. When we do that as feminists, we ourselves turn the canon into a male edifice.

Question 4: Today we are seeing women produce literary, philosophical, and psychoanalytical theory of recognized importance, and, parallel to this, we are also seeing a new fluidity in the borderlines among disciplines and genres of writing. Will this parallelism lead only to women being welcomed alongside men, or to a definitive blurring of these categories?

—First, I do not think this process is specifically linked to women. Second, I think the disciplines, on the contrary, have strengthened their boundaries.

[1] Monique Wittig chose not to answer this question. Her statements in "The Straight Mind" may help to explain her position. See *Feminist Issues* (1980), 1:103–11.

Question 5: Given the problematic and the politics of the categories of the canon, and given the questions we've been dealing with, do you think your oeuvre will be included in the twentieth-century canon, and if so, how will it be presented? In your opinion, what will the content of the canon be?

—That's a provocative question to which no writer with any modesty can respond.

Question 6: Deciding the content of the canon is a classification process that is doubly complicated in your case.

First, given the positive way The Opoponax *with its stylistic innovations was received in France, one can imagine that a category will be proposed in order to include it in the canon. But when one adds to this formal experimentation an even more radically other exploration of sexuality, as in* Les Guérillères *and* The Lesbian Body, *one can expect to see a complete refusal of your work on the part of the guardians of the dominant culture.*

Second, to make this process even more problematic, especially in relation to the questions we have asked you, you refuse the category of woman and declare that you are instead a lesbian. What do you think about the fact that you have been so successful at disconcerting these efforts at categorization?

—First, the question of the canon is a question for literary criticism, not for fiction writers.

Second, there is confusion created when a purely sociological matter is carried over into literary criticism. For example, women are a sociological group whose very existence vis-à-vis the sociological group of men is barely accepted. The fact that these two groups exist in a conflictual political situation is not yet taken seriously, so it is important not to jump ahead, past this essential fact. Lesbians, by their very existence, are fugitive women—people trying to escape their class. It is true that the notion of woman is the ideological aspect, the alienated representation of oneself that seems to emanate from the group but is in fact imported from outside. That is to say: women exist as a class while woman is an imaginary formation (to use an expression by Guillaumin).[2] These are

---

[2] Colette Guillaumin is a sociologist whose work deals with racism and the appropriation of women. She has served on the editorial boards of the French journal *Questions féministes* and its English-language edition *Feminist Issues*. Her comments on imaginary formations occur in "Race and Nature: The System of Marks. The Idea of a Natural Group and Social Relationships," *Feminist Issues* (1988), 8(2):25–43. Among Guillaumin's

sociological issues. Now to return to the literary problem: I can no more say I am a lesbian writer than I can say I am a woman writer. I am simply a writer. Writing is what is important, not sociological categories. I do think some changes of form are more open to history than others; but working, writing—for the writer—is an individual process, never a collective one.

---

many articles in *Feminist Issues,* see "The Practice of Power and Belief in Nature": Part 1, "The Appropriation of Women" (1981), 1(2):3–28; Part 2, "The Naturalist Discourse" (1981), 1(3):87–109.

Selected Bibliography

Chawaf, Chantal. *Blé de semences*. Paris: Mercure de France, 1976.
—— *Cercoeur*. Paris: Mercure de France, 1975.
—— *Chair chaude: Suivi de l'écriture: Théâtre*. Paris: Mercure de France, 1976.
—— *Crépusculaires*. Paris: Ramsay, 1981.
—— *L'Eclaircie*. Paris: Flammarion, 1990.
—— *Elwina, le roman fée*. Paris: Flammarion, 1985.
—— *Fées de toujours*. Paris: Plon, 1988.
—— *L'Intérieur des heures*. Paris: Des femmes, 1987.
—— *Landes*. Paris: Stock, 1980.
—— *Maternité*. Paris: Stock, 1979.
—— *Rédemption*. Paris: Flammarion, 1989.
—— *Rétable: La Rêverie*. Paris: Des femmes, 1974.
—— *Rougeâtre*. Paris: Pauvert, 1978.
—— *Le Soleil et la terre*. Paris: Pauvert, 1977.
—— *Les Surfaces de l'orage*. Paris: Ramsay, 1982.
—— *La Vallée incarnate*. Paris: Flammarion, 1984.

TRANSLATIONS IN ENGLISH:

Chawaf, Chantal. *Mother Love; Mother Earth,* trans. Monique Nagem. New York: Garland, 1990.

Cixous, Hélène. *Ananké.* Paris: Des femmes, 1979.
—— *Angst.* Paris: Des femmes, 1977.
—— *La Bataille d'Arcachon: Un Conte.* Quebec: Trois, 1986.
—— *Les Commencements.* Paris: Grasset, 1970.
—— *Dedans.* Paris: Grasset, 1969.
—— *Double page.* Paris: Théâtre du soleil, 1987.
—— *Entre l'écriture.* Paris: Des femmes, 1986.
—— *L'Exil de James Joyce ou l'art du remplacement.* Paris: Grasset, 1968.
—— *L'Heure de Clarice Lispector, précédé de Vivre l'orange.* Paris: Des femmes, 1989.
—— *L'Histoire terrible mais inachevée de Norodom Sihanouk, roi du Cambodge.* Paris: Théâtre du soleil, 1985.
—— *Illa.* Paris: Des femmes, 1980.
—— *L'Indiade, ou, L'Inde de leurs rêves, et quelques écrits sur le théâtre.* Paris: Théâtre du soleil, 1987.
—— *La Jeune née* (with Catherine Clément). Paris: Union générale, 1975.
—— *Jours de l'an.* Paris: Des Femmes, 1990.
—— *Là.* Paris: Gallimard, 1976.
—— *Limonade tout était si infini.* Paris: Des femmes, 1982.
—— *Le Livre de Prométhéa.* Paris: Gallimard, 1983.
—— *Un K incompréhensible: Pierre Goldmann.* Paris: Bourgois, 1975.
—— *Manne: Aux Mandelstams, aux Mandelas.* Paris: Des femmes, 1988.
—— *Neutre.* Paris: Grasset, 1972.
—— *Le Nom d'Oedipe: Opéra tiré de chant du corps interdit.* Paris: Des femmes, 1978.
—— *Partie.* Paris: Des femmes, 1976.
—— *Portrait de Dora.* Paris: Des femmes, 1976.
—— *Portrait de Dora, et la prise de l'école de Madhubaï.* Paris: Des femmes, 1986.
—— *Portrait du soleil.* Paris: Denoël, 1974.
—— *Le Prénom de dieu.* Paris: Grasset, 1967.
—— *Prénoms de personne.* Paris: Seuil, 1974.
—— *Préparatifs de noces au-delà de l'abîme.* Paris: Des femmes, 1978.
—— *La Pupille.* Paris: Gallimard, 1972.
—— *Révolutions pour plus d'un Faust.* Paris: Seuil, 1975.
—— *Souffles.* Paris: Des femmes, 1975.
—— *Tombe.* Paris: Seuil, 1973.
—— *La Venue à l'écriture.* Paris: Union générale, 1977.
—— *Vivre l'orange.* Paris: Des femmes, 1979.
—— *Le Vrai jardin.* Paris: Herne, 1971.
—— *With, ou l'art de l'innocence.* Paris: Des femmes, 1981.
Cixous, Hélène, et al. *Rykiel: Textes de Madeleine Chapsal, Hélène Cixous, Sonia Rykiel.* Paris: Herscher, 1985.

TRANSLATIONS IN ENGLISH

Cixous, Hélène *Angst*. Trans. Jo Levy. New York: Riverrun Press, 1985.
—— *Benmussa Directs: Portrait of Dora by Hélène Cixous*. Trans. Anita Barrows. *The Singular Life of Albert Nobbs by Simone Benmussa*. Trans. Barbara Wright. New York: Riverrun Press, 1979.
—— *The Book of Promethea*. Trans. Betsy Wing. Lincoln: Nebraska University Press, 1991.
—— *The Exile of James Joyce*. Trans. Sally A.J. Purcell. New York: D. Lewis, 1972.
—— *Inside*. Trans. Carol Barko. New York: Schocken, 1986.
—— *The Newly Born Woman* (with Catherine Clément). Trans. Betsy Wing. Minneapolis: University of Minnesota Press, 1986.
—— *Reading with Clarisse Lispector*. Ed. and trans. Verena Andermatt Conley. London: Harvester Wheatsheaf, 1990.
—— *Writing Differences: Readings from the Seminar of Hélène Cixous*. Ed. Susan Sellers. Milton Keyes: Open University Press, 1988.

Clément, Catherine. *Bildoungue roman: une vie de Freud?* Paris: Bourgois, 1978.
—— *Bleu panique*. Paris: Grasset, 1986.
—— *Claude Lévi-Strauss*. Paris: Gallimard, 1979.
—— *Les Fils de Freud sont fatigués*. Paris: Grasset, 1978.
—— *Le Goût de miel*. Paris: Grasset, 1987.
—— *La Jeune née* (with Hélène Cixous). Paris: Union générale, 1975.
—— *Le Maure de Venise*. Paris: Grasset, 1983.
—— *Miroirs du sujet*. Paris: Union générale, 1975.
—— *L'Opéra ou la défaite des femmes*. Paris: Grasset, 1979.
—— *Le Pouvoir des mots: Symbolique et idéologique*. Paris: Mame, 1974.
—— *Rêver chacun pour l'autre: Sur la politique culturelle*. With the participation of Costa Gavras et al. and replies from the President of the Republic and the Minister of Culture. Paris: Fayard, 1982.
—— *La Sultane*. Paris: Grasset, 1981.
—— *La Syncope: Philosophie du ravissement*. Paris: Grasset, 1990.
—— *Torero d'or* (with François Coupry). Paris: Hachette, 1981.
—— *Vies et légendes de Jacques Lacan*. Paris: Grasset, 1981.
Clément, Catherine, et al. *Pour une critique marxiste de la théorie psychanalytique*. Paris: Sociales, 1977.
—— *Vladimir Jankélévitch*. Aix-en-Provence: L'Arc, 1979.

TRANSLATIONS IN ENGLISH

Clément, Catherine. *The Lives and Legends of Jacques Lacan*. Trans. Arthur Goldhammer. New York: Columbia University Press, 1983.
—— *The Newly Born Woman* (with Hélène Cixous). Trans. Betsy Wing. Minneapolis: University of Minnesota Press, 1986.
—— *Opera, or The Undoing of Women*. Trans. Betsy Wing. Minneapolis: University of Minnesota Press, 1988.
—— *The Weary Sons of Freud*. Trans. Nicole Ball. New York: Verso, 1987.

Collin, Françoise. *Le Jour fabuleux*. Paris: Seuil, 1960.
—— *Maurice Blanchot et la question de l'écriture*. Paris: Gallimard, 1971.

—— *Le Rendez-vous.* Paris: Tierce, 1988.

—— *Rose qui peut.* Paris: Seuil, 1962.

—— *Trois-cent-trente et un W vingt: lection du Président.* Paris: Transédition, 1975.

Duras, Marguerite. *Abahn, Sabana, David.* Paris: Gallimard, 1970.

—— *Agatha.* Paris: Minuit, 1981.

—— *Ah Ernesto!* Paris: François Ruy-Vidal et Harlin Quist, 1971.

—— *L'Amant.* Paris: Minuit, 1984.

—— *L'Amante anglaise.* Paris: Gallimard, 1967.

—— *L'Amour.* Paris: Gallimard, 1971.

—— *L'Après-midi de Monsieur Andesmas.* Paris: Gallimard, 1962.

—— *Une Aussi longue absence.* En collaboration avec Gérard Jarlot. Paris: Gallimard, 1961.

—— *Un Barrage contre le Pacifique.* Paris: Gallimard, 1950.

—— *Le Camion suivi de Entretien avec Michelle Porte.* Paris: Minuit, 1977.

—— *Détruire dit-elle.* Paris: Minuit, 1969.

—— *Dix heures et demie du soir en été.* Paris: Gallimard, 1960.

—— *La Douleur.* Paris: POL, 1985.

—— *L'Eden cinéma.* Paris: Mercure de France, 1977.

—— *Emily L.* Paris: Minuit, 1987.

—— *L'Eté 80.* Paris: Minuit, 1980.

—— *Les femmes, les soeurs* (with Erica Lennard). Paris: Des femmes, 1976.

—— *Hiroshima mon amour.* Paris: Gallimard, 1960.

—— *L'Homme assis dans le couloir.* Paris: Minuit, 1980.

—— *L'Homme atlantique.* Paris: Minuit, 1982.

—— *Les Impudents.* Paris: Plon, 1943.

—— *India Song.* Paris: Gallimard, 1973.

—— *Des Journées entières dans les arbres. Suivi de Le Boa, Madame Dodin, Les Chantiers.* Paris: Gallimard, 1954.

—— *Les Lieux de Marguerite Duras,* ed. Michelle Porte. Paris: Minuit, 1977.

—— *La Maladie de la mort.* Paris: Minuit, 1982.

—— *Marguerite Duras* (collection Ça/Cinéma). Paris: Albatros, 1979.

—— *Marguerite Duras à Montréal.* Texts collected and introduced by Suzanne Lamy and André Roy. Montréal: Spirales, 1981.

—— *Le Marin de Gibraltar.* Paris: Gallimard, 1952.

—— *Moderato cantabile.* Paris: Minuit, 1958.

—— *La Musica deuxième.* Paris: Gallimard, 1985.

—— *Nathalie Granger. Suivi de La Femme du Gange.* Paris: Gallimard, 1973.

—— *Le Navire Night. Césarée. Les Mains négatives. (Aurélia Steiner. Aurélia Steiner. Aurélia Steiner.)* Paris: Mercure de France, 1979.

—— *Outside: papiers d'un jour.* Paris: Albin Michel, 1981.

—— *Les Parleuses* (with Xavière Gauthier). Paris: Minuit, 1974.

—— *Les Petits chevaux de Tarquinia.* Paris: Gallimard, 1953.

—— *La Pluie d'été.* Paris: POL, 1990.

—— *La Pute de la côte normande.* Paris: Minuit, 1986.

—— *Le Ravissement de Lol V. Stein.* Paris: Gallimard, 1964.

—— *Savannah Bay.* Paris: Minuit, 1982.

—— *Savannah Bay.* Nouvelle édition augmentée. Paris: Minuit, 1983.

—— *Le Square.* Paris: Gallimard, 1955.

—— *Théâtre I, II, III.* Paris: Gallimard, 1965, 1968, 1984.

—— *Vera Baxter ou Les Plages de l'Atlantique.* Paris: Albatros, 1980.

—— *Les Viaducs de la Seine-et-Oise.* Paris: Gallimard, 1959.
—— *Le Vice-consul.* Paris: Gallimard, 1966.
—— *La Vie matérielle: Marguerite Duras parle à Jérôme Beaujour.* Paris: POL, 1987.
—— *La Vie tranquille.* Paris: Gallimard, 1944.
—— *Les Yeux bleus cheveux noirs.* Paris: Minuit, 1986.
—— *Les Yeux verts.* Paris: Cahiers du cinéma, 1980.

TRANSLATIONS IN ENGLISH

Duras, Marguerite. *L'Amante anglaise.* Trans. Barbara Bray. New York: Grove Press, 1968.
—— *Blue Eyes, Black Hair.* Trans. Barbara Bray. New York: Pantheon Books, 1987.
—— *Destroy, She Said and Destruction and Language: An Interview with Marguerite Duras.* Trans. Barbara Bray and Helen Lane Cumberford. New York: Grove Press, 1970.
—— *Eden Cinéma.* Bilingual Edition. Paris: Actes Sud-Papiers, 1988
—— *Emily L.* Trans. Barbara Bray. New York: Pantheon Books, 1989.
—— *Four Novels.* Intro. Germaine Brée. Trans. Sonia Pitt-Rivers et al. Includes *The Afternoon of Mr. Andesmas, Ten-Thirty on a Summer Night, Moderato Cantabile, The Square.* New York: Grove Press, 1982.
—— *Hiroshima Mon Amour.* Text by Marguerite Duras for the film by Alain Resnais. Trans. Richard Seaver. New York: Grove Press, 1976.
—— *India Song.* Trans. Barbara Bray. New York: Grove Press, 1976.
—— *The Lover.* Trans. Barbara Bray. New York: Pantheon Books, 1985.
—— *Little Horses of Tarquinia.* Trans. Peter DuBerg. New York: Riverrun, 1986.
—— *The Malady of Death.* Trans. Barbara Bray. New York: Grove Press, 1986.
—— *Marguerite Duras by Marguerite Duras.* Trans. Edith Cohen and Peter Connor et al. San Francisco: City Lights, 1987.
—— *Moderato Cantabile.* Trans. Richard Seaver. New York: Grove Press, 1960.
—— *Outside: Selected Writings.* Trans. Arthur Goldhammer. Boston: Beacon Press, 1986.
—— *Practicalities: Marguerite Duras Speaks to Jérôme Beaujour.* Trans. Barbara Bray. New York: Grove Weidenfeld, 1990.
—— *The Ravishing of Lol Stein.* Trans. Richard Seaver. New York: Pantheon Books, 1986.
—— *The Sailor from Gibraltar.* Trans. Barbara Bray. New York: Grove Press, 1967.
—— *The Sea Wall.* Trans. Herma Briffault. New York: Pellegrini, 1952.
—— *The Square.* Trans. Sonia Pitt-Rivers and Irina Murdoch. New York: Grove Press, 1959.
—— *Suzanna Andler; La Musica; L'Amante anglaise.* Trans. Barbara Bray. London: Calder, 1975.
—— *Ten Thirty on a Summer Night.* Trans. Anne Borchardt. New York: Grove Press, 1963.
—— *Three Plays: The Square, Days in the Trees,* and *The Viaducts of Seine-et-Oise.* Trans. Barbara Bray and Sonia Orwell. London: Calder, 1967.
—— *The Vice-Consul.* Trans. Eileen Ellenbogen. New York: Pantheon, 1987.
—— *The War: A Memoir.* Trans. Barbara Bray. New York: Pantheon Books, 1986.
—— *Whole Days in the Trees and Other Stories.* Trans. Anita Barrows. New York: Riverrun Press, 1984.
—— *Woman to Woman* (with Xavière Gautier). Trans. Katharine Jensen. Lincoln: University of Nebraska Press, 1987.

Herrmann, Claudine. *Le Cavalier des steppes.* Paris: Gallimard, 1963.
—— *Le Diplôme.* Paris: Gallimard, 1965.

—— *L'Etoile de David*. Paris: Gallimard, 1958.
—— *Maître Talmon*. Paris: Gallimard, 1961.
—— *Le Rôle judiciare et politique des femmes sous la République romaine*. Bruxelles: Latomus, 1964.
—— *Souvenirs de Louise Elisabeth Vigée-Lebrun (1755–1842): une édition féministe de Claudine Herrmann*. Paris: Des femmes, 1984.
—— *Les Voleuses de langue*. Paris: Des femmes, 1976.

TRANSLATIONS IN ENGLISH

Herrmann, Claudine. *The Tongue Snatchers*. Trans. Nancy Kline. Lincoln: University of Nebraska Press, 1989.

Hyvrard, Jeanne. *Auditions musicales certains soirs d'été*. Paris: Des femmes, 1984.
—— *La Baisure suivi de Que se partagent encore les eaux*. Paris: Des femmes, 1984.
—— *Canal de la Toussaint*. Paris: Des femmes, 1985.
—— *Le Cercan: Essai sur un long et douloureux dialogue de sourds*. Paris: Des femmes, 1987.
—— *Le Corps défunt de la comédie: Traité d'économie politique*. Paris: Seuil, 1982.
—— *Les Doigts du figuier*. Paris: Minuit, 1977.
—— *Mère la mort*. Paris: Minuit, 1976.
—— *La Pensée corps*. Paris: Des femmes, 1989.
—— *La Meurtritude*. Paris: Minuit, 1977.
—— *Les Prunes de Cythère*. Paris: Minuit, 1975.
—— *Le Silence et l'obscurité: Requiem littoral pour corps polonais, 13–28 décembre 1981*. Paris: Montalba, 1982.

TRANSLATIONS IN ENGLISH

Hyvrard, Jeanne. *Mother Death*. Trans. Laurie Edson. Lincoln: University of Nebraska Press, 1988.

Irigaray, Luce. *Amante marine: De Friedrich Nietzsche*. Paris: Minuit, 1980.
—— *Ce sexe qui n'en est pas un*. Paris: Minuit, 1977.
—— *Le Corps-à-corps avec la mère*. Paris: Pleine lune, 1981.
—— *La Croyance même*. Paris: Galilée, 1983.
—— *Et l'une ne bouge pas sans l'autre*. Paris: Minuit, 1979.
—— *Ethique de la différence sexuelle*. Paris: Minuit, 1984.
—— *Le Langage des déments*. The Hague: Mouton, 1973.
—— *L'Oubli de l'air: Chez Martin Heidegger*. Paris: Minuit, 1983.
—— *Parler n'est jamais neutre*. Paris: Minuit, 1985.
—— *Passions élementaires*. Paris: Minuit, 1982.
—— *Sexes et parentés*. Paris: Minuit, 1987.
—— *Spéculum de l'autre femme*. Paris: Minuit, 1974.
—— *Le Temps de la différence: Pour une révolution pacifique*. Paris: Librairie générale française, 1989.

TRANSLATIONS IN ENGLISH

Irigaray, Luce. *Speculum of the Other Woman.* Trans. Gillian Gill. Ithaca, N.Y.: Cornell University Press, 1985.
—— *This Sex Which Is Not One.* Trans. Catherine Porter and Carolyn Burke. Ithaca, N.Y.: Cornell University Press, 1985.

Kofman, Sarah. *Aberrations: Le Devenir-femme d'Auguste Comte.* Paris: Flammarion, 1978.
—— *Autobiogriffures.* Paris: Bourgois, 1976.
—— *Autobiogriffures du "Chat Murr" d'Hoffmann.* Paris: Galilée, 1984.
—— *Caméra obscura: De l'idéologie.* Paris: Galilée, 1973.
—— *Comment s'en sortir.* Paris: Galilée, 1983.
—— *Conversions: Le Marchand de Venise sous le signe de Saturne.* Paris: Galilée, 1987.
—— *L'Enfance de l'art: Une Interprétation de l'esthéthique freudienne.* Paris: Galilée, 1985.
—— *L'Enigme de la femme: La Femme dans les textes de Freud.* Paris: Galilée, 1980.
—— *Lectures de Derrida.* Paris: Galilée, 1984.
—— *Mélancolie de l'art.* Paris: Galilée, 1985.
—— *Un Métier impossible: Lecture de "Construction en analyse."* Paris: Galilée, 1983.
—— *Nerval: Le charme de la répétition. Lecture de Sylvie.* Lausanne: L'Age d'homme, 1979.
—— *Nietzsche et la métaphore.* Paris: Galilée, 1983.
—— *Nietzsche et la scène philosophique.* Paris: Galilée, 1986.
—— *Paroles suffoquées.* Paris: Galilée, 1987.
—— *Pourquoi rit-on? Freud et le mot d'esprit.* Paris: Galilée, 1986.
—— *Quatre romans analytiques.* Paris: Galilée, 1974.
—— *Le Respect des femmes: Kant et Rousseau.* Paris: Galilée, 1982.
—— *Séductions: de Sartre à Heraclite.* Paris: Galilée, 1990.
—— *Socrate(s).* Paris: Galilée, 1989.

TRANSLATIONS IN ENGLISH

Kofman, Sarah. *The Childhood of Art: An Interpretation of Freud's Aesthetics.* Trans. Winifred Woodhull. New York: Columbia University Press, 1988.
—— *The Enigma of Woman: Woman in Freud's Writings.* Trans. Catherine Porter. Ithaca, N.Y.: Cornell University Press, 1985.

Kristeva, Julia. *Au Commencement était l'amour: Psychanalyse et foi.* Paris: Hachette, 1985.
—— *Des Chinoises.* Paris: Des femmes, 1974.
—— *Etrangers à nous-mêmes.* Paris: Fayard, 1988.
—— *Folle vérité: Vérité et vraisemblance du texte psychotique.* Paris: Seuil, 1979.
—— *Histoires d'amour.* Paris: Denoël, 1983.
—— *Le Langage, cet inconnu: Une Initiation à la linguistique.* Paris: Seuil, 1981.
—— *Polylogue.* Paris: Seuil, 1977.
—— *Pouvoirs de l'horreur: Essai sur l'abjection.* Paris: Seuil, 1980.
—— *La Révolution du langage poétique. L'Avant-garde à la fin du xixe siècle: Lautréamont et Mallarmé.* Paris: Seuil, 1974.
—— *Langage, discours, société: Pour Emile Benveniste.* Sous la direction de Julia Kristeva. Paris: Seuil, 1975.
—— *Les Samouraïs.* Paris: Fayard, 1990.
—— *Séméiotiké: Recherches pour une sémanalyse.* Paris: Seuil, 1969.

—— *Soleil noir: Dépression et mélancholie.* Paris: Gallimard, 1987.
—— *Le Texte du roman: Approche sémiologique d'une structure discursive transformationelle.* The Hague: Mouton, 1970.
—— *La Traversée des signes.* Paris: Seuil, 1975.

TRANSLATIONS IN ENGLISH

Kristeva, Julia. *About Chinese Women.* Trans. Anita Barrows. New York: Urizen Books, 1977.
—— *Black Sun: Depression and Melancholia.* Trans. Leon S. Roudiez. New York: Columbia University Press, 1989.
—— *Desire in Language: A Semiotic Approach to Literature and Art.* Ed. Leon S. Roudiez. Trans. Thomas Gora, Alice Jardine, and Leon S. Roudiez. New York: Columbia University Press, 1980.
—— *In the Beginning Was Love: Psychoanalysis and Faith.* Trans. Arthur Goldhammer. New York: Columbia University Press, 1987.
—— *Language, The Unknown: An Initiation into Linguistics.* Trans. Anne M. Menke. New York: Columbia University Press, 1989.
—— *Powers of Horror: An Essay on Abjection.* Trans. Leon S. Roudiez. New York: Columbia University Press, 1982.
—— *Revolution in Poetic Language.* Trans. Margaret Waller. Introd. Leon S. Roudiez. New York: Columbia University Press, 1984.
—— *Tales of Love.* Trans. Leon S. Roudiez. New York: Columbia University Press, 1987.
Kristeva, Julia et al. *The Kristeva Reader.* Ed. Toril Moi. New York: Columbia University Press, 1986.

Lemoine-Luccioni, Eugénie. *Marches.* Paris: Des femmes, 1977.
—— *Partage des femmes.* Paris: Seuil, 1976.
—— *Psychanalyse pour la vie quotidienne.* Paris: Navarin, 1987.
—— *Un Questionnement du réel.* Paris: Navarin, 1984.
—— *Le Rêve du cosmonaute.* Paris: Seuil, 1980.
—— *La Robe: Essai psychanalytique sur le vêtement. Entretien avec André Couréges.* Paris: Seuil, 1983.

TRANSLATIONS IN ENGLISH

Lemoine-Luccioni, Eugénie. *The Dividing of Women, or Woman's Lot.* Trans. Marie-Laure Davenport and Marie-Christine Reguis. London: Free Association Books, 1987.

Marini, Marcelle. *Lacan.* Paris: Belfond, 1986.
—— *Territoires du féminin: Avec Marguerite Duras.* Paris: Minuit, 1977.

Montrelay, Michele. *L'Ombre et le nom: Sur la féminité.* Paris: Minuit, 1977.

Rochefort, Christiane. *Archaos ou Le Jardin étincelant.* Paris: Grasset, 1972.
—— *C'est bizarre l'écriture.* Paris: Grasset, 1970.

—— *Encore heureux qu'on va vers l'été*. Paris: Grasset, 1975.

—— *Les Enfants d'abord*. Paris: Grasset, 1976.

—— *Journal de printemps: Recit d'un livre*. Montréal: Editions l'étincelle, 1977.

—— *Ma vie revue et corrigée par l'auteur: A partir d'entretiens avec Maurice Chavardès*. Paris: Stock, 1978.

—— *Le Monde est comme deux chevaux*. Paris: Grasset, 1984.

—— *Les Petits enfants du siècle*. Paris: Grasset, 1961.

—— *La Porte du fond*. Paris: Grasset, 1988.

—— *Printemps au parking*. Paris: Grasset, 1969.

—— *Quand tu vas chez les femmes*. Paris: Grasset, 1982.

—— *Le Repos du guerrier*. Paris: Grasset, 1958.

—— *Une Rose pour Morrison*. Paris: Grasset, 1966.

—— *Les Stances à Sophie*. Paris: Grasset, 1963.

TRANSLATIONS IN ENGLISH

Rochefort, Christiane. *Josyane and the Welfare*. Trans. Edward Hyams. London: Vacdonald, 1963.

—— *The Warrior's Rest*. Trans. Lowell Bair. London: Hamilton, 1960.

Wittig, Monique. *Brouillon pour un dictionnaire des amantes*. Avec Sande Zeig. Paris: Grasset, 1976.

—— *Le Corps lesbien*. Paris: Minuit, 1973.

—— *Les Guérillères*. Paris: Minuit, 1969.

—— *L'Opoponax*. Paris: Minuit, 1964.

—— *Virgile, non*. Paris: Minuit, 1985.

—— *Le Voyage sans fin*. Paris: Vlasta, 1985.

TRANSLATIONS IN ENGLISH

Wittig, Monique. *Across the Acheron*. Trans. David Le Vay and Margaret Crosland. Dufour, 1987.

—— *Les Guérillères*. Trans. David Le Vay. London: Women's Press, 1979.

—— *The Lesbian Body*. Trans. David Le Vay. Boston: Beacon Press, 1986.

—— *The Opoponax*. Trans. Helen Weaver. New York: Simon & Schuster, 1966. Trans. David Le Vay. New York: Viking, 1971.

Wittig, Monique and Sande Zeig. *Lesbian Peoples: Material for a Dictionary*. New York: Avon, 1979.

The Contributors

EDITORS

ALICE A. JARDINE is Professor of Romance Languages and Literatures at Harvard University. She is the author of *Gynesis: Configurations of Woman and Modernity;* coeditor of *The Future of Difference* (with Hester Eisenstein) and *Men in Feminism* (with Paul Smith); and co-translator of Julia Kristeva's *Desire in Language* (with Thomas Gora and Leon S. Roudiez). She is currently working on a manuscript entitled *Of Bodies and Technologies: Woman and the Machine.*

ANNE M. MENKE is Assistant Professor of French at Swarthmore College. She is the author of articles on Francophone literature, and the translator of Julia Kristeva's *Language, the Unknown.* She is currently completing a manuscript entitled *Fictions of Sexual Intitiation: Readings in French Erotic Fiction, 1655–1809.*

CONTRIBUTORS

CHANTAL CHAWAF studied at the Ecole du Louvre and the Ecole Pratique des Hautes Etudes. Much of her work concerns writing and the body, maternity, and the linguistic transposition of women's domestic roles, as in *Chair chaude* and *Maternité*. She has also written several books inspired by fairy tales and the oral tradition (particularly as transmitted between mothers and children), including *Cercoeur* and *Elwina, le roman fée*.

HÉLÈNE CIXOUS graduated from the Lycée Bugeaud in Algiers in 1954 and emigrated to France in 1955, where she became a *professeur agrégé* in English in 1959 and *Docteur ès lettres* in 1968. In 1968 she was named *chargé de mission* to found the Université de Paris VIII at Vincennes, now at St. Denis, and she established the Centre de Recherches en Etudes Féminines in 1974. Her first text, *Le Prénom de dieu*, was published in 1967. More than thirty other works of fiction, theater, and essays have followed. Since 1983 two of her plays have been produced at the experimental Théâtre du Soleil: *L'Histoire terrible mais inachevée de Norodom Sihanouk* and *L'Indiade ou l'Inde de leurs rêves*. Her most recent projects include the screenplay for the televised film "La Nuit miraculeuse" and a play on the French Resistance. Despite the remarkable breadth of Cixous's writings, she is best known in the United States for her essay "The Laugh of the Medusa,"in *New French Feminisms*, eds. Elaine Marks and Isabelle de Courtivron (New York: Schocken, 1981).

CATHERINE CLÉMENT holds an *agrégation* in philosophy. She has been a cultural editor and writer for the socialist newspaper *Le Matin*, a diplomat in charge of cultural exchanges at the French Ministry of External Relations, and a coeditor with Hélène Cixous of *Féminin Futur*, and she has taught at the University of Paris I and at Vincennes. Her work spans diverse subjects and fields including cultural and visual criticism from a Marxist perspective; numerous books on psychoanalysis as practice and phenomenon *(The Weary Sons of Freud* and *The Lives and Legends of Jacques Lacan);* and a study on women and opera. In the United States she is particularly known for her essay and "exchange" with Hélène Cixous, her coauthor, in *The Newly Born Woman*. She currently lives in New Delhi.

FRANÇOISE COLLIN holds a doctorate in philosophy. She teaches in Brussels, although she now lives in Paris. She is best known as the director of the interdisciplinary independent journal *Les Cahiers du GRIF*, which she founded in 1973. She wrote the first book-length study on Blanchot *(Maurice Blanchot et la question de l'écriture)*, and has since written many essays on women's writing as a contestation of patriarchal and national economies of writing. She has also written about practical issues of feminism as a form of social and political grouping. An excerpt from her writing has been translated in *French Connections*. She has also written *Le Rendez-Vous*.

MARGUERITE DURAS (pseud. Marguerite Donnadieu) is a novelist, screenwriter, playwright, journalist, and film director. She emigrated to Paris at age seventeen after graduating from the Lycée de Saigon in Indochina with a baccalaureate in both Vietnamese and French. She holds *licence* degrees in law and political science from the University of Paris. She began writing in 1943 and has written more than fifty books, including the internationally acclaimed *The Lover*. She is also known in the United States for her screenplay *Hiroshima Mon Amour*, and for the "India" cycle, a group of three novels *(The Ravishing of Lol V. Stein, The Vice-Consul, L'Amour)* and three films *(La Femme du Gange, India Song, Son Nom de Venise dans Calcutta Désert)* interwoven in a process of remembering and forgetting aspects of one story. She has discussed her life in several texts, including *The War: A Memoir*. She has written for the French periodical *Sorcières* and speaks with Xavière Gautier of her involvement with feminism in *Woman to Woman*.

CLAUDINE HERRMANN is a practicing lawyer and has taught literature at the University of Paris VIII and at a number of universities in the United States. She has also been an editor at Editions Des femmes. She has written a book on the political and judicial role of women in ancient Rome as well as several novels, including *L'Etoile de David* and *Le Diplôme*. In *The Tongue Snatchers* she presents feminist critiques of the judicial system and explores the spatial and temporal "coordinates" of women's position within traditional linguistic and cultural dichotomies.

JEANNE HYVRARD (pseud.) has been *professeur de sciences économiques* since 1968. Her pen name is the name of an admired great-aunt. Much of her work concerns economic, philosophical, and social issues and blurs the boundaries between the scientific and the literary. (Her first book, *Les Prunes de Cythère,* was intended as an economic and social report on the French Antilles, where she taught for two years, but has been received as a literary work.) She writes from the point of departure of a transnational identity within a political, feminist, and intellectual discourse. Her work addresses many problems, including colonialism, physical illness, and linguistic constraints. She is best known in the United States for her novel *Mother Death.*

LUCE IRIGARAY is a psychoanalyst in Paris. She holds doctorates in both linguistics and philosophy. The publication of her book *Speculum of the Other Woman,* in which she critiques Platonic and Freudian representations of women, prompted her expulsion from the Lacanian Ecole freudienne and the loss of her teaching position at Vincennes. She is currently a director of research at the Centre National de la Recherche Scientifique in Paris. Her writing in the 1980s includes work on the pathological cultural repression of the mother-child bond *(Le Corps-à-corps avec la mère)* and on the consequences of the repression of the feminine in Christian faith structures *(La Croyance même).* In the United States her work is often discussed in the debate on essentialism, as for example in *Differences* (summer 1989), vol. 1.

SARAH KOFMAN holds a *doctorat d'état* in philosophy. She has taught as a *maître de conférences* at the University of Paris I since 1970 and frequently lectures in the United States. She has written dozens of books on Freud, Comte, Nietzsche, Kant, and others and is best known in the United States for her book on Freud's writings on women, *The Enigma of Woman,* and for a book of visual criticism, *The Childhood of Art.* She has also written on Auschwitz in *Paroles suffoquées.* An excerpt of her autobiographical writings is published in *Sub-Stance 49.*

JULIA KRISTEVA came from Bulgaria to Paris on a doctoral fellowship in 1966. She became a member of the editorial board of the journal *Tel Quel* in 1970. Since the 1970s she has divided her time between her psychoanalytic practice, teaching at the University of Paris VII, and writing. In *Revolution in Poetic Language* the well-known concepts of the semiotic and the symbolic and the phenotext and the genotext were developed. Her psychoanalytically inspired works include *Powers of Horror, Tales of Love,* and *Black Sun,* in which she writes about Marguerite Duras. In her book *In the Beginning Was Love: Psychoanalysis and Faith* she discusses psychoanalytic transference and the postulates of the Catholic faith. She also addresses the social and political problems of living with difference in *Etrangers à nous-mêmes.* Her stance toward feminism and the concept of the feminine are discussed most directly in the essay "Women's Time." Her first novel, *Les Samouraïs,* appeared in 1990.

EUGÉNIE LEMOINE-LUCCIONI is a Lacanian psychoanalyst and a member of the Ecole de la cause freudienne. She has written about maternity from the point of departure of Lacanian clinical testimony in *The Dividing of Women* and about desire for the Other in *Le Rêve du cosmonaute.* In the United States she is best known for her review of Luce Irigaray's *Speculum of the Other Woman* (in *Esprit,* March 1975), later discussed by Jane Gallop in *The Daughter's Seduction.*

MARCELLE MARINI teaches at the University of Paris VII. Much of her work focuses on language and politics; she is associated with the journal *34/44: Cahiers de recherches STD.* She has written a well-known study of Marguerite Duras *(Territoires du féminin: Avec Marguerite Duras)* and has also published articles about Jeanne Hyvrard and in defense of Luce Irigaray against the criticisms of the Ecole freudienne. Her most recent book is *Lacan.*

MICHÈLE MONTRELAY was an "analyste de l'Ecole Freudienne," and has practiced analysis independently since its dissolution. She is best known for her book *L'Ombre et le nom,* which includes her review of *Female Sexuality: New Psychoanalytic Views* (edited by Janine Chasseguet-Smirgel), translated as "Inquiry into Femininity" in Toril Moi, ed., *French Feminist Thought. L'Ombre et le nom* also discusses the work of Marguerite Duras. She has published work on a variety of psychological subjects, including narcissism and telepathy. Jane Gallop writes of her views of male and female sexuality in *The Daughter's Seduction.*

CHRISTIANE ROCHEFORT studied medicine and psychiatry before beginning a varied career as a teacher, journalist, film specialist, and novelist. Her first novel, *The Warrior's Rest,* was made into a film by Roger Vadim. Probably her most famous book remains *Les Petits enfants du siècle. Les Stances à Sophie,* in which she humorously critiques marriage, was adapted for a film by Moshé Mizrahi in 1970. A utopian novel, *Archaos ou le jardin étincelant,* is discussed in *Feminist Utopias* by Frances Bartkowski.

MONIQUE WITTIG is best known in the United States for her novels *The Opoponax, Les Guérillères,* and *The Lesbian Body.* Early in the 1970s she was a founder of the group Féministes Révolutionnaires and was briefly its spokeswoman; she gained public visibility when, with other women such as Christiane Rochefort, she placed a wreath on the Tomb of the Unknown Soldier dedicated to "the unknown wife of the soldier." Her other work includes *Lesbian Peoples: Material for a Dictionary* (with Sande Zeig), the play *Le Voyage sans fin,* and a recent novel, *Across the Acheron.* She is advisory editor and a frequent contributor to *Feminist Issues* and has taught at the University of Southern California and other universities.

Index